10649893

Warfighting

Maxims of Maneuver Warfare

1. MISSION TACTICS

2. FOCUS OF EFFORT

3. SPEED AND SURPRISE

4. RECONNAISSANCE PULL

5. SURFACES AND GAPS

6. FIREPOWER

7. CAMOUFLAGE, CONCEALMENT AND DECEPTION

8. THE CONCEPT OF RESERVE

9. COMMAND AND CONTROL SYSTEMS

10. CENTER OF GRAVITY

11. COMBAT SERVICE SUPPORT

– Lt. Col. H.T. Hayden

Warfighting

Maneuver Warfare in the U.S. Marine Corps

Edited by Lt. Col. H.T. Hayden

Greenhill Books, London
Stackpole Books, Pennsylvania

TO MY WIFE SHEILA
AND OUR DAUGHTER ALESSANDRA

Warfighting: Maneuver Warfare in the U.S. Marine Corps
first published 1995 by Greenhill Books,
Lionel Leventhal Limited, Park House, 1 Russell Gardens,
London NW11 9NN
and
Stackpole Books, 5067 Ritter Road, Mechanicsburg, PA 17055, USA

British Library Cataloguing in Publication Data available

ISBN 1–85367–198–3

Library of Congress Cataloging-in-Publication Data available

Publishing History
Warfighting: Maneuver Warfare in the U.S. Marine Corps reproduces
the complete and unabridged text of FMFM 1 *Warfighting*, FMFM 1-1 *Campaigning*,
and FMFM 1-3 *Tactics*, first published by the Department of the Navy,
Headquarters United States Marine Corps, Washington D.C., 1989, 1990 and 1991
respectively. New material by H.T. Hayden is provided for this edition: the Preface,
Introduction, Epilogue, Bibliography and additional Notes.

Typeset by DP Photosetting, Aylesbury, Bucks
Printed and bound in Great Britain by
Clays Ltd, St Ives plc

Contents

List of Maps

The Department of Defense and the U.S. Marine Corps have not authorized Lt. Col. Hayden to present the Marine Corps' positions on the subjects discussed. The views expressed are his own, and not those of the DoD or the Marine Corps.

Note: American titles, colloquialisms, phrases, and interpretations are employed throughout this book. Official American usage, especially for titles, reflects the American preference in the late 18th and early 19th centuries for French rather than English or German forms.

Preface

The creation of an effective military force depends upon more than the provision of adequate resources, the building of advanced weapons, or the availability of manpower. Military force must be organized, equipped, and trained properly. Doctrine is the substance that binds them together and makes them effective.

> Robert Allan Doughty
> *The Seeds of Disaster:*
> *The Development of French*
> *Army Doctrine, 1919–1939*

In March 1994, the first Navy and Marine Corps capstone publication in 218 years appeared: Naval Doctrine Publication 1 (NDP 1), *Naval Warfare*. The complete series of planned NDPs will form a bridge linking strategic level thinking in the joint Navy/Marine Corps white paper, '*Forward . . . From the Sea: The Strategic Concepts for the Employment of Naval Forces,*' to specific tactics, techniques and procedures contained in existing Naval Warfare Publications (NWPs) and Fleet Marine Force Manuals (FMFMs).

The major themes in NDP 1 include:

1. Naval Forces extend U.S. influence in the world through forward presence and crisis response
2. Naval Forces confront aggression using the offensive, emphasising combat power projection and the Navy/Marine Corps role in maintaining maritime superiority
3. Naval Forces favor the use of maneuver warfare, focusing high tempo operations on enemy weaknesses
4. Naval Forces contribute an array of distinct operational capabilities to the theater commander, operating as a Navy/Marine joint task force or as Navy and Marine components of joint or combined operations

There is now an opportunity, with the doctrine expressed in NDP 1, *Naval Warfare*, to construct a more cost-effective use of sea based military power than before, when a great deal of money had to be spent on defensive weapons protecting the American fleet from its only blue-water enemy, the Soviet navy. The national security strategic implication is that the U.S. can adopt a concept of operational maneuver from the sea combining amphibious ships with Marines, if needed, to fully exploit the capabilities of the Marine Corps and their maneuver warfare doctrine, tactics, techniques, and procedures.

What follows in this book is a collection of three Fleet Marine Force Manuals (FMFMs) and commentaries. FMFM 1, *Warfighting*, FMFM 1–1, *Campaigning*, and FMFM 1–3, *Tactics*, are published together as one book, with my commentaries, by permission of the Commandant of the Marine Corps, General Carl E. Mundy, Jr. FMFM 1–2, *The Role of the Marine Corps in the National Defense*, is not included because it is more a technical publication and does not greatly contribute to the theme of this book – maneuver warfare as practiced by the U.S. Marine Corps.

It must be emphasized that maneuver warfare, to the U.S. Marine Corps, is more than just a new doctrine. It is a way of thinking. It is a culture. It is a concept of how to cope with the fog of war, chaos, and friction of war, which cause confusion, death, and injuries to men on the battlefield.

'Synchronization' has long been a basic tenet of U.S. Army doctrine. Since the publication of FMFM 1, *Warfighting*, the U.S. Marine Corps has debated the extent to which synchronization concepts apply in Marine Corps maneuver warfare doctrine. The *Marine Corps Gazette* and the Army's *Military Review* and *Parameters* have published in-depth articles on the two schools of thought. My view is that it is neither a black-and-white nor an either/or issue. Most U.S. Marine Corps commanders are constantly synchronizing their forces at the same time as they continue their attack under their maneuver warfare doctrine.

The new Marine Corps culture of maneuver warfare has moved the Marine Corps away from battles of annihilation and savage force by balancing American capabilities for attrition with maneuver. Additionally, it has added the concept of the operational level of war with increased emphasis on campaign planning and improved coordination of joint and combined forces.

According to Major John Schmitt, USMCR, author of FMFM 1, in an article for the *Marine Corps Gazette*, August 1994, 'synchronization reflects an extremely deterministic and methodical approach to military operations. We can understand the appeal it has for the American [or UK] mind. It is organized, orderly and logical.' He continues that 'FMFM 1 tells us that war is inherently uncertain, unpredictable, frictional, fluid, disorderly, imprecise, and somewhat random. The problem is that these truths do not sit well with Americans [or the British] in their current culture.'

By trying to create order in an inherently chaotic battlefield, synchronization may hamper rather than enhance performance. Major Schmitt says: 'Make no mistake about it, the [U.S.] Army and Marine Corps philosophies as described in their keystone doctrine manuals are fundamentally different. It all comes down to your fundamental view of the inherent nature of war.' Western military establishments' most critical consideration in the aftermath of the Cold

War is to combine emerging technologies with new doctrine and new combat organizations to achieve and maintain decisive superiority. The techniques and procedures used to concentrate and focus combat power in time and space are not tools of synchronization. However, these concepts are inherent in the culture of maneuver warfare. If you believe in the offensive as the primacy of combat power, you synchronize your forces as you attack, probe for strengths and weaknesses and concentrate your focus of effort where the enemy is unprepared to react in time and space.

Today we face a major revolution in military affairs. Most obvious is the revolution in military technology. However, at the heart of the matter is the adoption of the culture of maneuver warfare, designed to collapse the enemy's will and lead to victory. All the high technology, exotic equipment, and brave troops cannot overcome weak warfighting doctrine.

Not since the National Security Act (1947) with the Key West Agreement (1948), which established the American Joint Chiefs of Staff (JCS) and the Goldwater-Nichols Act (1987) which firmly established the Chairman of the JCS as the principal advisor to the Secretary of Defense and the President, has there been a broader review of the national security process than with the 1995 Commission on Roles and Missions of the Armed Forces. The 25 'issues' that the Commission has reviewed provide major, wide-ranging implications for all the Services. It remains to be seen how Congress and the Administration will carry the Commission's recommendations into law.

My personal thanks to General Carl E. Mundy, Jr., Commandant of the Marine Corps, Major General P.K. Van Riper, Colonel John Shotwell, Colonel David Hague, Major John Schmitt, Major Mike Keegan, Captain Scott Shoemaker, Ms Evy Englander, and Mrs Martha Sisson.

H.T. Hayden
Quantico, VA
1995

Introduction
The History and Execution of
Marine Corps Doctrine

'It is not big armies that win battles. It is the good ones.'
Count Maurice de Saxe
Marshal of France, 1732

The formal study of land warfare was first identified in ancient China about 500 B.C. Western military academies were first established in Prussia and France in the 17th Century. Such formal study began in the British Isles at Woolwich (later the Royal Military Academy at Sandhurst) in 1764, and in America at West Point in 1802. The U.S. Naval Academy was founded in 1845 to 'cope with steam.'

Originally, before the academies existed, regimental training at the hands of a tough sergeant major, and on-the-job training, taught the prospective ensign or second lieutenant field craft, that is, the skills of warfare. Theory, doctrine, and tactics was the province of generals.

Early History of American Warfighting Doctrine

In the colonial Americas the first printed manual on the subject of how to fight a war was a reprint of a British publication: *The Words of Command and Direction for Exercising the Musket, Bayonet, and Cartridge* (Boston, 1733; first published by William Breton and printed in London). This manual may well have been the primary source for the colonial militia in the French and Indian War (1754–1763, the American part of the Seven Years' War), and later the American Revolution (1775–1783).

The first 'American' doctrine on warfighting was contained in the *Regulations for the Order and Discipline of the Troops of the United States*, by Baron de Steuben, Major General and Inspector-General of the Army of the United States (Albany, 1807). This was no more than the standard European tactics of the time with American terminology. During the War of 1812, Major General Winfield Scott drilled the troops under his command according to Baron de Steuben and French regulations of 1791 (noted by Professor Steven T. Ross, in a lecture to the U.S. Air Force Academy). In 1815 the U.S. Government appointed Scott to head a board charged with revising the Army's drill. Ultimately, using the translated 1791 French manual, de Steuben's manual and his own experiences in the Mexican War, Scott wrote *Infantry Tactics: Or, Rules for the Exercise and Manoeuvres of the United States Infantry*. The Army used the Scott manual, and other translations of the French, until the American 'War Between the States' (1861–1865). Great American military thinkers did not blossom until almost 100 years after the French and Indian War.

The reputation of Alfred Thayer Mahan (*The Influence of Sea Power Upon History: 1660–1805*) as a military theorist has tended to obscure the earlier fame of his father, Dennis Hart Mahan. The elder Mahan, after graduating from West Point, two years of teaching and four years of study in France, was appointed a professor at West Point in 1830. He was principally an engineering professor but it was the art of war that most interested him. His analysis of the battles of Napoleon and the writings of Antoine Henri Baron de Jomini became the basis of the only course on warfighting (doctrine, tactics, and techniques) taught at West Point. His most famous work (*Advanced Guard, Outpost and Detached Service of Troops, with the Essential Principles of Strategy and Ground Tactics*), simply called 'Outpost' by the cadets, was the premier warfighting textbook on military doctrine studied by top leaders wearing union blue or confederate grey during the American War Between the States, according to *The Encyclopedia of Military History*, by Ernest Dupuy and Trevor Dupuy. Lieutenant General Thomas 'Stonewall' Jackson once said that he learned warfighting from Dennis Hart Mahan and the only military book he carried in his saddlebags was Napoleon's *Maxims of War*.

The next major American manual on the doctrine of warfighting was 'Upton's Infantry Tactics', officially called *Infantry Tactics: Double and Single Rank (Adopted to American Topography and Improved Fire Arms)*, by Brevet Major General Emory Upton, U.S. Army (D. Appleton Co., New York, 1868). For the first time, the Army used the tactics of the previous war to train for the next.

While the Cavalry and Infantry School at Fort Leavenworth, Kansas, had been in existence for some time, Marine officers learned their trade through their regiment. It was not until May 1, 1891, that Marine Corps General Order No. 1 announced the establishment of the now famous Marine Corps 'School of Application'. In the School's Department of Military Art, the course was divided into minor tactics, grand tactics, and strategy. The major textbooks were Mayne's *Infantry Fire Tactics*, Batchelor's *Infantry Fire, Its Use in Battle*, and, later, Wagner's *Organization of Tactics*.

Since the establishment of the General Board of the Navy in 1900 and the General Staff of the Army as part of the Elihu Root military reforms in 1903, the United States had possessed the roots of a strategic planning organization. However, when the U.S. committed the American Expeditionary Force to

World War I (WW I) there was little opportunity to offer an alternative strategy to the war, and the French tactics of linear defense were readily accepted by the Americans – attrition warfare became the mainstay of the U.S. Army. With few exceptions, the major military thinkers in America and Europe paid little attention to the lessons of the American War Between the States, the Franco-Prussian War, or the Russo-Japanese War, all of which illustrated the futility of linear defenses. Factors such as the increasing deadliness of weapons and the improvements in the defense persuaded some German generals in WW I to look for an alternative to suicidal frontal attacks and to resort to tactical maneuver in seeking a decision. The Germans tried General Oscar von Hutier's formations of 'storm troopers' to rout the Russian Twelfth Army, September 1, 1917, by-passing strongpoints and attacking rear units. Similarly at Caporetto, October 24 to November 12, 1917, 'Hutier tactics' crushed the Italian Second Army. Fortunately for the allies on the Western Front, General Erich F.W. Ludendorff, in the Somme Offensive of 1918 (not to be confused with the First Battle of The Somme, 1916), instigated the German return to frontal assaults. However, without logistical mobility or tactical fire support for the Germans, the Allies moved reserves into the gap and restored the linear front.

Post World War I Warfighting Doctrine

Even before WW I, American armed forces had lacked unity of doctrine, unity of tactics, and unity of basic military principles. Each Service, and indeed different regiments of the same Service, had different basic essentials of tactics. In an attempt to apply some form of 'scientific' concepts of war and develop a unified military doctrine, the War Department published its first list of the principles of war, in War Department Training Regulations No. 10–5, 1921:

1. The principle of the objective
2. The principle of the offensive
3. The principle of mass
4. The principle of economy of force
5. The principle of movement
6. The principle of surprise
7. The principle of security
8. The principle of simplicity
9. The principle of co-operation

Colonel Mike Wyly, in William S. Lind's *Maneuver Warfare Handbook*, credits Major General J.F.C. Fuller, British Army, as the original author of these nine principles of war adopted by the U.S. Army.

While the writings of General Carl von Clausewitz were studied in Prussia and most of Europe from the 1830s onward, his writings were not widely distributed in the United States. According to Roger Nye, in *The Patton Mind*, Captain George S. Patton, Jr., during a visit to Great Britian, bought a copy of *General Carl von Clausewitz On War* published in 1909, which was a translation by a Miss Maguire and was perhaps only one-quarter of Clausewitz's *On War*. On a later visit he purchased a three-volume edition of *On War* (published in 1918 by E.P. Dutton and Company, translated by Colonel J.J. Graham, with notes by Colonel F.N. Maude).

Nye reported that Captain Patton did not always agree with General Clausewitz: 'Clausewitz suggested that if the object of combat is not the destruction of the enemy force, but merely shaking the enemy's feeling of security, "we go so far in the destruction of his forces as is sufficient." Captain Patton wrote in the margin, "Bunk – always go the limit."'

However, for the vast majority of American military leaders, Clausewitz was not readily available until World War II. Clausewitz's essay, *The Principles of War*, was translated and edited in America by Hans W. Gatzke (Military Service Publishing Co., 1942). The first complete edition of Clausewitz's *On War* to be printed in, and distributed throughout, America was a translation by O.J. Matthijs Jolles (Random House, 1943). Prior to this, the major foreign influence on American warfighting doctrine from the War Between the States and through World War I was Jomini's *The Art of War*.

According to Christopher Bassford, *Clausewitz in English: The Reception of Clausewitz in Britian and America, 1815–1945*; 'Because much British writing on Clausewitz during the interwar period was hostile and seemed to indicate little real understanding of his ideas, it has generally been assumed that Clausewitz had had no positive impact on that nation [the UK]. In this view, Clausewitz exercised no meaningful influence in either country [U.S. or UK] until after World War II ...'

The Development of Marine Corps Warfighting Doctrine

When the U.S. Marine Corps was developing its written doctrine of warfighting, it had already established its reputation. After the Spanish American War, Admiral Dewey said: 'If there had been 5,000 Marines under my command at Manila Bay, the city would have surrendered to me on May 1, 1898 ... and there would have been no insurrection.' (quoted in *Soldiers of the Sea* by Colonel Robert Heinl, Jr.).

Throughout World War I the Marines had followed Army doctrine and French training on warfighting. However, the Banana Wars (a term applied to the U.S. interventions against bandits or guerrillas in Latin America), and the expeditions in the Far East, showed that the Marines needed something different to cover what Capt Alfred Thayer Mahan, USN, called maritime expeditions – later known as amphibious operations.

Thanks to Admiral Dewey and a fortunate accident at Guantanamo, Cuba, where a Marine Battalion became an instrument for offensive work ashore, the U.S. Marine Corps began to develop doctrine, tactics, and techniques for amphibious warfare. Other nations facing the same problem failed to reach a sound solution to amphibious operations. The Royal Marines and other British forces involved were subordinated to the British line Navy at the Dardanelles in 1915, which they failed to take due to faulty doctrine, ineffective tactics and techniques, poor leadership and a complete lack of coordination between the Navy and Army.

Reorganization of formal Marine Corps officer training began in May 1917, with the establishment of the Marine Officers' Training School. By 1920 the Marines had a Field Officers' Course and a Company Officers' Course. Naturally, Army doctrine and Marine treatises were the source documents for the study of warfighting. A vast amount of uncorrelated information had accumulated, but no attempt was made to undertake a comprehensive study until Major S.M. Harrington prepared a pamphlet entitled *The Strategy and Tactics of Small Wars* (he may have borrowed the term 'small wars' from the great work by Colonel, later Major General, C.E. Callwell, British Army, but in fairness to Harrington, when reading the two works one quickly sees that the two authors wrote about doctrine, tactics, and techniques that were continents apart, figuratively and literally).

The U.S. Marine Corps' experiences in the 1920s and 1930s taught them that they needed two separate manuals: one for their increasing role as the policeman of the western hemisphere (small wars) and another for amphibious operations (opposed landings on a hostile shore).

On October 30, 1933, the Commandant of the Marine Corps directed that a manual on doctrine for landing operations be completed; it was first known as the *Tentative Manual for Landing Operations*. Under its official title, the *Tentative Landing Operations Manual* was initially published in 1934, but was later revised and reissued as *Fleet Training Publication (FTP) #167* (also known as *Landing Operations Doctrine, U.S. Navy 1938*).

The *Tentative Landing Operations Manual* was perhaps the most important contribution to military science made by the U.S. Marine Corps until their current attempts to adopt a culture of maneuver warfare. It was U.S. Marine Corps amphibious doctrine, tested and developed in the 1930s, that paved the way in North Africa, Italy, and France — not to mention the Pacific Theater — during WW II, and later in Korea, Vietnam, and Kuwait. Concurrently with the *Tentative Landing Operations Manual*, in 1935, a 'Restricted' book entitled *Small Wars Operations* was published for use only within Marine Corps Schools. In 1940, a revised and corrected edition, called *Small Wars Manual*, was published for the Marine Corps general use by the Government Printing Office. Of course the *Small Wars Manual* was not used extensively during World War II, but it was read by counterinsurgency practitioners during Vietnam and copies were even ordered for certain parties advising the Nicaragua Resistance (Contra) as late as 1988.

A third book used by the 1930s Marines (*The Marines Handbook*, 1934, by First Lieutenant L.A. Brown) is still being printed today, in a re-edited and reissued version, *Guidebook for Marines* (published by the Marine Corps Association, Quantico, Virginia, 1990). The *Guidebook* can be found in any Marine bookstore on any Marine Corps Base in America. Doctrine and tactics are not addressed in this book, but basic individual combat measures are included with customs and traditions of the Marine Corps. The official Marine Corps 'handbook', the *Marine Battle Skills Training (MBST) Handbook*, is a series of five books on the basic tasks of individual combat for privates through gunnery sergeants. The purpose of these publications is to establish individual training standards for combat and is used to train and assess enlisted Marines' proficiency. The MBSTs are published by the Marine Corps Institute.

In the late 1940s and 1950s, a series of Landing Force Manuals (LFMs) tried to combine doctrine, tactics, and techniques for amphibious operations and sustained operations ashore. In 1964, the first edition of a Fleet Marine Force Manual (FMFM) 6–1, *Marine Division*, brought the organization, doctrine, and tactics of how to fight as a Marine Division into one publication. FMFMs soon replaced some LFMs, and new concepts of 'Combat Service Support', 'Fire Support Coordination', 'Marine Aviation', etc., added new publications to basic warfighting documents.

According to Brigadier General E.H. Simmons, *The United States Marines: The First Two Hundred Years, 1775–1975*, the Marines who fought in the Banana Wars following World War I were the first to use the airplane as a close air support weapon, in coordination with infantry, dropping bombs on enemy targets during the Civil War in Nicaragua, 1927 (Colonel Robert Heinl states in *The Marine Officer's Guide* that the techniques of dive bombing were invented by Marine aviators in Haiti in 1919). Since that time, 'in every clime and place where Marines could carry a gun,' Marine air has been an integral part of the Marine Air–Ground Task Force (MAGTF).

Modern Marine Corps Warfighting Doctrine

Today, within the Joint Doctrine/Joint Tactics, Techniques, and Procedures (JTTP), Landing Force Manuals have been redesignated as Joint Publications. In addition to the new series of Naval Doctrine Publications, beginning with NDP 1, *Naval Warfare*, doctrinal and associated publications for the Marine Corps are called Fleet Marine Force Manuals (FMFMs), Operational Handbooks (OHs) or Fleet Marine Force Reference Publications (FMFRPs). Army Field Manuals (FMs), Naval Warfare Publications (NWPs), and Air Force Manuals (AFMs) are the principal other Service doctrinal publications. Marine Corps Bulletin 5600, 'Marine Corps Doctrinal Publications Status', is published each year and is a quarter-inch thick. It almost boggles the mind to see list after list of publications on 'how to ...' conduct *Close Air Support and Close-In Fire Support* (FMFM 5–4A), *Counterintelligence* (FMFM 3–25), *Command and Staff Action* (FMFM 3–1), etc. However, until FMFM 1, *Warfighting*, FMFM 1–1, *Campaigning*, and FMFM 1–3, *Tactics*, not one publication taught a Marine how to think about war. Not one produced a theory of war. In the first sentence of the Foreword of FMFM 1, *Warfighting*, General A.M. Gray writes: 'This book describes my philosophy on warfighting.' He explains that the theory of war derived from an understanding of the characteristics, problems, and demands of war in turn provides the foundation for how Marines wage war – maneuver warfare.

Maneuver warfare, always controversial and demanding operational and tactical innovation, presents the most important doctrinal questions currently facing the conventional and unconventional military forces of the United States.

Through the articulation of Mr William S. Lind, Colonel John R. Boyd, USAF (Ret), Colonel Michael D. Wyly, USMC (Ret), and a number of other far-sighted Marine and civilian writers and lecturers, maneuver warfare was introduced in all Marine Corps Schools in the mid 1980s.

Bill Lind wrote a *Maneuver Warfare Handbook* (Westview Press, Boulder, Co, 1984), one of the first printed volumes to use the Marine Corps as a model in the theory of maneuver warfare. The book contains the lectures of Colonel Mike Wyly on the 'Fundamentals of Tactics'. Both men credit Colonel John Boyd, with a study of air-to-air combat that he conducted at Nellis Air Force Base in 1974, as the godfather of maneuver warfare in the U.S. Marine Corps. Boyd later studied ground combat to see if there were any valid comparisons, and found that in battles and campaigns like Cannae, Agincourt, Austerlitz, Chancellorsville, Midway, Khe Sanh, and Kuwait, a similar phenonenon seemed to occur: one side had presented the other with a sudden, unexpected change, or a series of changes, to which the other side could not adjust in a timely manner. Colonel Boyd developed a lecture for the Marine Corps Command and Staff College, 'Patterns of Conflict,' to explain his theory, which he took five hours to do. The essence of his theory could be seen as a time-competitive observation–orientation–decision–action cycle, sometimes called the 'Boyd Cycle' or the 'OODA Loop'.

If one side in a conflict can consistently and quickly go through the Boyd Cycle faster than the other, that side gains a significant advantage over the other.

Bill Lind explains that if the objective in maneuver warfare is to move through the OODA Loop faster than the enemy, a general theory is worth considering:

1. Only a decentralized military force can have a fast OODA Loop.

2. Maneuver warfare requires that you will not only accept confusion and disorder and operate successfully within it, through decentralization, you will also generate confusion and disorder and thrive on it.
3. All patterns, formulas and standard operating procedures must be avoided – the enemy must not be able to predict your actions.

Therefore, one of the first principles of maneuver warfare has to be that there can be no fixed patterns of battle drills. Bill Lind provides a useful definition of tactics in maneuver warfare: it is a process of combining two elements – techniques and education – through three mental reference points: mission-type orders, the focus of effort (*Schwerpunkt*), and the search for enemy surfaces and gaps (strengths and weaknesses), with the object of producing an unas-sailable approach for the specific enemy, time and place.

All of this is explained in more detail in the three FMFMs that are the centerpiece of this book. Each FMFM must be read in sequence, for one must understand the concepts of the first manual in order to appreciate the arguments of the second and third in turn.

U.S. Army and U.S. Marine Corps Warfighting

As Bill Lind makes clear, the U.S. Army and the U.S. Marine Corps have a basic difference of opinion on the philosophy of warfighting. To the U.S. Army warfighting is a system of fire and movement in an attrition context – the focus is inward, on the process (operational plan, synchronization, etc.). To the U.S. Marine Corps, warfighting is fire and movement in a maneuver context – the focus is outward, on results. The Marine Corps uses fire and maneuver to attack the enemy, i.e. a combined arms attack (air, artillery, infantry, etc.) – while the Army uses fire as a basis for maneuver to establish a base of fire and then maneuver.

According to FM 100–5, *Operations*, Headquarters Department of the Army, June 1983, pp. 2–10: 'Maneuver is the movement of combat forces to gain positional advantage, usually in order to deliver – or threaten delivery of – direct and indirect fires. Maneuver is the means of positioning forces at decisive points to achieve surprise, psychological shock, physical momentum, massed effects, and moral dominance. Successful maneuver requires anticipation and mental agility.'

U.S. Army forces maneuver to bring firepower on the enemy, and bring firepower on the enemy in order to maneuver. The U.S. Marine Corps sees combined arms fire and maneuver as a single process. There is no 'step one – then step two,' there is only one step for the Marine Corps.

The U.S. Army says that maneuver refers to the employment of forces through offensive or defensive operations to achieve relative positional advan-tage over an enemy force to achieve tactical, operational, or strategic objectives.

To the U.S. Marine Corps, maneuver would not only be the employment of forces to achieve 'relative positional advantage over an enemy,' but could also be an attack to develop a positional advantage after identifying the 'surfaces and gaps' in the enemy positions, or it could be a seemingly static defensive position, making a feint of weakness, in order to encourage the enemy to attack for the Marines to maneuver in a more favorable position.

Maneuver warfare is an element of combat power, a principle of war and a state of mind. It is a culture that has to be developed in the first officers' basic course (for the Marines it is called The Basic School), and continues through the war colleges.

Contemporary Concepts of Warfighting

It is generally accepted that there are only three theories of warfare: attrition warfare theory, maneuver warfare theory, and revolutionary warfare theory (unconventional warfare, guerrilla operations and insurgency/counter-insurgency). In revolutionary warfare – unconventional warfare (low intensity conflict or operations other than war) against guerrillas – one can use decentralization, mission-type orders, focus of effort and search for surface and gaps, in running down guerrilla units, by using Small Independent Action Forces (SIAF) who stay in the field until the last guerrilla or bandit is captured or killed.

Robert Leonhard, in his book *The Art of Maneuver: Maneuver-Warfare Theory and AirLand battle*, states that while national strategy seeks to use armed forces to accomplish national goals, revolutionary warfare, also known as low intensity conflict, tends to blur the distinction between military and civil policy when armed forces are matched with civilian policy. Such conflicts often see tactical decisions being weighed against national policy. In Vietnam there was no distinction between military policy and civil policy on the part of the North Vietnamese.

An important lesson from Vietnam and revolutionary warfare (low intensity conflict) is the definition of the 'center of gravity.' Most military leaders would define the center of gravity in terms of the focus of enemy power or the main combatant forces on a battlefield. However, during Vietnam, the Americans misjudged the North Vietnamese center of gravity (believing it to be the North Vietnamese Army), whereas the North Vietnamese correctly judged the American center of gravity to be the will of the American people. When the President and the Congress failed to convince the American population that South Vietnam had some national security interest to the United States, success on the battlefield in Vietnam was irrelevant. In South Vietnam the U.S. never understood that the center of gravity of the NVA was in Hanoi and in Ho Chi Minh, and General Vo Nguyen Giap and their political infrastructure. It was only after President Richard Nixon used the China–USSR trump card (opening diplomatic and economic channels with the USSR and China, thus weakening the North Vietnamese position with their two major communist supporters) and initiated operation Linebacker II, almost destroying Hanoi with day-and-night bombing of the political and economic infrastructure, that the North Vietnamese Communist Party was brought to sign the Paris Peace Accords of 1973. Popular unrest at home caused the administration to settle for something less than many expected.

Colonel Harry G. Summers, Jr., USA (Ret) in his book *On Strategy II: A Critical Analysis of the Gulf War*, reported that the North Vietnamese commander for the 'Final Offensive,' General Van Tien Dung, had an overall 5.5 to 1 personnel advantage in the initial Battle at Ban Me Thuot – 5 South Vietnamese divisions against 15 North Vietnamese divisions. Summers quoted from General Dung's book, *Great Spring Victory*, that the 'NVA General staff charged with planning the maneuver of General Dung's four army corps worked beside a large poster that read: "Lightning speed, more lightning speed; boldness, more boldness." '

In counterinsurgency warfare (fighting revolutionary warfare) the focus of effort is the people. Flexibility is the key – decentralization is important so that a local commander can work with a local village chief, under a mission-type order (such as 'provide security for the people and help render government services'), and then find surfaces and gaps in the insurgent tactics and their operational art. Only a competently trained, on-scene commander can evaluate and react to events with the requisite force or nation-building assistance.

Maneuver warfare during the Vietnam War was not a concept easily understood and had mixed results when applied to military operations. Maneuver warfare should have been better understood and applied in Vietnam since similar concepts were readily accessible in Sun Tzu and Mao Tse-tung when studying insurgency/counterinsurgency warfare. Two of the most significant concepts of land warfare (maneuver warfare and revolutionary warfare) both find their origins in the writings of Sun Tzu.

Using the three basic elements of maneuver warfare – mission-type orders, focus of effort and the search for surface and gaps – many of us brought an extensive study of the British experience in Malaya and the American experiences fighting the Indians in America, the Banana Wars, the French-Indochina War, and the Huks in the Philippines, to our assignments in Vietnam. Many military advisors brought only conventional warfare training to their assignments and never bothered to educate themselves further. They did not realise that the tactics and techniques for something like the anticipated battle for the Fulda Gap (USSR vs USA) had no application to the tactics and techniques needed for the battle with the Viet Cong.

A Personal Experience

In Vietnam, as a Province Senior Advisor, MACV/CORDS, I had two parts of a mission-type order – to provide security for a given area and conduct nation-building programs. The focus of effort was the people. I sought surface and gaps in the enemy's combat tactics and the agitation–propaganda campaign he used to terrorize or win over the people.

The first gap to exploit was to take the sea (the people) away from the fish (the Viet Cong) – to paraphrase Mao Tse-tung, who said the communists were like fish swimming in a sea of the people and would only live as long as they swam in the sea. This was done physically and psychologically. Physical security was first and foremost before nation-building. Winning the hearts and minds of the people was secondary. No one will ever follow a government that cannot provide security, whether it be in Vietnam or Washington, D.C. Security of the people is the first responsibility of government. I learned that to fight the Viet Cong militarily was easy. First you take away the night, by night-time ambushes, booby traps and spoiling attacks, and then you take away the day by aggressive patrolling, running the enemy into the ground when you find him and letting no one escape. In revolutionary warfare (counterinsurgency, counterguerrilla warfare – whatever you want to call it) you have to master the environment (jungle, desert, mountains, etc.) and out-guerrilla the guerrillas. Boldness – always boldness!

I learned that to fight the Viet Cong politically and psychologically was more difficult. To fight an idea, I had to have a better idea to offer, and democracy was a foreign concept to the Vietnamese. So the worldwide struggle (at that time) between communism and democracy was of no concern. The idea that was sellable was that if they joined with the government of the Republic of Vietnam, their children would have a better life, health, education, and some measure of prosperity.

Only in rare cases was it possible to fight the Viet Cong militarily and politically/psychologically at the same time. I had one great success 59 days after the TET Offensive of 1968.

My provincial capital of Vinh Binh, a peninsula with major Mekong River tributaries north and south and the Pacific ocean to the west, had been cut off from the rest of the country, as the Viet Cong had blown all bridges and cut trenches across the only major road leading into the province from the outside – the major markets of Can Tho, My Tho and Saigon. The people needed to get their rice and other products to market and we needed to open the road and drive the Viet Cong out of their positions blocking the road.

Working for weeks, we repaired the bridges, rebuilt the road, and reestablished the Popular Force platoons in their mud forts to protect the bridges and the uncovered sections of the road.

Militarily I arranged a 'penetration' element of two armored commando vehicles and two truck mounted infantry units to lead the way. Next I arranged a 'suppression element' consisting of U.S. Army helicopter gunships, on-call

USAF air support, and preselected artillery targets all along the road. For the 'exploitation element,' I arranged the civilian convoy full protection, fore and aft, by armored commando vehicles and truck mounted infantry. Additionally, throughout the convoy, I placed heavy trucks with .50 cal. machine guns mounted on the cab and troops in the rear of the trucks.

The Vietnamese civilians had been told for a week to be ready for a one or two hour notice: 'Have your trucks packed with your rice bags or your products, all tied down and ready to roll.'

Late one morning in March 1968, my counterpart, Major Nguyen Qui Than, walked into my office and said he was ready to go. A quick check with the U.S. Army MACV Combat Operations Center, to make sure our suppression element was available, and we gave the civilians a one hour notice – no time for the Viet Cong to move reinforcements.

We did not slow down for snipers – preselected artillery targets were well chosen. Our first ambush caused a halt in the convoy. We did not fully dismount, but returned fire and called in gunships. The second ambush (halfway to our objective) destroyed an armored commando vehicle and a civilian truck. An air strike destroyed the enemy position. We by-passed the snipers and the remnants of fleeing Viet Cong. The last ambush before we reached the adjacent province, where the road was already cleared of Viet Cong, was the worst. No USAF fixed wing or Army gunships were available and we were out of range of the artillery.

We made the decision to dismount and fight and cover the civilian trucks as they rolled through the ambush site. We did incur some civilian casualties, including the wife of the Regional Force company commander who commanded the rifle company with our main force – but we did not lose one civilian truck.

As the last civilian truck broke through the linear ambush (no 'L' shaped ambushes encountered) the Viet Cong began to abandon their fighting positions. A short pursuit proved futile due to booby traps and mines. However, without ever knowing it at the time, using modern maneuver warfare tactics, we broke the siege of Vinh Binh and won back our province. The Viet Cong never recovered from their losses in the TET Offensive and the 60 day campaign we initiated to regain the initiative and defeat the Viet Cong proved a great military and political/psychological defeat for the enemy.

The above example may be too simple an illustration of maneuver warfare in a revolutionary war context. What I have not mentioned is the weeks of counterguerrilla operations, meetings with village and hamlet leaders to learn the population grievances, assisting in nation-building programs (roads, bridges, schools, dispensaries, etc.) and sometimes organizing, training, and equipping Popular Self-Defense Forces. On the one hand we had to out-guerrilla the guerrilla and on the other we had the political/economic/social/

psychological/informational aspects of nation-building. As a general rule, actions spoke louder than words, and where the US/GVN lived up to their word and genuinely cared for the security, health, and well-being of a village and its hamlets, the US/GVN won. Where incompetence, graft or corruption predominated, the US/GVN lost. By 1970 the counterinsurgency war had been won by the GVN and their allies. How can I say this? The answer is that there were two separate wars being fought in South Vietnam: one was the counterinsurgency war against the Viet Cong from 1965 to 1973 (many indigenous South Vietnamese in 1965, but mostly North Vietnamese after 1968) and the other was a conventional war against the North Vietnamese Army (1968–1975).

We never really understood our enemy. The Viet Cong, indigenous South Vietnamese, practiced a classic Mao Tse-tung insurgency from 1961–1968. However, the Viet Cong never recovered from their participation in the ill-fated TET Offensive of 1968 – the North Vietnamese took over former Viet Cong units and continued to field conventional North Vietnamese Army units. In the 1972 Easter Offensive, the North Vietnamese made a conventional attack, but were defeated by South Vietnam, with U.S. air support. Then in the Final Offensive of 1975, the South Vietnamese Army lost because the U.S. government failed to provide any combat support whatsoever against a North Vietnamese conventional warfare campaign.

The North Vietnamese, in their Final Offensive, practiced a modified form of maneuver warfare from January to April 1975. The American Army and the Marine Corps conducted attrition warfare during their involvement in Vietnam and that is what they taught the South Vietnamese. An American-trained attrition warfare army fought a Chinese-trained (i.e. according to Sun Tzu and Mao Tse-tung) maneuver warfare army, and history knows the results. Revolutionary warfare was irrelevant to the 1975 North Vietnamese campaign.

Warfighting in the 1990s

Whatever the moral or political basis for a decision, great powers are not going to refrain from intervention in conflicts or trouble spots when they see their 'vital national security interest' threatened. Nor will they hesitate when they can gain an advantage or secure a position, before the world press can react. For the United States the most recent examples are Grenada, Panama, and to some extent the Kuwaiti Theater of Operation (KTO). Generally speaking, 'massive intervention by organized forces seems to be at best overly costly, and at worst disastrous' (see *Race To The Swift: Thoughts on Twenty-First Century Warfare* by Brigadier Richard Simpkin). Such was not the case in Saudi Arabia and the Gulf War, but this was an anomaly. Had the Iraqis invaded Saudi Arabia from August to November 1990, there would have been massive casualties. Our next enemy may not sit and wait for our build-up of combat power.

Early in the Marine deployment to Saudi Arabia during Operation Desert Shield the 7th Marine Amphibious Brigade, under Major General John I. Hopkins, with only a regiment of infantry, an artillery battalion, light armored vehicle (LAV) company, tank company, and a High Mobility Multi-purpose Wheeled Vehicle (Tracked Optical Wire Guided Missile) (HMMWV (TOW)) company, stood against the Iraqi seven divisions poised near the Saudi/Kuwait border. Disallowing a static defensive posture and capitalizing on terrain channeling features, Major General Hopkins formed a light mobile screen for early warning and then formed three battalion landing teams, mobile strike forces composed of an equal mixture of the ground forces with Marine air (which had self-deployed) – Marine air often provided flank security. Using maneuver warfare tactics each task force would trade space for time until the main thrust of an enemy attack was drawn into a 'fire sack' (almost like an ambush where all combined arms have preselected targets if an enemy stumbles into the trap) where the Marine combined arms team could use maximum maneuver with firepower to halt the enemy attack. A brigade of the Army's 82d Airborne Division was just as 'gung ho' and ready to join the fight from their defensive position protecting the principal Saudi communication and transportation assets, if they were needed.

The First Marine Division attack into Kuwait, during the Gulf War, accepted a light screening force of LAVs and HMMWVs (TOW) on their right. The coalition forces coming up the Kuwaiti coast could not keep up with the operational tempo of the Marines. An Iraqi counterattack against the First Marine Division right flank was defeated by rapidly adjusting the forces available turning to meet the attack, defeating it and then quickly turning back to their main focus of effort.

The counterattack by the Iraqis against the 1st Marine Division occurred on G + 1, February 25, 1991, when the Iraqis began from the east with a feint against the 1st Marine Division left flank followed by large-scale assaults against the Division's right flank and center. Major General Mike Myatt, Commanding General, 1st Marine Division, had just completed adjustments to the Division's defenses. He concluded that the Division command post was too far forward (a result of the maneuver warfare tenet of the commander leading from the front), being just behind Task Force Ripper, one of the two leading assault task forces, and with only Company C, 1st Battalion, 1st Marines, protecting the avenue of approach to the Division command post from the east. General Myatt decided to reinforce Company C with the nearest unit available, a Light Armored Vehicle (LAV) company from Task Force Shepherd. Accordingly, Company B, Task Force Shepherd, linked up with Company C at 0645. The Company B Commander was so upset about his assignment that he approached the Assistant Division Commander, Brigadier General Tom Draude and asked if his company could be returned to the line. As things turned out Company B was put in a position to be the centerpiece of one of the most important engagements fought by the 1st Marine Division during the war.

The first Iraqi attack struck Task Force Shepherd (1st Light Armored Infantry Battalion (Rein)) and Task Force Ripper (7th Marine Regimental Landing Team). The Iraqi 26th Armored Brigade hit the main Marine forward units from the northeast. The Iraqi 22d Mechanized Brigade unknowingly drove straight at the 1st Marine Division (Forward) command post from the east.

At one point Colonel Rich Hodory, Commanding Officer, 1st Marine Regimental Combat Team (Task Force Papa Bear), just south of the 1st Marine Division CP, was holding a staff meeting just outside his command Assault Amphibious Vehicle (AAV) when a T-55 tank three Type-63 armored personnel carriers emerged from the fog smoke and stopped less than 50 meters from where Hodory stood. The T-55 cannon pointed straight at the standing Marines, but never fired – instead the brigade commander came forward to surrender, but said the rest of the 22d Brigade, 5th Mechanized, Division of the Iraqi army was attacking.

With only a mission-type order (to cover the Division's right flank) Captain Ray's Company B maneuvered their LAVs against five T-55s, 33 armored personnel carriers and dismounted infantry. Company B and Company C, 1st Battalion, 1st Marines, along with Marines assigned to the division forward command element, had only TOW, AT-4 (antitank infantry weapon) and the 25 MM guns on the LAVs. After an hour of fighting, burning enemy vehicles littered the battlefield and the Iraqis withdrew to reorganize and attack again. This time AH-1J, Cobra, helicopter gunships, firing TOW missiles, had arrived to help repulse the enemy. Stopped again, the enemy force finally disintegrated with the loss of 320 Iraqi soldiers captured, and 27 armored personnel vehicles and three tanks destroyed. As soon as the Iraqi pressure eased General Myatt repositioned the division and resumed the offensive hunt for the surfaces and gaps in the enemy positions.

The Marine Corps performance was somewhat different from that of the Army in character and results in a number of areas. The operational decision in keeping a large amphibious force embarked at sea contributed to the overall Central Command (CENTCOM) and I Marine Expeditionary Force (I MEF) maneuver warfare plan. The amphibious Marines floated off Kuwait, while the 1st and 2d Marine Divisions drove a dagger straight at Kuwait City, presenting a dilemma for the Iraqi command. Which was the main attack? The speed and boldness of the Marine ground attack got inside the 'Boyd Cycle' or 'OODA Loop' of the Iraqis and created a total collapse of Iraqi command and control.

Some Marine regiments, using decentralization of command, mission-type orders, thrust vectors (instead of phase lines) and a high operational tempo, were highly successful. Fortunately, the Commanding General, I MEF, Lieutenant General Walter E. Boomer, USMC, was a maneuver warfare practitioner who led from the front and constantly adjusted his focus of effort as he discovered surfaces and gaps in the Iraqi defenses.

Maneuver warfare is often confused as basically only an offensive philosophy – principally a tank warfare philosophy. In fact it is a way of thinking about how to conduct a defense as much as an attack. In my own personal case as the Commanding Officer of Headquarters and Service Battalion, 1st Force Service Support Group, I MEF, my battalion had the mission to defend the I MEF rear area. To accomplish this mission, I had my battalion military police company, a security company from the other three headquarters and service companies of my HQSVC Battalion, and until sufficient combat power was established ashore (after off-loading the Maritime Prepositioned Ships), I was augmented by two infantry companies from the rotating infantry battalions as they collected their rolling stocks, ammo and supplies from the MPSs. In October, I received a Navy Port Security and Harbor Defense Group which included above and under water surveillance equipment with a U.S. Coast Guard Patrol Boat Unit. All units inside the perimeter of the Al Jubail Vital Area had point security responsibility. This permitted a minimum perimeter security force, a checkerboard defense force (all point security forces) and a strong mobile strike force in reserve to counter-attack any enemy penetration of our perimeter.

Regardless of the fact that there were infantry, armor, artillery, aircraft wing, and logistics units in the Al Jubail Vital Area, the Commanding General had decentralized the responsibility for the defense of the area to one command – mine. I had a mission-type order: to defend the port (as a matter of fact, besides the Commanding General's direct verbal instructions I had only a one-page message order). Once the surface and gaps had been located our 'focus of effort' could be established. Gate entry check points, observation posts, unscheduled mobile patrols (no set patterns), rapid reaction drills, and continual command interest (mine) were the orders of the day. Intelligence reports from the Saudi police and Saudi intelligence agencies informed me that enemy agents were reporting that the port was too well defended and softer targets should be sought elsewhere.

In mid-October, 1990, when the 1st Marine Division was fully established ashore, and in mobile defensive positions north of Al Jubail, the Commanding General of the 1st Force Service Support Group (1st FSSG), Brigadier General Jim Brabham, gave me a new mission-type order and released all infantry units to the 1st Marine Division. He instructed me to reduce my guard force as much as possible (so they could do their normal logistics/combat service support duties) and secure the port.

No message order, only verbal instruction, which substantially changed the mission. Still a mission-type order. There is a big difference between defending an area and providing security for an area. Maintaining my focus of effort, using cover and deception, increasing mobile patrols with a well rehearsed reinforcement plan, counterintelligence always had surveillance intercepts reporting the same information: Al Jubail was too strongly defended. No one but the Americans and the Saudi security heads knew anything had changed.

General H. Norman Schwarzkopf, in *It Doesn't Take a Hero*, does not say much about his education and study of maneuver warfare. However, he does state: 'Saddam was ... an enemy center of gravity – an aspect of the opposing force that, if destroyed, will cause the enemy to lose its will to fight. (Clausewitz, the great Prussian philosopher of war, defined the concept of a center of gravity in his 1832 book, *Vom Kriege*.)' When General Schwarzkopf told his XVIII and VII Corps commanders that he wanted them to move over 100 miles to their left, both Corps commanders are reported to have initially complained, not grasping the operational art that Schwarzkopf was initiating. When the U.S. Army, French and British forces were finally in place, prior to the initiation of the ground war on February 25, 1991, Schwarzkopf had, by maneuver, already won the war (as Napoleon had done at Ulm and Austerlitz.) It was really only a question of how long and how many casualties before the destruction of the Iraqi forces. You cannot argue with success. The U.S. Army, in the personification of General Schwarzkopf, followed some of the major tenets of maneuver warfare during the Gulf War. He provided superb examples of deception, pre-emption, dislocation, and disruption.

While the VII Corps commander stopped his forces on the night of Sunday, February 24, to synchronize the VII Corps, the XVIII Airborne Corps, after its initial objections to the far left displacement, moved out smartly – apart from a late start from some 101st Airmobile Division helicopters due to the weather – and would have done more if it had been given mission-type orders.

Unfortunately, across the board for the U.S. Army, detailed and centralized planning, vertical communications, recon-push tactics and so on, were the order of the day for many division and brigade commanders.

One of the most interesting aspects of Operation Desert Storm was the decision to launch an air campaign in January, long before, and independent of, a ground assault. Normally, alliances of the type assembled during the Gulf War mitigate against the use of strategic pre-emption in war.

It needs to be said again that the decision (defeat of the Iraq forces in the KTO) was won prior to February 24, 1991. While too many credit airpower, the logistics of Operations Desert Shield and Desert Storm reveal more about the ability of the American armed forces to conduct maneuver warfare than any other aspect of the campaign.

The overall military campaign in the KTO during Operation Desert Storm clearly demonstrated some of the cultural differences between the U.S. Army and the U.S. Marine Corps in the application of maneuver warfare theory and practice. It was clear to many that there was more to maneuver warfare than the ability to execute a carefully planned, centrally-directed, methodical maneuver – 'synchronization.' The absence of a total understanding of maneuver warfare was dramatically demonstrated when the Army VII Corps defended its inability to close the Basrah road due to their having to slow down to synchronize their forces. Bill Lind would say that synchronization is the very essence of the 1939–1940 French-style methodical battle – the diametrical opposite of maneuver warfare.

Synchronizing fire with maneuver is important if it can be done. No Marine commander is going to wait, like chess pieces that have to be established in place on the chess board before a checkmate, if time and space are of the essence.

Lieutenant General Franz Uhle-Wettler, Army of the Federal Republic of Germany (Ret), wrote in Richard D. Hooker's book, *Maneuver Warfare: An Anthology*, that 'maneuver warfare' was not a phrase in German military terminology but various experts recommended the adoption of the German system which was called *Auftragstaktik* (literally, mission tactics, translated in America as 'mission-type orders'). Uhle-Wettler noted that *Auftragstaktik* was created in Prussia in the Army in the mid-19th century, where there was a long tradition of unusual devotion to professionalism and devotion to duty. Uhle-Wettler commented that an English author remarked at the turn of the century that 'nowhere in this world is independence of thought and freedom of decision as much groomed and supported as in the German army, from the corps commanders down to the last NCO.' One must keep in mind that he was talking about Prussia, although the Bundeswehr and the Wehrmacht have some comparisons in the philosophy of military leadership.

In the past a review of all western military commanders would have found that they went through the same process in developing an operations plan: appreciation of the situation, courses of action, and a battle plan; then the subordinates receive the commander's battle plan and their mission (and so on down the line). But, says Uhle-Wettler, in the German, and earlier Prussian armies, there seems to have been a difference: 'the importance of the mission . . . was reduced. The importance of the commander's intent was very much more emphasized.'

Uhle-Wettler's final comment on *Auftragstaktik* is that it means the readiness to act independently and the capability to do so sensibly. 'If you try to introduce *Auftragstaktik* . . . you are bound to fail. Instead, create an army in which independence has become a life-style, and in which a high level of professionalism prevails as well as a cocky, well-founded self-confidence.'

In the Gulf War, the 1st and 2d Marine Divisions launched their attacks on Saturday, February 23, 1991, at 4 AM (local Saudi time). Parts of the XVIII Airborne Corps with the French Daguet Division began to cover the allied left flank at the same time. The main U.S. Army flanking attack to the west began Sunday morning, February 24, with the VII Corps and the British 1st Armored Division lunging into Iraq. Originally, the main attack was not to have begun until 26 hours later, on Monday when the allied center, with VII Corps, was to head north toward the Republican Guards in the so-called 'Left Hook,' after the Marines had been used as bait for the entire Iraqi army in Kuwait.

Three hours into the Marines' attack, CENTCOM realized that Lieutenant General Boomer was approximately eight hours ahead of schedule. The Marine maneuver warfare tactics were rapidly establishing a salient that exposed both their left and right flanks. Still, VII Corps, with the 24th Mech Division and the 3rd Armored Cavalry Regiment were not scheduled to attack until G + 26 hours, 6 AM on February 25th.

To the American press it looked like the Marines would be on the outskirts of Kuwait before the VII Corps ever got into the battle. Finally, the CinC passed the word to his VII Corps that their attack would begin fifteen hours ahead of schedule, at 3 PM, Sunday, February 24th. At 9 AM Wednesday morning Arab forces entered Kuwait. By then few Iraqi forces remained in the city, having fled for their lives the day before. For Lieutenant General Boomer, and the Marines of I Marine Expeditionary Force, their mission was completed.

The 'synchronization matrix' of the VII Corps and their failure to close the door completely on the Basrah road notwithstanding, General Schwarzkopf's maneuver warfare operational art allowed the President of the United States, after consultation with the allies, to end the war at 8 AM, Thursday (Saudi time) exactly one hundred hours after the ground war had begun.

Rick Atkinson, in *Crusade: The Untold Story of the Persian Gulf War* (and confirmed by Lieutenant General de la Billière, UK Army, in *Storm Command: A Personal Account of the Gulf War*), states that the British 'fretted over high casualties if his [de la Billière's] forces were required to remain with Lieutenant General Boomer's Marines. The Marines struck him [de la Billière] as 'mustard keen' to press the attack regardless of how stout the Iraqi defenses.' Atkinson cites Boomer's retort as: 'Marines are gung-ho, but they're not stupid.'

The 2d Marine Division captured an Iraqi colonel and his entire staff. According to Rick Atkinson, the colonel's operations officer stated: 'We're very disappointed today . . . This is not going well for us. The shock of you coming through our flank disoriented me. I could not make good decisions.' No higher compliment could have been paid to the Marines and their maneuver warfare philosophy.

In assessing the Gulf War, too much has been made of the 'dominance of air power' or, as some have foolishly called it, the 'victory of airpower.' The U.S. Air Force won the battle of public relations and had the press believing that air power had won the war. The Air Force deserves credit for attempting in its targeting to isolate the battlefield first and then to strike all critical command

and control nodes. Overall, airpower achieved the same results it had obtained since WW II. Deep interdiction strikes against Iraqi civilian and military war-making capabilities and civilian infrastructure were extensively damaged. High altitude bombing of dug-in Iraqi forces in Kuwait has, subsequent to initial euphoria, proved to have had little effect. Ground 'after-action reports' (not airpower battle damage assessments) indicate little damage to Iraqi ground defensive positions and no evidence of 'massive casualties.' Once the ground assault began, airpower was very effective against columns moving in the open.

Warfighting into Print

FMFM 1, *Warfighting*, introduced in March of 1989, was inspired and championed by the then Commandant, General A.M. Gray, Jr., USMC, who sought a vehicle by which he could infuse his maneuver warfare doctrine into the Marine Corps. FMFM 1, *Warfighting*, was actually written over a five-month period by the then Captain John F. Schmitt, who also wrote the companion piece, FMFM 1–1, *Campaigning*, which applied maneuver warfare concepts to the operational level of war.

Gray and Schmitt met face to face for some eight hours over two sessions, in which Gray did not discuss the book directly, but rather described his vision of the nature of war and his maneuver warfare philosophy. Gray left the accomplishment of the mission, the organization and substance of the book, entirely up to Schmitt.

Schmitt immersed himself in the military classics, relying most heavily on Clausewitz and Sun Tzu. He also relied on a group that included military reformer Bill Lind and military officers, Generals P.K. Van Riper and Anthony Zinni, Colonels John Boyd, Michael Wyly, and Ray Cole, Captain Bruce Audmundsson, and many other Marines.

After receiving Gray's guidance, Schmitt and his group made several practical decisions about the book. The first was that as a symbol of the new doctrine, *Warfighting* should be short and to the point so that Marines of all grades could grasp its meaning; the book should be readable in a couple of sittings – the original aim (successfully met) was to stay under one hundred pages; and that the manual should be small and handy, so that it could fit into the map pocket of a pair of utility (battle dress) trousers and could be easily carried around. Finally, the book should be easy and interesting reading. The intent was to create a doctrine with a cohesive flow from beginning to end.

Schmitt was responsible for the final product, and the only person he had to satisfy was the Commandant. In the end, Gray signed off on the end product without changing a word.

The same approach was used in the writing of FMFM 1–3, *Tactics*, the tactical-level companion, written later by Captain Scott Shoemaker. FMFM 1–2,

The Role of The Marine Corps in The National Defense, does not concern maneuver warfare and is omitted from this book.

Today JCS Pub 3-02, *Joint Doctrine for Amphibious Operations*, with Change 5, is the basic joint document for amphibious doctrine while the three FMFMs printed in this book are the Marine Corps basic doctrine for Warfighting.

The world is still a dangerous place and the recent publication of the 'Military Doctrine of the Russian Federation,' as reported in *Defense News*, November 8–14, 1993, p. 3, somewhat analogous to a defense White Paper, identifies 'local wars and armed conflicts' and 'internal threats' as the main area of interest for the Russian army. Additionally, the 'doctrine' no longer rules out the first use of nuclear weapons, and 'the rights, freedoms and lawful interest of Russian citizens in foreign states,' attacks on Russian military facilities in foreign states, armed provocation and incursions over Russian borders, or those of her allies taken together give a number of excuses for armed intervention outside Russia.

A coalition of radical Islamic states, a new expansionist Russia, or current hot spots such as Korea, Iran, and Iraq, remind the major western powers to keep their powder dry. Another war on the scale of the Gulf War of 1991 is not beyond possibility. Yet all the NATO partners, except Norway, want to down size their military. What will save the western powers if they have demilitarized beyond their former capabilities? Better trained and equipped troops will not win against a vastly superior enemy unless there is a better doctrine or a philosophy of warfighting that is superior to that of the enemy. This book provides that philosophy for those who are not so blind as to refuse to see.

BOOK ONE

FMFM 1 Warfighting

Book One reproduces, in a new setting, the complete and unabridged original text and notes of FMFM 1 *Warfighting*, first published March 1989 by the Department of the Navy, Headquarters United States Marine Corps, Washington D.C.

New, additional notes by Lt. Col. H.T. Hayden are set in italics.

Foreword

This book describes my philosophy on warfighting. It is the Marine Corps' doctrine and, as such, provides the authoritative basis for how we fight and how we prepare to fight.

By design, this is a small book and easy to read. It is not intended as a reference manual, but is designed to be read from cover to cover. There is a natural progression to its four chapters. Chapter 1 describes our understanding of the characteristics, problems, and demands of war. Chapter 2 derives a theory about war based on that understanding. This theory in turn provides the foundation for how we prepare for war and how we wage war, chapters 3 and 4 respectively.

You will notice that this book does not contain specific techniques and procedures for conduct. Rather, it provides broad guidance in the form of concepts and values. It requires judgment in application.

I expect every officer to read – and reread – this book, understand it, and take its message to heart. The thoughts contained here represent not just guidance for actions in combat, but a way of thinking in general. This manual thus describes a philosophy for action which, in war and in peace, in the field and in the rear, dictates our approach to duty.

A.M. GRAY
General, U.S. Marine Corps
Commandant of the Marine Corps

CHAPTER 1

The Nature of War

'Everything in war is simple, but the simplest thing is difficult. The difficulties accumulate and end by producing a kind of friction that is inconceivable unless one has experienced war.'[1]

— Carl von Clausewitz

'In war the chief incalculable is the human will.'[2]

— B.H. Liddell Hart

'Positions are seldom lost because they have been destroyed, but almost invariably because the leader has decided in his own mind that the position cannot be held.'[3]

— A.A. Vandegrift

To understand the Marine Corps' philosophy of war-fighting, we first need an appreciation for the nature of war itself – its moral and physical characteristics and demands.[4] A common view among Marines of the nature of war is a necessary base for the development of a cohesive doctrine.

War Defined

War is a state of hostilities that exists between or among nations, characterized by the use of military force. The essence of war is a violent clash between two hostile, independent, and irreconcilable wills, each trying to impose itself on the other.

Thus, the object of war is to impose our will on our enemy. The means to that end is the organized application or threat of violence by military force.

When significant disagreements cannot be settled through peaceful means, such as diplomacy, nations resort to war. Nations not at war with one another can be said to be at peace. However, absolute war and peace rarely exist in practice. Rather, they are extremes between which exist the relations among most nations. The need to resort to military force of some kind may arise at any point within these extremes, even during periods of relative peace. Thus, for our purposes war may range from intense clashes between large military forces – backed by an official declaration of war – to covert hostilities which barely reach the threshold of violence.[5]

37

Friction

So portrayed, war appears a simple enterprise. But in practice, because of the countless factors that impinge on it, the conduct of war becomes extremely difficult. These factors collectively have been called *friction*, which Clausewitz described as 'the force that makes the apparently easy so difficult.'[6] Friction is the force that resists all action. It makes the simple difficult and the difficult seemingly impossible.

The very essence of war as a clash between opposed wills creates friction. It is critical to keep in mind that the enemy is not an inanimate object but an independent and animate force. The enemy seeks to resist our will and impose his own will on us. It is the dynamic interplay between his will and ours that makes war difficult and complex. In this environment, friction abounds.

Friction may be mental, as in indecision over a course of action. Or it may be physical, as in effective enemy fire or a terrain obstacle that must be overcome. Friction may be external, imposed by enemy action, the terrain, weather, or mere chance. Or friction may be self-induced, caused by such factors as lack of a clearly defined goal, lack of coordination, unclear or complicated plans, complex task organizations or command relationships, or complicated communication systems. Whatever form it takes, because war is a human enterprise, friction will always have a psychological as well as a physical impact.

While we should attempt to minimize self-induced friction, the greater requirement is *to fight effectively within the medium of friction*. The means to overcome friction is the will; we prevail over friction through persistent strength of mind and spirit. While striving to overcome the effects of friction ourselves, we must attempt at the same time to raise our enemy's friction to a level that destroys his ability to fight.

We can readily identify countless examples of friction, but until we have experienced it ourselves, we cannot hope to appreciate it fully. Only through experience can we come to appreciate the force of will necessary to overcome friction and to develop a realistic appreciation for what is possible in war and what is not. While training should attempt to approximate the conditions of war, we must realize it can never fully duplicate the level of friction of real combat.

Uncertainty

The next attribute of the environment of war is uncertainty. We might argue that uncertainty is just one of many sources of friction, but because it is such a pervasive trait of war we will treat it singly.

All actions in war take place in an atmosphere of uncertainty – the *fog of war*. Uncertainty pervades battle in the form of unknowns about the enemy, about the environment, and even about the friendly situation. While we try to reduce these unknowns by gathering information, we must realize we cannot eliminate them. The very nature of war makes absolute certainty impossible; all actions in war will be based on incomplete, inaccurate, or even contradictory information.

At best, we can hope to determine probabilities. This implies a certain standard of military judgment: what is probable and what is not? Through this judgment of probability we make an estimate of our enemy's designs and act accordingly. But, having said this, we also realize that it is precisely those actions which fall outside the realm of probability that often have the greatest impact on the outcome of war.

We must learn to fight in an environment of uncertainty, which we can do by developing simple, flexible plans; planning for contingencies; developing standing operating procedures; and fostering initiative among subordinates.

By its nature, uncertainty invariably involves the estimation and acceptance of risk. Risk is inherent in war and is involved in every mission. Risk is also related to gain; normally, greater potential gain requires greater risk. Further, risk is equally common to action and inaction. The practice of concentrating combat power at the focus of effort necessitates the willingness to accept prudent risk. However, we should clearly understand that the acceptance of risk does not equate to the imprudent willingness to gamble the entire likelihood of success on a single improbable event.

Part of risk is the ungovernable element of chance. The element of chance is a universal characteristic of war and a continuous source of friction. Chance consists of turns of events that cannot reasonably be foreseen and over which we and our enemy have no control. The uncontrollable *potential* for chance alone creates psychological friction. We should remember that chance favors neither belligerent exclusively. Consequently, we must view chance not only as a threat but also as an opportunity, which we must be ever ready to exploit.

Fluidity

Like friction and uncertainty, fluidity is an integral attribute of the nature of war. Each episode in war is the temporary result of a unique combination of circumstances, requiring an original solution. But no episode can be viewed in isolation. Rather, each merges with those that precede and follow it – shaped by the former and shaping the conditions of the latter – creating a continuous, fluctuating fabric of activity replete with fleeting opportunities and unforeseen events. Success depends in large part on the ability to adapt to a constantly changing situation.

It is physically impossible to sustain a high tempo of activity indefinitely, although clearly there will be times when it is advantageous to push men and equipment to the limit. Thus, the tempo of war will fluctuate – from periods of intense activity to periods in which activity is limited to information gathering, replenishment, or redeployment. Darkness and weather can influence the tempo of war but need not halt it. A competitive rhythm will develop between the opposing wills, with each belligerent trying to influence and exploit tempo and the continuous flow of events to suit his purposes.

Disorder

In an environment of friction, uncertainty, and fluidity, war gravitates naturally toward disorder. Like the other attributes of the environment of war, disorder is an integral characteristic of war; we can never eliminate it. In the heat of battle, plans will go awry, instructions and information will be unclear and mis-interpreted, communications will fail, and mistakes and unforeseen events will be commonplace. It is precisely this natural disorder which creates the conditions ripe for exploitation by an opportunistic will.

Each encounter in war will usually tend to grow increasingly disordered over time. As the situation changes continuously, we are forced to improvise again and again until finally our actions have little, if any, resemblance to the original scheme.

By historical standards, the modern battlefield is particularly disorderly. While past battlefields could be described by linear formations and unin-terrupted linear fronts, we cannot think of today's battlefield in linear terms. The range and lethality of modern weapons has increased dispersion between units. In spite of communications technology, this dispersion strains the limits of positive control. The natural result of dispersion is unoccupied areas, gaps, and exposed flanks which can and will be exploited, blurring the distinction between front and rear and friendly- and enemy-controlled areas.

The occurrences of war will not unfold like clockwork. Thus, we cannot hope to impose precise, positive control over events. The best we can hope for is to impose a general framework of order on the disorder, to prescribe the general flow of action rather than to try to control each event.

If we are to win, we must be able to operate in a disorderly environment. In fact, we must not only be able to fight effectively in the face of disorder, we should seek to generate disorder for our opponent and use it as a weapon against him.

The Human Dimension

Because war is a clash between opposing human wills, the human dimension is central in war. It is the human dimension which infuses war with its intangible moral factors. War is shaped by human nature and is subject to the com-plexities, inconsistencies, and peculiarities which characterize human behavior. Since war is an act of violence based on irreconcilable disagreement, it will invariably inflame and be shaped by human emotions.

War is an extreme trial of moral and physical strength and stamina. Any view of the nature of war would hardly be accurate or complete without consideration of the effects of danger, fear, exhaustion, and privation on the men who must do the fighting.[7] However, these effects vary greatly from case to case. Individuals and peoples react differently to the stress of war; an act that may break the will of one enemy may only serve to stiffen the resolve of another.

No degree of technological development or scientific calculation will overcome the human dimension in war. Any doctrine which attempts to reduce warfare to ratios of forces, weapons, and equipment neglects the impact of the human will on the conduct of war and is therefore inherently false.

Violence and Danger

War is among the greatest horrors known to mankind; it should never be romanticized. The means of war is force, applied in the form of organized violence. It is through the use of violence – or the credible threat of violence, which requires the apparent willingness to use it – that we compel our enemy to do our will. In either event, violence is an essential element of war, and its immediate result is bloodshed, destruction, and suffering. While the magnitude of violence may vary with the object and means of war, the violent essence of war will never change.[8] Any study of war that neglects this characteristic is misleading and incomplete.

Since war is a violent enterprise, danger is a fundamental characteristic of war. And since war is a human phenomenon, fear – the human reaction to danger – has a significant impact on the conduct of war. All men feel fear. Leadership must foster the courage to overcome fear, both individually and within the unit. Courage is not the absence of fear; rather, it is the strength to overcome fear.[9]

Leaders must study fear, understand it, and be prepared to cope with it. Like fear, courage takes many forms, from a stoic courage born of reasoned calculation to a fierce courage born of heightened emotion. Experience under fire generally increases courage, as can realistic training by lessening the mystique of combat. Strong leadership which earns the respect and trust of subordinates can limit the effects of fear. Leaders should develop unit cohesion and esprit and the self-confidence of individuals within the unit. In this environment a Marine's unwillingness to violate the respect and trust of his peers will overcome personal fear.

Moral and Physical Forces

War is characterized by the interaction of both moral and physical forces. The physical characteristics of war are generally easily seen, understood, and measured: hardware, technology, physical objectives seized, force ratios, losses of materiel or life, terrain lost or gained, prisoners or materiel captured. The moral characteristics are less tangible. (The term *moral* as used here is not restricted to ethics – although ethics are certainly included – but pertains to those forces of psychological rather than tangible nature, to include the mental aspects of war.[10]) Moral forces are difficult to grasp and impossible to quantify. We cannot easily gauge forces like national and military resolve, national or individual conscience, emotion, fear, courage, morale, leadership, or esprit. Yet moral forces exert a greater influence on the nature and outcome of war than do physical.[11] This is not to lessen the importance of physical forces, for the physical forces in war can have a significant impact on the moral. For example, the greatest effect of fires on the enemy is generally not the amount of physical destruction they cause, but the effect of that physical destruction on his moral strength.

Because the moral forces of war are difficult to come to grips with, it is tempting to exclude them from our study of war. However, any doctrine or theory of war that neglects these factors ignores the greater part of the nature of war.[12]

The Evolution of War

War is both timeless and ever changing. While the basic nature of war is constant, the means and methods we use evolve continuously. These changes may be gradual in some cases and drastic in others. Drastic changes in the nature of war are the result of developments that dramatically upset the equilibrium of war, such as the rifled bore and the railroad.

One major catalyst of change is the advancement of technology. As the physical hardware of war improves through technological development, so must the tactical, operational, and strategic usage of those means adapt to the improved capabilities – both to maximize our own capabilities and to counteract our enemy's.[13]

We must stay abreast of this process of change, for the belligerent who first exploits a development in the art and science of war gains a significant, if not decisive, advantage. Conversely, if we are ignorant of the changing face of war, we will find ourselves unequal to its challenges.

Art and Science of War

From the discussion to this point, we can conclude that war demonstrates characteristics of both art and science. Various aspects of war, particularly its technical aspects, fall principally in the realm of science, which we will describe as the methodical application of the empirical laws of nature. The science of war includes those activities directly subject to the laws of physics, chemistry, and like disciplines; for example, the application of fires, the effects of weapons, and the rates and methods of movement and resupply. However, these are among the components of war; they do not describe the whole phenomenon. Owing to the vagaries of human behavior and the countless other intangible factors which contribute to it, there is far more to the conduct of war than can be explained by science. The science of war stops short of the need for military judgment, the impact of moral forces, the influence of chance, and other similar factors. We thus conclude that the conduct of war is ultimately an art, an activity of human creativity and intuition powered by the strength of the human will. The art of war requires the intuitive ability to grasp the essence of a unique battlefield situation, the creative ability to devise a practical solution, and the strength of purpose to execute the act.

Conclusion

At first glance, war seems a rather simple clash of interests. But at closer examination, it takes shape as one of the most demanding and trying of man's endeavors. Fog, friction, and chaos are its natural habitat. Each episode is the unique product of the dynamic interaction of myriad moral and physical forces. While founded on the laws of science, war demands, ultimately, the intuition and creativity of art.

NOTES

1. Carl von Clausewitz, *On War*, trans. and ed. M. Howard and P. Paret (Princeton, NJ: Princeton University Press, 1984) p. 119.
2. B.H. Liddell Hart, as quoted in *Encyclopedia Britannica*, 1929.
3. A.A. Vandegrift, 'Battle Doctrine for Front Line Leaders,' (Third Marine Division, 1944) p. 7.
4. For the definitive treatment of the nature and theory of war, see the unfinished classic, *On War*, by Clausewitz. All Marine officers should consider this book essential reading. Read the Princeton University Press edition, the best English translation available. This version also includes several valuable essays on the book and author and a useful guide to reading *On War*.
5. In the strict legal sense, the United States enters a state of war only by formal declaration of Congress, which possesses the sole constitutional power to do so. The United States has declared war on five occasions: with Britain (1812); with Mexico (1846); with Spain (1898); with Germany and Austria-Hungary (1917); and with Japan, Germany, Italy, Bulgaria, Hungary, and Rumania (1941–2). A President, as commander in chief, may commit U.S. Forces to military action without a declaration of war when the circumstances do not warrant or permit time for such a declaration. Militarily there will be little if any distinction between war and military action short of war. Within this context, this book will focus on the military aspects of war, and the term *war* as discussed here will apply to that state of hostilities between or among nations regardless of the existence of a declaration of war.
6. Clausewitz, *On War*, p. 121.
7. For a first-hand description of human experience and reaction in war, read Guy Sajer's *The Forgotten Soldier* (Annapolis, MD: Nautical and Aviation Publishing Co., 1988), a powerful account of the author's experience as a German infantryman on

the eastern front during the Second World War and ultimately a tribute to the supremacy of the human will.

8. Clausewitz: 'Kind-hearted people might, of course, think there was some inge- nious way to disarm or defeat an enemy without too much bloodshed, and might imagine this is the true goal of the art of war. Pleasant as it sounds, it is a fallacy that must be exposed: war is such a dangerous business that the mistakes which come from kindness are the very worst ...

   'This is how the matter must be seen. It would be futile – even wrong – to try to shut one's eyes to what war really is from sheer distress at its brutality.' *On War*, pp. 75–76.

9. For an insightful study of the reaction of men to combat, see S.L.A. Marshall's *Men Against Fire* (New York: William Morrow and Co., 1961).

10. *The American Heritage Dictionary*, (New York: Dell Publishing Co., 1983).

11. In his often-quoted maxim, Napoleon assigned an actual ratio: 'In war, the moral is to the material as three to one.'

12. *This is a grave understatement and needs serious discussion in warfighting. H.T.H.*

13. *The nature of man has not changed in over 10,000 years, whether the weapon is a caveman's club or a Stealth Fighter/Bomber. Man's 'hierarchy of needs' – not the least of which is the need to avoid letting your fellow Marines down on the battlefield – is a constant that should be remembered. H.T.H.*

CHAPTER 2

The Theory of War

'The political object is the goal, war is the means of reaching it, and the means can never be considered in isolation from their purposes.'[1]
— Carl von Clausewitz

'Invincibility lies in the defense; the possibility of victory in the attack. One defends when his strength is inadequate; he attacks when it is abundant.'[2]
— Sun Tzu

'Battles are won by slaughter and manoeuvre. The greater the general, the more he contributes in manoeuvre, the less he demands in slaughter.'[3]
— Winston Churchill

Having arrived at a common view of the nature of war, we proceed to develop from it a theory of war. Our theory of war will in turn be the foundation for the way we prepare for and wage war.

War as an Instrument of Policy

War does not exist for its own sake.[4] It is an extension of policy with military force.[5] The policy aim that is the motive for war must also be the foremost determinant for the conduct of war. The single most important thought to understand about our theory is that war *must serve policy*. As the policy aims of war may vary from resistance against aggression to complete annihilation of the enemy, so must the application of violence vary in accordance with those aims. Of course, we may also have to adjust our policy objectives to accommodate our means; we must not establish goals outside our capabilities.

When the policy motive of war is intense, such as the annihilation of an enemy, then policy and war's natural military tendency toward destruction will coincide, and the war will appear more military and less political in nature. On the other hand, the less intense the policy motive, the more the military tendency toward destruction will be at variance with that motive, and the more political and less military the war will appear.[6]

The aim in war is to achieve our will. The immediate requirement is to overcome our enemy's ability to resist us, which is a product of the physical means at his disposal and the strength of his will.[7] We must either eliminate his physical ability to resist or, short of this, we must destroy his will to resist. In

military terms, this means the defeat of the enemy's fighting forces, but always
in a manner and to a degree consistent with the national policy objective.

Means in War

At the national level, war involves the use of all the elements of national power,
including diplomacy, military force, economics, ideology, technology, and
culture.[8] Our primary concern is with the use of *military force* as an instrument
of policy. But while we will focus on the use of military force, we must not
consider it in isolation from the other elements of national power. The use of
military force may take any number of forms, from intense warfare with
sophisticated weaponry to mere demonstrations. The principal means for the
application of military force is combat – violence in the form of armed conflict
between military or paramilitary forces.

The Spectrum of Conflict

Conflict can take a wide range of forms, constituting a spectrum which reflects
the magnitude of violence involved.[9] At one end are those conflicts of low
intensity in which the application of military power is restrained and selective.
The other end of the spectrum represents conflicts of high intensity, such as
nuclear war. The place on the spectrum of a specific conflict depends on several
factors. Among them are policy objectives, military means available, national
will, and density of fighting forces or combat power on the battlefield. In
general, the greater the density, the more intense the conflict. As a result, we
may witness relatively intense actions within a low-intensity conflict or relatively quiet sectors or phases in an intense war.

Low-intensity conflicts are more probable than high-intensity conflicts.[10]
Many nations simply do not possess the military means to wage war at the high
end of the spectrum. And, unless national survival is at stake, nations are
generally unwilling to accept the risks associated with wars of high intensity.
However, a conflict's intensity may change over time. Belligerents may escalate
the level of violence if the original means do not achieve the desired results.
Similarly, wars may actually de-escalate over time; for example, after an initial
pulse of intense violence, the belligerents may continue to fight on a lesser level,
unable to sustain the initial level of intensity.

The Marine Corps, as the nation's force in readiness, must have the versatility
and flexibility to deal with military and paramilitary situations across the entire
spectrum of conflict. This is a greater challenge than it may appear; conflicts of
low intensity are not simply lesser forms of high-intensity war. A modern
military force capable of waging a war of high intensity may find itself ill-
prepared for a 'small' war against a poorly equipped guerrilla force.

Levels of War

War takes place simultaneously at several correlated levels, each with differing ends, means, characteristics, and requirements.

Activities at the *strategic* level focus directly on national policy objectives. Strategy applies to peace as well as war. Within strategy we distinguish between *national strategy*, which coordinates and focuses all the components of national power to attain the policy objective,[11] and *military strategy*, which is the application of military force to secure the policy objective.[12] Military strategy thus is subordinate to national strategy. Strategy can be thought of as the art of winning wars. Strategy establishes goals in theaters of war. It assigns forces, provides assets, and imposes conditions on the use of force. Strategy derived from national policy must be clearly understood to be the sole authoritative basis of all operations.

Activities at the *tactical* level of war focus on the application of combat power to defeat an enemy in combat at a particular time and place.[13] Tactics can be thought of as the art and science of winning engagements and battles. It includes the use of firepower and maneuver, the integration of different arms, and the immediate exploitation of success to defeat the enemy. Included within the tactical level of war is the sustainment of forces during combat. The tactical level also includes the *technical* application of combat power, which consists of those techniques and procedures for accomplishing specific tasks *within* a tactical action. These techniques and procedures deal primarily with actions designed to enhance the effects of fires or reduce the effects of enemy fires – methods such as the call for fire, techniques of fire, the technical operation of weapons and equipment, or tactical movement techniques. There is a certain overlap between tactics and techniques. We make the point only to draw the distinction between tactics, which are the product of judgment and creativity, and techniques and procedures, which are generally performed by repetitive routine.

The *operational* level of war links the strategic and tactical levels. It is the use of tactical results to attain strategic objectives.[14] The operational level includes deciding when, where, and under what conditions to engage the enemy in battle – and when, where, and under what conditions to *refuse* battle – with reference to higher aims. Actions at this level imply a broader dimension of time and space than do tactics. As strategy deals with wars and tactics with battles and engagements, the operational level of war is the art of winning campaigns. Its means are tactical results, and its end is the military strategic objective.

Offense and Defense

Regardless of its type and nature or the level at which it is fought, combat manifests itself in two different but complementary forms: the offense and the defense. The offense and defense are neither mutually exclusive nor clearly distinct; as we will see, each includes elements of the other.

The offense contributes *striking power*. The offense generally has as its aim some positive gain; it is through the offense that we seek to impose some design on the enemy. The defense, on the other hand, contributes *resisting power*, the ability to preserve and protect oneself. Thus, the defense generally has a negative aim, that of resisting the enemy's will.[15]

The defense is inherently the stronger form of combat. Were this not the case, there would be no reason ever to assume the defensive. The offense, with its positive aim, would always be preferable.[16] But in fact, if we are weaker than our enemy, we assume the defensive to compensate for our weakness. Similarly, if we are to mount an offensive to impose our will, we must develop enough force to overcome the inherent superiority of the enemy's defense.

At least one party to a conflict must have an offensive intention, for without the desire to impose upon the other there would be no conflict. Similarly, the second party must at least possess a defensive desire, for without the willingness to resist there again would be no conflict. We can imagine a conflict in which both parties possess an offensive intention. But after the initial clash one of them must assume a defensive posture out of weakness until able to resume the offensive.

This leads us to the conclusion that while the defense is the stronger form of combat, the offense is the preferred form, for only through the offense can we truly pursue a positive aim. We resort to the defensive when weakness compels.[17]

While opposing forms, the offense and defense are not mutually exclusive. In fact, they cannot exist separately. For example, the defense cannot be purely passive resistance. An effective defense must assume an offensive character, striking at the enemy at the moment of his greatest vulnerability. It is 'not a simple shield, but a shield made up of well-directed blows.'[18] The truly decisive element of the defense is the counterattack. Thus, the offense is an integral component of the concept of the defense.

Similarly, the defense is an essential component of the offense.[19] The offense cannot sustain itself indefinitely. At some times and places, it becomes necessary to halt the offense to replenish, and the defense automatically takes over. Furthermore, the requirement to concentrate forces at the focus of effort for the offense often necessitates assuming the defensive elsewhere. Therefore, out of necessity we must include defensive considerations as part of our concept of the offense.

This brings us to the concept of the *culminating point*,[20] without which our understanding of the relationship between the offense and defense would be incomplete. Not only can the offense not sustain itself indefinitely, it generally grows weaker as it advances. Certain moral factors, such as morale or boldness, may increase with a successful attack, but these generally cannot compensate for the physical losses involved in sustaining an advance in the face of resistance.

We advance at a cost – lives, fuel, ammunition, physical and sometimes moral strength – and so the attack becomes weaker over time. Eventually, the superiority that allowed us to attack and forced our enemy to defend in the first place dissipates and the balance tips in favor of our enemy. We have reached the culminating point, at which we can no longer sustain the attack and must revert to the defense. It is precisely at this point that the defensive element of the offense is most vulnerable to the offensive element of the defense, the counterattack.

This relationship between offense and defense exists simultaneously at the various levels of war. For example, we may employ a tactical defense as part of an offensive campaign, availing ourselves of the advantages of the defense tactically while pursuing an operational offensive aim.

We conclude that there exists no clear division between the offense and defense. Our theory of war should not attempt to impose one artificially. The offense and defense exist simultaneously as necessary components of each other, and the transition from one to the other is fluid and continuous.

Styles of Warfare

Just as there are two basic forms of combat, there are two essential components: fire and movement. Of all the countless activities in combat, we can distill them to these.[21]

It would seem in theory that fire and movement represent opposite ends of a spectrum. But in reality, one cannot exist without the other, for fire and movement are complementary and mutually dependent. It is movement that allows us to bring our fires to bear on the enemy just as it is the protection of fires that allows us to move in the face of the enemy. It is through movement that we exploit the effects of fires while it is the destructive force of fires that adds menace to our movements.

Although all warfare uses both fire and movement, these components provide the foundation for two distinct styles of warfare: an *attrition* style, based on firepower, and a *maneuver* style, based on movement.[22] The different styles can exist simultaneously at different levels. For example, the island-hopping campaign in the Pacific during the Second World War was a maneuver campaign comprising a series of attrition battles.

Warfare by attrition seeks victory through the cumulative destruction of the enemy's material assets by superior firepower and technology. An attritionist sees the enemy as targets to be engaged and destroyed systematically. Thus, the focus is on efficiency, leading to a methodical, almost scientific, approach to war. With the emphasis on the efficient application of massed, accurate fires, movement tends to be ponderous and tempo relatively unimportant. The attritionist gauges progress in quantitative terms: battle damage assessments, 'body counts,' and terrain captured. He seeks battle under any and all conditions, pitting strength against strength to exact the greatest toll from his enemy. Results are generally proportionate to efforts; greater expenditures net greater results – that is, greater attrition. The desire for volume and accuracy of fire tends to lead toward centralized control, just as the emphasis on efficiency tends to lead to an inward focus on procedures and techniques. Success through attrition demands the willingness and ability also to withstand attrition, because warfare by attrition is costly. The greatest necessity for success is numerical superiority,[23] and at the national level war becomes as much an industrial as a military problem. Victory does not depend so much on military competence as on sheer superiority of numbers in men and equipment.

In contrast, warfare by maneuver stems from a desire to circumvent a problem and attack it from a position of advantage rather than meet it straight on. The goal is the application of strength against selected enemy weakness. By definition, maneuver relies on speed and surprise, for without either we cannot concentrate strength against enemy weakness. Tempo is itself a weapon – often the most important. The need for speed in turn requires decentralized control. While attrition operates principally in the physical realm of war, the results of maneuver are both physical and moral. The object of maneuver is not so much to destroy physically as it is to shatter the enemy's cohesion, organization, command, and psychological balance. Successful maneuver depends on the ability to identify and exploit enemy weakness, not simply on the expenditure of superior might. To win by maneuver, we cannot substitute numbers for skill. Maneuver thus makes a greater demand on military judgment. Potential success by maneuver – unlike attrition – is often disproportionate to the effort made. But for exactly the same reasons, maneuver incompetently applied carries with it a greater chance for catastrophic failure, while attrition is inherently less risky.

Because we have long enjoyed vast numerical and technological superiority, the United States has traditionally waged war by attrition. However, Marine Corps doctrine today is based on warfare by maneuver, as we will see in the fourth chapter, 'The Conduct of War.'[24]

Combat Power

Combat power is the total destructive force we can bring to bear on our enemy at a given time.[25] Some factors in combat power are quite tangible and easily measured, such as superior numbers, which Clausewitz called 'the most common element in victory.'[26] Some may be less easily measured, such as the effects of maneuver, tempo, or surprise; the advantages established by geography or climate; the relative strengths of the offense and defense; or the relative merits of striking the enemy in the front, flanks, or rear. And some may be wholly intangible, such as morale, fighting spirit, perseverance, or the effects of leadership.

It is not our intent to try to list or categorize all the various components of combat power, to index their relative values, or to describe their combinations and variations; each combination is unique and temporary. Nor is it even desirable to be able to do so, since this would lead us to a formulistic approach to war.

Construction and Speed

Of all the consistent patterns we can discern in war, there are two concepts of such significance and universality that we can advance them as principles: *concentration* and *speed*.[27]

Concentration is the convergence of effort in time and space. It is the means by which we develop superiority at the decisive time and place. Concentration does not apply only to combat forces. It applies equally to all available resources: fires, aviation, the intelligence effort, logistics, and all other forms of combat support and combat service support. Similarly, concentration does not apply only to the conduct of war, but also to the preparation for war.

Effective concentration may achieve decisive local superiority for a numerically inferior force. The willingness to concentrate at the decisive place and time necessitates strict economy and the acceptance of risk elsewhere and at other times. To devote means to unnecessary efforts or excessive means to necessary secondary efforts violates the principle of concentration and is counterproductive to the true objective.

Since war is fluid and opportunities fleeting, concentration applies to time as well as to space. We must concentrate not only at the decisive location, but also at the decisive moment. Furthermore, physical concentration — massing — makes us vulnerable to enemy fires, necessitating dispersion. Thus, a pattern develops: disperse, concentrate, disperse again.

Speed is rapidity of action. Like concentration, speed applies to both time and space. And, like concentration, it is *relative* speed that matters. Speed over time is tempo – the consistent ability to operate fast.[28] Speed over distance, or space, is velocity – the ability to move fast. Both forms are genuine sources of combat power. In other words, *speed is a weapon*. Superior speed allows us to seize the initiative and dictate the terms of combat, forcing the enemy to react to us. Speed provides security. It is a prerequisite for maneuver and for surprise. Moreover, speed is necessary in order to concentrate superior strength at the decisive time and place.

Since it is relative speed that matters, it follows that we should take all measures to improve our own tempo and velocity while degrading our enemy's. However, experience shows that we cannot sustain a high rate of velocity or tempo indefinitely. As a result, another pattern develops: fast, slow, fast again. A competitive rhythm develops in combat, with each belligerent trying to generate speed when it is to his advantage.

The combination of concentration and speed is momentum.[29] Momentum generates impetus. It adds 'punch' or 'shock effect' to our actions. It follows that we should strike the decisive blow with the greatest possible combination of concentration and speed.

Surprise and boldness

We must now acknowledge two additional considerations that are significant as multipliers of combat power: *surprise* and *boldness*.

By surprise we mean striking the enemy at a time or place or in a manner for which he is unprepared. It is not essential that we take the enemy unaware, but only that he become aware too late to react effectively. The desire for surprise is 'more or less basic to all operations, for without it superiority at the decisive point is hardly conceivable.'[30] But, while a necessary condition for superiority, surprise is also a genuine multiplier of strength in its own right because of its psychological effect. Surprise can decisively affect the outcome of combat far beyond the physical means at hand.

Surprise is the paralysis, if only partial and temporary, of the enemy's ability to resist.[31] The advantage gained by surprise depends on the degree of surprise and the enemy's ability to adjust and recover.[32] Surprise is based on speed, secrecy, and deception. It means doing the unexpected thing, which in turn normally means doing the more difficult thing in the hope that the enemy will not expect it. In fact, this is the genesis of maneuver – to circumvent the enemy's strength to strike him where he is not prepared. Purposely choosing the more difficult course because it is less expected necessarily means sacrificing efficiency to some degree. The question is: Does the anticipated advantage gained compensate for the certain loss of efficiency that must be incurred?[33]

While the element of surprise is often of decisive importance, we must realize that it is difficult to achieve and easy to lose. Its advantages are only temporary and must be quickly exploited. Friction, a dominant attribute of war, is the constant enemy of surprise. We must also recognize that while surprise is always desirable, the ability to achieve it does not depend solely on our own efforts. It depends at least as much on our enemy's susceptibility to surprise – his expectations and preparedness. Our ability to achieve surprise thus rests on our ability to appreciate and then dislocate our enemy's expectations. Therefore, while surprise can be decisive, it is a mistake to depend on it alone for the margin of victory.

Boldness is a multiplier of combat power in much the same way that surprise is, for 'in what other field of human activity is boldness more at home than in war?'[34] Boldness 'must be granted a certain power over and above successful calculations involving space, time, and magnitude of forces, for wherever it is superior, it will take advantage of its opponent's weakness. In other words, it is a genuinely creative force.'[35] Boldness is superior to timidity in every instance and is at a disadvantage only in the face of nervy, calculating patience which allows the enemy to commit himself irrevocably before striking – a form of boldness in its own right. Boldness must be tempered with judgment lest it border on recklessness. But this does not diminish its significance.

Exploiting Vulnerability and Opportunity

It is not enough simply to generate superior combat power. We can easily conceive of superior combat power dissipated over several unrelated efforts or concentrated on some indecisive object. To win, we must concentrate combat power toward a decisive aim.[36]

We obviously stand a better chance of success by concentrating strength against enemy weakness rather than against strength. So we seek to strike the enemy where, when, and how he is most vulnerable. This means that we should generally avoid his front, where his attention is focused and he is strongest, and seek out his flanks and rear, where he does not expect us and where we can also cause the greatest psychological damage. We should also strike at that moment in time when he is most vulnerable.

Of all the vulnerabilities we might choose to exploit, some are more critical to the enemy than others. It follows that the most effective way to defeat our enemy is to destroy that which is most critical to him. We should focus our efforts on the one thing which, if eliminated, will do the most decisive damage to his ability to resist us. By taking this from him we defeat him outright or at least weaken him severely.

Therefore, we should focus our efforts against a *critical enemy vulnerability*. Obviously, the more critical and vulnerable, the better.[37] But this is by no means an easy decision, since the most critical object may not be the most vulnerable. In selecting an aim, we thus recognize the need for sound military judgment to compare the degree of criticality with the degree of vulnerability and to balance both against our own capabilities. Reduced to its simplest terms, *we should strike our enemy where and when we can hurt him most.*

This concept applies equally to the conflict as a whole – the war – and to any episode of the war – any campaign, battle, or engagement. From this we can conclude that the concept applies equally to the strategic, operational, and tactical levels. At the highest level a critical vulnerability is likely to be some intangible condition, such as popular opinion or a shaky alliance between two countries, although it may also be some essential war resource or a key city. At the lower levels a critical vulnerability is more likely to take on a physical nature, such as an exposed flank, a chokepoint along the enemy's line of operations, a logistics dump, a gap in enemy dispositions, or even the weak side armor of a tank.

In reality, our enemy's most critical vulnerability will rarely be obvious, particularly at the lower levels. We may have to adopt the tactic of exploiting any and all vulnerabilities until we uncover a decisive opportunity.

This leads us to a corollary thought: exploiting opportunity. Decisive results in war are rarely the direct result of an initial, deliberate action. Rather, the initial action creates the conditions for subsequent actions which develop from it. As the opposing wills interact, they create various, fleeting opportunities for either foe. Such opportunities are often born of the disorder that is natural in war. They may be the result of our own actions, enemy mistakes, or even chance. By exploiting opportunities, we create in increasing numbers more opportunities for exploitation. It is often the ability and the willingness to ruthlessly exploit these opportunities that generate decisive results. The ability to take advantage of opportunity is a function of speed, flexibility, boldness, and initiative.

Conclusion

The theory of war we have described will provide the foundation for the discussion of the conduct of war in the final chapter. The warfighting doctrine which we derive from our theory is one based on maneuver. This represents a change since, with a few notable exceptions – Stonewall Jackson in the Valley, Patton in Europe, MacArthur at Inchon – the American way of war traditionally has been one of attrition. This style of warfare generally has worked for us because, with our allies, we have enjoyed vast numerical and technological superiority. But we can no longer presume such a luxury. In fact, an expeditionary force in particular must be prepared to win quickly, with minimal casualties and limited external support, against a physically superior foe. This requirement mandates a doctrine of maneuver warfare.

NOTES

1. Clausewitz, *On War*, p. 87.
2. Sun Tzu, *The Art Of War*, trans. S.B. Griffith (New York: Oxford University Press, 1982) p. 85. Like *On War*, *The Art of War* should be on every Marine officer's list of essential reading. Short and simple to read, *The Art of War* is every bit as valuable today as when it was written about 400 B.C.
3. Winston S. Churchill, *The World Crisis* (New York: Charles Scribner's Sons, 1923) vol. II, p. 5. The passage continues: 'Nearly all battles which are regarded as masterpieces of the military art, from which have been derived the foundation of states and the fame of commanders, have been battles of manoeuvre in which the enemy has found himself defeated by some novel expedient or device, some queer, swift, unexpected thrust or strategem. In many battles the losses of the victors have been small. There is required for the composition of a great commander not only massive common sense and reasoning power, not only imagination, but also an element of legerdemain, an original and sinister touch, which leaves the enemy

puzzled as well as beaten. It is because military leaders are credited with gifts of this order which enable them to ensure victory and save slaughter that their profession is held in such high honour . . .

'There are many kinds of manoeuvre in war, some only of which take place upon the battlefield. There are manouevres far to the flank or rear. There are man-oeuvres in time, in diplomacy, in mechanics, in psychology; all of which are removed from the battlefield, but react often decisively upon it, and the object of all is to find easier ways, other than sheer slaughter, of achieving the main pur-pose.'

4. *War has existed for many different reasons. In 1993 there was no state in Somalia – clans killed clans; in Afghanistan clans fought for power; in Bosnia-Herzegovina ethnic groups kill other ethnic groups out of fear and hatred. The Clausewitz quotation (see note 1) presupposes that states have a monopoly of power. There are some parts of countries where the state is irrelevant. H.T.H.*

5. Clausewitz, *On War*, p. 87. We prefer the phrase *with military force* rather than *by military force* as translated since military force does not replace the other elements of national power, but supplements them.

6. *Ibid.*, pp. 87–88.

7. Clausewitz, *On War*, p. 77.

8. The *National Security Strategy of the United States* (Washington: The White House, 1988), pp. 7–8, lists the elements of national power as moral and economic example, military strength, economic vitality, alliance relationships, public diplomacy, security assistance, development assistance, science and technology cooperation, international organizations, and diplomatic mediation.

9. *There is no violence in an economic war or an informational war. The 'spectrum of conflict' in the U.S. military lexicon now has a category called 'operations other than war.' H.T.H*

10. *'Low intensity conflict' to many of the direct participants is a life and death struggle. In the 34 wars and 112 'civil disputes' currently raging around the world the term LIC often belittles the struggle and makes the Third World think that the First World is condescending to their troubles. H.T.H.*

11. Also referred to as *grand* strategy or the *policy* level. From JCS Pub. 1-02: '**National Strategy** – (*DOD, IADB*) The art and science of developing and using the political, economic, and psychological powers of a nation, together with its armed forces, during peace and war, to secure national objectives.'

12. JCS Pub. 1-02: '**Military Strategy** – (*DOD, IADB*) The art and science of employing the armed forces of a nation to secure the objectives of national policy by the application of force or the threat of force.'

13. JCS Pub. 1-02: '**Tactical Level of War** – (*DOD*) The level of war at which battles and engagements are planned and executed to accomplish military objectives assigned to tactical units or task forces. Activities at this level focus on the ordered arrangement and maneuver of combat elements in relation to each other and to the enemy to achieve combat objectives.'

14. JCS Pub. 1-02: '**Operational Level of War** – (*DOD*) The level of war at which campaigns and major operations are planned, conducted, and sustained to accomplish strategic objectives within theaters or areas of operations. Activities at

this level link tactics and strategy by establishing operational objectives needed to accomplish the strategic objectives, sequencing events to achieve the operational objectives, initiating actions, and applying resources to bring about and sustain these events. These activities imply a broader dimension of time or space than do tactics; they ensure the logistic and administrative support of tactical forces, and provide the means by which tactical successes are exploited to achieve strategic objectives.'

15. *The defense is also used to lure the enemy into a false assumption of the current situation. Defense can be a ruse, it can be a trap, it can be a holding action while another force strikes elsewhere. 'Resisting power' is for a weak military unit. In maneuver warfare, if you're on the defense you have lost or may be losing the initiative. Most Great Captains of history have used the defense to draw out their enemy – not 'to preserve and protect' themselves. H.T.H.*

16. Clausewitz, *On War*, pp. 84, 357–359.

17. *The Iraqi defense in the Gulf War was originally thought to be one of the strongest in the world. The Marine Corps, using maneuver warfare tactics – identifying surfaces and gaps – went through the 'Iron and Fire Wall' in short order. The metal of the defenders or the attackers determines the 'stronger form of combat.' H.T.H.*

18. Clausewitz, *On War*, p. 357.

19. Clausewitz argued (p. 524) that while the offense is an integral component of the concept of defense, the offense is conceptually complete in itself. The introduction of the defense into the concept of the offense, he argued, is a necessary evil and not an integral component.

20. Clausewitz, *On War*, p. 528.

21. *This equation lacks the elements of cover and deception. You can 'move, shoot, and communicate' all day but it will do you no good if you have been deceived. There are styles of combat other than 'fire and movement.' H.T.H.*

22. *There is also the revolutionary style of warfare. H.T.H.*

23. *This was manfestly not the case for the North Vietnamese or the Armenians or the Georgians. H.T.H.*

24. The United States Army has also adopted a doctrine based on maneuver, called 'AirLand Battle.' The principal doctrinal source is Field Manual 100-5, *Operations* (1986).

25. JCS Pub. 1-02: '**Combat Power** – (*DOD, NATO*) The total means of destructive and/or disruptive force which a military unit/formation can apply against the opponent at a given time.'

26. Clausewitz, *On War*, p. 194.

27. *Ibid.*, p. 617.

28. Tempo is often associated with a mental process known variously as the 'Decision Cycle,' 'OODA Loop,' or 'Boyd Cycle,' after retired Air Force Colonel John Boyd who pioneered the concept in his lecture, 'The Patterns of Conflict.' Boyd identified a four-step mental process: observation, orientation, decision, and action. Boyd theorized that each party to a conflict first observes the situation. On the basis of the observation, he orients; that is, he makes an estimate of the situation. On the basis of the orientation, he makes a decision. And, finally, he implements the decision – he acts. Because his action has created a new situation, the process

begins anew. Boyd argued that the party that consistently completes the cycle faster gains an advantage that increases with each cycle. His enemy's reactions become increasingly slower by comparison and therefore less effective until, finally, he is overcome by events.

29. From basic physics, momentum is the product of mass and velocity: $M = mv$.

30. Clausewitz, *On War*, p. 198.

31. Edward N. Luttwak, *Strategy: The Logic of War and Peace* (Cambridge, MA: Belknap Press of Harvard University Press, 1987) p. 8.

32. *Surprise doesn't always mean doing the unexpected. Surprise is truly achieved in maneuver warfare when your fire and maneuver makes it impossible for the enemy to react in time. When you can get inside the enemy's OODA Loop he will be 'surprised' at every turn. H.T.H.*

33. Luttwak, *Strategy: The Logic of War and Peace*, pp. 8–10.

34. Clausewitz, *On War*, p. 190.

35. *Ibid.*

36. We should note that this concept is meaningless in attrition warfare in its purest form, since the identification of critical vulnerability by definition is based on selectivity, which is a foreign thought to the attritionist. In warfare by attrition, any target is as good as any other as long as it contributes to the cumulative destruction of the enemy.

37. Sometimes known as the *center of gravity*. However, there is a danger in using this term. Introducing the term into the theory of war, Clausewitz wrote (p. 485): 'A center of gravity is always found where the mass is concentrated the most densely. It presents the most effective target for a blow; furthermore, the heaviest blow is that struck by the center of gravity.' Clearly, Clausewitz was advocating a climactic test of strength against strength 'by daring all to win all' (p. 596). This approach is consistent with Clausewitz' historical perspective. But we have since come to prefer pitting strength against weakness. Applying the term to modern warfare, we must make it clear that by the enemy's center of gravity we do not mean a source of strength, but rather a critical vulnerability.

CHAPTER 3

Preparing for War

'The essential thing is action. Action has three stages: the decision born of thought, the order or preparation for execution, and the execution itself. All three stages are governed by the will. The will is rooted in character, and for the man of action character is of more critical importance than intellect. Intellect without will is worthless, will without intellect is dangerous.'[1]

— Hans von Seekt

'The best form of welfare for the troops is first-class training, for this saves unnecessary casualties.'[2]

— Erwin Rommel

'Untutored courage {is} useless in the face of educated bullets.'[3]

— George S. Patton. Jr.

During times of peace the most important task of any military is to prepare for war. As the nation's rapid-response force, the Marine Corps must maintain itself ready for immediate employment *in any clime and place* and in any type of conflict. All peacetime activities should focus on achieving combat readiness. This implies a high level of training, flexibility in organization and equipment, qualified professional leadership, and a cohesive doctrine.

Planning

Planning plays as important a role in the preparation for war as in the conduct of war. The key to any plan is a clearly defined objective, in this case a required level of readiness. We must identify that level of readiness and plan a campaign to reach it. A campaign is a progressive sequence of attainable goals to gain the objective within a specified time.[4]

The plan must focus all the efforts of the peacetime Marine Corps, including training, education, doctrine, organization, and equipment acquisition. Unity of effort is as important during the preparation for war as it is during the conduct of war. This systematic process of identifying the objective and planning a course to gain it applies to all levels.

Organization

The Fleet Marine Forces must be organized to provide forward-deployed or rapidly-deployable forces capable of mounting expeditionary operations in any environment. This means that, in addition to maintaining their unique amphibious capability, the Fleet Marine Forces must maintain a capability to deploy by whatever means is appropriate to the situation.

The active Fleet Marine Forces must be capable of responding immediately to most types of conflict. Missions in sustained high-intensity warfare will require augmentation from the Reserve establishment.

For operations and training, Fleet Marine Forces – active and Reserve – will be formed into Marine Air-Ground Task Forces (MAGTFs). MAGTFs are task organizations consisting of ground, aviation, combat service support, and command components. They have no standard structure, but rather are constituted as appropriate for the specific situation. The MAGTF provides a single commander the optimum combined-arms force for the situation he faces. As the situation changes, it may of course be necessary to restructure the MAGTF.

To the greatest extent practicable, Fleet Marine Forces must be organized for warfighting and then adapted for peacetime rather than vice versa. Tables of organization of Fleet Marine Force units should reflect the two central requirements of *deployability* and *the ability to task-organize according to specific situations*. Units should be organized according to type only to the extent dictated by training, administrative, and logistic requirements. Further, we should streamline our headquarters organizations and staffs to eliminate bureaucratic delays in order to add tempo.

Commanders should establish habitual relationships between supported and supporting units to develop operational familiarity among those units. This does not preclude nonstandard relationships when required by the situation.

Doctrine

Doctrine is a teaching advanced as the fundamental beliefs of the Marine Corps on the subject of war, from its nature and theory to its preparation and conduct.[5] Doctrine establishes a particular way of thinking about war and a way of fighting, a philosophy for leading Marines in combat, a mandate for professionalism, and a common language. In short, it establishes the way we practice our profession. In this manner, doctrine provides the basis for harmonious actions and mutual understanding.

Marine Corps doctrine is made official by the Commandant and is established in this manual. Our doctrine does not consist of procedures to be applied in specific situations so much as it establishes general guidance that requires judgment in application. Therefore, while authoritative, doctrine is not prescriptive.

Leadership

Marine Corps doctrine demands professional competence among its leaders. *As military professionals charged with the defense of the nation, Marine leaders must be true experts in the conduct of war.* They must be men of action and of intellect both, skilled at 'getting things done' while at the same time conversant in the military art. Resolute and self-reliant in their decisions, they must also be energetic and insistent in execution.[6]

The military profession is a thinking profession. Officers particularly are expected to be students of the art and science of war at all levels – tactical, operational, and strategic – with a solid foundation in military theory and a knowledge of military history and the timeless lessons to be gained from it.

Leaders must have a strong sense of the great responsibility of their office; the resources they will expend in war are human lives.

The Marine Corps' style of warfare requires intelligent leaders with a penchant for boldness and initiative down to the lowest levels. Boldness is an essential moral trait in a leader, for it generates combat power beyond the physical means at hand.[7] Initiative, the willingness to act on one's own judgment, is a prerequisite for boldness. These traits carried to excess can lead to rashness, but we must realize that errors by junior leaders stemming from overboldness are a necessary part of learning. We should deal with such errors leniently; there must be no 'zero defects' mentality.[8] Not only must we not stifle boldness or initiative, we must continue to encourage both traits *in spite of mistakes.* On the other hand, we should deal severely with errors of inaction or timidity. We will not accept lack of orders as justification for inaction; it is each Marine's *duty* to take initiative as the situation demands.

Consequently, trust is an essential trait among leaders – trust by seniors in the abilities of their subordinates and by juniors in the competence and support of their seniors. Trust must be earned, and actions which undermine trust must meet with strict censure. Trust is a product of confidence and familiarity. Confidence among comrades results from demonstrated professional skill. Familiarity results from shared experience and a common professional philosophy.

Relations among all leaders – from corporal to general – should be based on honesty and frankness, regardless of disparity between grades. Until a commander has reached and stated a decision, each subordinate should consider it his duty to provide his honest, professional opinion – even though it may be in disagreement with his senior's. However, once the decision has been reached, the junior then must support it as if it were his own. Seniors must encourage candor among subordinates and must not hide behind their rank insignia. Ready compliance for the purpose of personal advancement – the behavior of 'yes-men' – will not be tolerated.

Training

The purpose of all training is to develop forces that can win in combat. Training is the key to combat effectiveness and therefore is the focus of effort of a peacetime military. However, training should not stop with the commencement of war; training must continue during war to adapt to the lessons of combat.

All officers and enlisted Marines undergo similar entry-level training which is, in effect, a socialization process. This training provides all Marines a common experience, a proud heritage, a set of values, and a common bond of comradeship. It is the essential first step in the making of a Marine.

Basic individual skills are an essential foundation for combat effectiveness and must receive heavy emphasis. All Marines, regardless of occupational specialty, will be trained in basic combat skills. At the same time, unit skills are extremely important. They are not simply an accumulation of individual skills; adequacy in individual skills does not automatically mean unit skills are satisfactory.

Commanders at each echelon must allot subordinates sufficient time and freedom to conduct the training necessary to achieve proficiency at their levels. They must ensure that higher-level demands do not deny subordinates adequate opportunities for autonomous training and that oversupervision does not prevent subordinate commanders from training their units as they believe appropriate.

In order to develop initiative among junior leaders, the conduct of training – like combat – should be decentralized. Senior commanders influence training by establishing goals and standards, communicating the intent of training, and establishing a focus of effort for training. As a rule, they should refrain from dictating how the training will be accomplished.

Training programs should reflect practical, challenging, and progressive goals beginning with individual and small-unit skills and culminating in a fully combined-arms MAGTF.

In general, the organization for combat should also be the organization for training. That is, units – including MAGTFs – should train with the full complement of assigned, reinforcing, and supporting forces they require in combat.

Collective training consists of drills and exercises. Drills are a form of small-unit training which stress proficiency by progressive repetition of tasks. Drills are an effective method for developing standardized techniques and procedures that must be performed repeatedly without variation to ensure speed and coordination, such as gun drill or immediate actions. In contrast, exercises are designed to train units and individuals in tactics under simulated combat conditions. Exercises should approximate the conditions of battle as much as possible; that is, they should introduce friction in the form of uncertainty, stress, disorder, and opposing wills. This last characteristic is most important; only in opposed, free-play exercises can we practice the art of war. Dictated or 'canned' scenarios eliminate the element of independent, opposing wills that is the essence of combat.

Critiques are an important part of training because critical self-analysis, even after success, is essential to improvement. Their purpose is to draw out the lessons of training. As a result, we should conduct critiques immediately after completing the training, before the memory of the events has faded. Critiques should be held in an atmosphere of open and frank dialogue in which all hands are encouraged to contribute. We learn as much from mistakes as from things done well, so we must be willing to admit and discuss them. Of course, a subordinate's willingness to admit mistakes depends on the commander's willingness to tolerate them. Because we recognize that no two situations in war are the same, our critiques should focus not so much on the actions we took as on why we took those actions and why they brought the results they did.

Professional Military Education

Professional military education is designed to develop creative, thinking leaders. A leader's career, from the initial stages of leadership training, should be viewed as a continuous, progressive process of development. At each stage of his career, he should be preparing for the subsequent stage.

Whether he is an officer or enlisted, the early stages of a leader's career are, in effect, his apprenticeship. While receiving a foundation in professional theory and concepts that will serve him throughout his career, the leader focuses on understanding the requirements and learning and applying the procedures and techniques associated with his field. This is when he learns his trade as an aviator, infantryman, artilleryman, or logistician. As he progresses, the leader should have mastered the requirements of his apprenticeship and should understand the interrelationship of the techniques and procedures within his field. His goal is to become an expert in the tactical level of war.

As an officer continues to develop, he should understand the interrelationship between his field and all the other fields within the Marine Corps. He should be an expert in tactics and techniques and should understand amphibious warfare and combined arms. He should be studying the operational level of war. At the senior levels he should be fully capable of articulating, applying, and integrating MAGTF warfighting capabilities in a joint and combined environment and should be an expert in the art of war at all levels.

The responsibility for implementing professional military education in the Marine Corps is three-tiered: it resides not only with the education establishment, but also with the commander and the individual.

The education establishment consists of those schools – administered by the Marine Corps, subordinate commands, or outside agencies – established to provide formal education in the art and science of war. In all officer education particularly, schools should focus on developing a talent for military judgment, not on imparting knowledge through rote learning. Study conducted by the education establishment can neither provide complete career training for an individual nor reach all individuals. Rather, it builds upon the base provided by commanders and by individual study.

All commanders should consider the professional development of their subordinates a principal responsibility of command. Commanders should foster a personal teacher-student relationship with their subordinates. Commanders are expected to conduct a continuing professional education program for their subordinates which includes developing military judgment and decision making and teaches general professional subjects and specific technical subjects pertinent to occupational specialties. Useful tools for general professional development include supervised reading programs, map exercises, war games, battle studies, and terrain studies. *Commanders should see the development of their subordinates as a direct reflection on themselves.*

Finally, every Marine has a basic responsibility to study the profession of arms on his own. A leader without either interest in or knowledge of the history and theory of warfare – the intellectual content of his profession – is a leader in appearance only. Self-study in the art and science of war is at least equal in importance – and should receive at least equal time – to maintaining physical condition. This is particularly true among officers; after all, an officer's principal weapon is his mind.

Equipping

Equipment should be easy to operate and maintain, reliable, and interoperable with other equipment. It should require minimal specialized operator training. Further, *equipment should be designed so that its usage is consistent with established doctrine and tactics*. Primary considerations are strategic and tactical lift – the Marine Corps' reliance on Navy shipping for strategic mobility and on helicopters and vertical/short takeoff and landing aircraft for tactical mobility from ship to shore and during operations ashore.

Equipment that permits overcontrol of units in battle is in conflict with the Marine Corps' philosophy of command and is not justifiable.

In order to minimize research and development costs and fielding time, the Marine Corps will exploit existing capabilities – 'off-the-shelf' technology – to the greatest extent possible.

Acquisition should be a complementary, two-way process. Especially for the long term, the process must identify combat requirements and develop equipment to satisfy these requirements. We should base these requirements on an analysis of critical enemy vulnerabilities and develop equipment specifically to exploit those vulnerabilities. At the same time, the process should not overlook existing equipment of obvious usefulness.

Equipment is useful only if it increases combat effectiveness. Any piece of equipment requires support: operator training, maintenance, power sources or fuel, and transport. The anticipated enhancement of capabilities must justify these support requirements and the employment of the equipment must take these requirements into account.

As much as possible, employment techniques and procedures should be developed concurrently with equipment to minimize delays between the fielding of the equipment and its usefulness to the operating forces. For the same reason, initial operator training should also precede equipment fielding.

We must guard against overreliance on technology.[9] Technology can enhance the ways and means of war by improving man's ability to wage it, but technology cannot and should not attempt to eliminate man from the process of waging war. Better equipment is not the cure for all ills; doctrinal and tactical solutions to combat deficiencies must also be sought. Any advantages gained by technological advancement are only temporary, for man will always find a countermeasure, tactical or itself technological, which will lessen the impact of the technology. Additionally, we must not become so dependent on equipment that we can no longer function effectively when the equipment becomes inoperable.

Conclusion

There are two basic military functions: waging war and preparing for war. Any military activities that do not contribute to the conduct of a present war are justifiable only if they contribute to preparedness for a possible future one. But, clearly, we cannot afford to separate conduct and preparation. They must be intimately related because failure in preparation leads to disaster on the battlefield.

NOTES

1. Hans von Seekt, *Thoughts of a Soldier*, trans. G. Waterhouse (London: Ernest Benn Ltd., 1930) p. 123.
2. Erwin Rommel, *The Rommel Papers*, ed. B.H. Liddell Hart, trans. P. Findlay (New York: Da Capo Press, Inc., 1985) p. 226.
3. George S. Patton, Jr., *Cavalry Journal*, April 1922, p. 167.
4. JCS Pub. 1-02: '**Campaign Plan** – (*DOD, IADB*) A plan for a series of related military operations aimed to accomplish a common objective, normally within a given time and space.' As defined, a campaign plan pertains to military operations, but the thought applies equally to preparations.
5. JCS Pub. 1-02: '**Doctrine** – (*DOD, IADB*) Fundamental principles by which the military forces or elements thereof guide their actions in support of national objectives. It is authoritative but requires judgment in application.'
6. Field Manual 100-5, *Tentative Field Service Regulations* (Washington: Government Printing Office, 1939) p. 31.

7. *Napoleon is reported to have said that to lose a battle is pardonable but to lose time is unforgivable. Boldness and timing must go together. H.T.H.*

8. Clausewitz: 'In a commander a bold act may prove to be a blunder. Nevertheless it is a laudable error, not to be regarded on the same footing as others. Happy the army where ill-timed boldness occurs frequently; it is a luxuriant weed, but indicates the richness of the soil. Even foolhardiness – that is, boldness without object – is not to be despised: basically it stems from daring, which in this case has erupted with a passion unrestrained by thought. Only when boldness rebels against obedience, when it defiantly ignores an expressed command, must it be treated as a dangerous offense; then it must be prevented, not for its innate qualities, but because an order has been disobeyed, and in war obedience is of cardinal importance.' *On War*, pp. 190–191.

9. *No statement could more truly illustrate 'triumph without victory' in the Gulf War. H.T.H.*

CHAPTER 4

The Conduct of War

'Now an army may be likened to water, for just as flowing water avoids the heights and hastens to the lowlands, so an army avoids strength and strikes weakness.'[1]

— Sun Tzu

'Speed is the essence of war. Take advantage of the enemy's unpreparedness; travel by unexpected routes and strike him where he has taken no precautions.'[2]

— Sun Tzu

'Many years ago, as a cadet hoping some day to be an officer, I was poring over the "Principles of War," listed in the old Field Service Regulations, when the Sergeant-Major came up to me. He surveyed me with kindly amusement. "Don't bother your head about all them things, me lad," he said. "There's only one principle of war and that's this. Hit the other fellow, as quick as you can, and as hard as you can, where it hurts him most, when he ain't lookin'!"'[3]

— Sir William Slim

The sole justification for the United States Marine Corps is to secure or protect national policy objectives by military force when peaceful means alone cannot. How the Marine Corps proposes to accomplish this mission is the product of our understanding of the nature and the theory of war and must be the guiding force behind our preparation for war.

The Challenge

The challenge is to identify and adopt a concept of warfighting consistent with our understanding of the nature and theory of war and the realities of the modern battlefield. What exactly does this require? It requires a concept of warfighting that will function effectively in an uncertain, chaotic, and fluid environment – in fact, one that will exploit these conditions to advantage. It requires a concept that, recognizing the time-competitive rhythm of war, generates and exploits superior tempo and velocity. It requires a concept that is consistently effective across the full spectrum of conflict, because we cannot attempt to change our basic doctrine from situation to situation and expect to

66

be proficient. It requires a concept which recognizes and exploits the fleeting opportunities which naturally occur in war. It requires a concept which takes into account the moral as well as the physical forces of war, because we have already concluded that moral forces form the greater part of war. It requires a concept with which we can succeed against a numerically superior foe, because we can no longer presume a numerical advantage. And, especially in expeditionary situations in which public support for military action may be tepid and short-lived, it requires a concept with which we can win quickly against a larger foe on his home soil, with minimal casualties and limited external support.

Maneuver Warfare

The Marine Corps concept for winning under these conditions is a warfighting doctrine based on rapid, flexible, and opportunistic maneuver. But in order to fully appreciate what we mean by *maneuver* we need to clarify the term. The traditional understanding of maneuver is a spatial one; that is, we maneuver in space to gain a positional advantage.[4] However, in order to maximize the usefulness of maneuver, we must consider maneuver *in time* as well; that is, we generate a faster operational tempo than the enemy to gain a temporal advantage. It is through maneuver in *both* dimensions that an inferior force can achieve decisive superiority at the necessary time and place.

> Maneuver warfare is a warfighting philosophy that seeks to shatter the enemy's cohesion through a series of rapid, violent, and unexpected actions which create a turbulent and rapidly deteriorating situation with which he cannot cope.

From this definition we see that the aim in maneuver warfare is to render the enemy incapable of resisting by shattering his moral and physical cohesion – his ability to fight as an effective, coordinated whole – rather than to destroy him physically through incremental attrition, which is generally more costly and time-consuming. Ideally, the components of his physical strength that remain are irrelevant because we have paralyzed his ability to use them effectively. Even if an outmaneuvered enemy continues to fight as individuals or small units, we can destroy the remnants with relative ease because we have eliminated his ability to fight effectively as a force.

This is not to imply that firepower is unimportant. On the contrary, the suppressive effects of firepower are essential to our ability to maneuver. Nor do we mean to imply that we will pass up the opportunity to physically destroy the enemy. We will concentrate fires and forces at decisive points to destroy enemy elements when the opportunity presents itself and when it fits our larger purposes. But the aim is not an unfocused application of firepower for the purpose of incrementally reducing the enemy's physical strength. Rather, it is the *selective* application of firepower in support of maneuver to contribute to the enemy's shock and moral disruption. The greatest value of firepower is not physical destruction – the cumulative effects of which are felt only slowly – but the moral dislocation it causes.

If the aim of maneuver warfare is to shatter the enemy's cohesion, the immediate object toward that end is to create a situation in which he cannot function. By our actions, we seek to pose menacing dilemmas in which events happen unexpectedly and faster than the enemy can keep up with them. The enemy must be made to see his situation not only as deteriorating, but deteriorating at an ever-increasing rate. The ultimate goal is panic and paralysis, an enemy who has lost the ability to resist.

Inherent in maneuver warfare is the need for speed to seize the initiative, dictate the terms of combat, and keep the enemy off balance, thereby increasing his friction. Through the use of greater tempo and velocity, we seek to establish a pace that the enemy cannot maintain so that with each action his reactions are increasingly late – until eventually he is overcome by events.

Also inherent is the need for violence, not so much as a source of physical attrition but as a source of moral dislocation. Toward this end, we concentrate strength against *critical* enemy vulnerabilities, striking quickly and boldly where, when, and how it will cause the greatest damage to our enemy's ability to fight. Once gained or found, any advantage must be pressed relentlessly and unhesitatingly. We must be ruthlessly opportunistic, actively seeking out signs of weakness, against which we will direct all available combat power. And when the *decisive* opportunity arrives, we must exploit it fully and aggressively, committing every ounce of combat power we can muster and pushing ourselves to the limits of exhaustion.

The final weapon in our arsenal is surprise, the combat value of which we have already recognized. By studying our enemy we will attempt to appreciate his perceptions. Through deception we will try to shape his expectations. Then we will dislocate them by striking at an unexpected time and place. In order to appear unpredictable, we must avoid set rules and patterns, which inhibit imagination and initiative. In order to appear ambiguous and threatening, we should operate on axes that offer several courses of action, keeping the enemy unclear as to which we will choose.

Philosophy of Command

It is essential that our philosophy of command support the way we fight. First and foremost, *in order to generate the tempo of operations we desire and to best cope with the uncertainty, disorder, and fluidity of combat, command must be decentralized.* That is, subordinate commanders must make decisions on their own initiative, based on their understanding of their senior's intent, rather than passing information up the chain of command and waiting for the decision to be passed down. Further, a competent subordinate commander who is at the point of decision will naturally have a better appreciation for the true situation than a senior some distance removed. Individual initiative and responsibility are of paramount importance. The principal means by which we implement decentralized control is through the use of mission tactics, which we will discuss in detail later.

Second, since we have concluded that war is a human enterprise and no amount of technology can reduce the human dimension, our philosophy of command must be based on human characteristics rather than on equipment or procedures. Communications equipment and command and staff procedures can enhance our ability to command, but they must not be used to replace the human element of command. Our philosophy must not only accommodate but must exploit human traits such as boldness, initiative, personality, strength of will, and imagination.

Our philosophy of command must also exploit the human ability to communicate *implicitly*.[5] We believe that *implicit communication* – to communicate through *mutual understanding*, using a minimum of key, well-understood phrases or even anticipating each other's thoughts – is a faster, more effective way to communicate than through the use of detailed, explicit instructions. We develop this ability through familiarity and trust, which are based on a shared philosophy and shared experience.

This concept has several practical implications. First, we should establish long-term working relationships to develop the necessary familiarity and trust. Second, key people – 'actuals' – should talk directly to one another when possible, rather than through communicators or messengers. Third, we should communicate orally when possible, because we communicate also in *how* we talk; our inflections and tone of voice. And fourth, we should communicate in person when possible, because we communicate also through our gestures and bearing.

A commander should command from well forward. This allows him to see and sense firsthand the ebb and flow of combat, to gain an intuitive appreciation for the situation which he cannot obtain from reports. It allows him to exert his personal influence at decisive points during the action. It also allows him to locate himself closer to the events that will influence the situation so that he can observe them directly and circumvent the delays and inaccuracies that result from passing information up the chain of command. Finally, we recognize the importance of personal leadership. Only by his physical presence – by demonstrating the willingness to share danger and privation – can the commander fully gain the trust and confidence of his subordinates.

We must remember that command from the front does not equate to oversupervision of subordinates.

As part of our philosophy of command we must recognize that war is inherently disorderly, uncertain, dynamic, and dominated by friction. Moreover, maneuver warfare, with its emphasis on speed and initiative, is by nature a particularly disorderly style of war. The conditions ripe for exploitation are normally also very disorderly. For commanders to try to gain certainty as a basis for actions, maintain positive control of events at all times, or shape events to fit their plans is to deny the very nature of war. We must therefore be prepared to cope – even better, to *thrive* – in an environment of chaos, uncertainty, constant change, and friction. If we can come to terms with those conditions and thereby limit their debilitating effects, we can use them as a weapon against a foe who does not cope as well.

In practical terms this means that we must not strive for certainty before we act for in so doing we will surrender the initiative and pass up opportunities. We must not try to maintain positive control over subordinates since this will necessarily slow our tempo and inhibit initiative. We must not attempt to impose precise order to the events of combat since this leads to a formulistic approach to war. And we must be prepared to adapt to changing circumstances and exploit opportunities as they arise, rather than adhering insistently to predetermined plans.

There are several points worth remembering about our command philosophy. First, while it is based on our warfighting style, this does not mean it applies only during war. We must put it into practice during the preparation for war as well.[6] We cannot rightly expect our subordinates to exercise boldness and initiative in the field when they are accustomed to being oversupervised in the rear. Whether the mission is training, procuring equipment, administration, or police call, this philosophy should apply.

Next, our philosophy requires competent leadership at all levels. A centralized system theoretically needs only one competent person, the senior commander, since his is the sole authority. But a decentralized system requires leaders at all levels to demonstrate sound and timely judgment. As a result, initiative becomes an essential condition of competence among commanders.

Our philosophy also requires familiarity among comrades because only through a shared understanding can we develop the implicit communication necessary for unity of effort. And, perhaps most important, our philosophy demands confidence among seniors and subordinates.

Shaping the Battle

Since our goal is not just the cumulative attrition of enemy strength, it follows that we must have some scheme for how we expect to achieve victory. That is, before anything else, we must conceive our vision of how we intend to win.

The first requirement is to establish our intent; what we want to accomplish and how. Without a clearly identified intent, the necessary unity of effort is inconceivable. We must identify that *critical* enemy vulnerability which we believe will lead most directly to accomplishing our intent.[7] Having done this, we can then determine the steps necessary to achieve our intent. That is, we must shape the battle to our advantage in terms of both time and space. Similarly, we must try to see ourselves through our enemy's eyes in order to identify our own vulnerabilities which he may attack and to anticipate how he will try to shape the battle so we can counteract him. Ideally, when the moment of engagement arrives, the issue has already been resolved: through our orchestration of the events leading up to the encounter, we have so shaped the conditions of war that the result is a matter of course. We have shaped the action decisively to our advantage.

To shape the battle, we must project our thoughts forward in time and space. This does not mean that we establish a detailed timetable of events. We have already concluded that war is inherently disorderly, and we cannot expect to shape its terms with any sort of precision. We must not become slaves to a plan. Rather, we attempt to shape the *general conditions* of war; we try to achieve a certain measure of ordered disorder. Examples include canalizing enemy movement in a desired direction, blocking or delaying enemy reinforcements so that we can fight a piecemealed enemy rather than a concentrated one, shaping enemy expectations through deception so that we can exploit those expectations, or attacking a specific enemy capability to allow us to maximize a capability of our own – such as launching a campaign to destroy his air defenses so that we can maximize the use of our own aviation. We should also try to shape events in such a way that allows us several options so that by the time the moment of encounter arrives we have not restricted ourselves to only one course of action.

The further ahead we think, the less our actual influence becomes. Therefore, the further ahead we consider, the less precision we should attempt to impose. Looking ahead thus becomes less a matter of influence and more a matter of interest. As events approach and our ability to influence them grows, we have already developed an appreciation for the situation and how we want to shape it.[8]

Also, the higher our echelon of command, the greater is our sphere of influence and the further ahead in time and space we must seek to impose our will. Senior commanders developing and pursuing military strategy look ahead weeks, months, or more, and their areas of influence and interest will encompass entire theaters. Junior commanders fighting the battles and engagements at hand are concerned with the coming hours, even minutes, and the immediate field of battle. But regardless of the spheres of influence and interest, it is essential to have some vision of the final result we want and how we intend to shape the action in time and space to achieve it.

Decision Making

Decision making is essential to the conduct of war since all actions are the result of decisions – or of nondecisions.[9] If we fail to make a decision out of lack of will, we have willingly surrendered the initiative to our foe. If we consciously postpone taking action for some reason, that is a decision. Thus, as a basis for action, any decision is generally better than no decision.

Since war is a conflict between opposing wills, we cannot make decisions in a vacuum. We must make our decisions in light of the enemy's anticipated reactions and counteractions, recognizing that while we are trying to impose our will on our enemy, he is trying to do the same to us.

Whoever can make and implement his decisions consistently faster gains a tremendous, often decisive advantage. Decision making thus becomes a time-competitive process, and timeliness of decisions becomes essential to generating tempo. Timely decisions demand rapid thinking, with consideration limited to essential factors. We should spare no effort to accelerate our decision-making ability.

A military decision is not merely a mathematical computation. Decision making requires both the intuitive skill to recognize and analyze the essence of a given problem and the creative ability to devise a practical solution. This ability is the product of experience, education, intelligence, boldness, perception, and character.

We should base our decisions on *awareness* rather than on mechanical *habit*. That is, we act on a keen appreciation for the essential factors that make each situation unique instead of from conditioned response.

We must have the moral courage to make tough decisions in the face of uncertainty – and accept full responsibility for those decisions – when the natural inclination would be to postpone the decision pending more complete information. To delay action in an emergency because of incomplete information shows a lack of moral courage. We do not want to make rash decisions, but we must not squander opportunities while trying to gain more information.

We must have the moral courage to make bold decisions and accept the necessary degree of risk when the natural inclination is to choose a less ambitious tack, for 'in audacity and obstinacy will be found safety.'[10]

Finally, since all decisions must be made in the face of uncertainty and since every situation is unique, there is no perfect solution to any battlefield problem. Therefore, we should not agonize over one. The essence of the problem is to select a promising course of action with an acceptable degree of risk, and to do it more quickly than our foe. In this respect, 'a good plan violently executed *now* is better than a perfect plan executed next week.'[11]

Mission Tactics

Having described the object and means of maneuver warfare and its philosophy of command, we will next discuss how we put maneuver warfare into practice. First is through the use of mission tactics. Mission tactics are just as the name implies: the tactic of assigning a subordinate mission without specifying how the mission must be accomplished.[12] We leave the manner of accomplishing the mission to the subordinate, thereby allowing him the freedom — and establishing the duty — to take whatever steps he deems necessary based on the situation. The senior prescribes the method of execution only to the degree that is essential for coordination. It is this freedom for initiative that permits the high tempo of operations that we desire. Uninhibited by restrictions from above, the subordinate can adapt his actions to the changing situation. He informs his commander what he has done, but he does not wait for permission.

It is obvious that we cannot allow decentralized initiative without some means of providing unity, or focus, to the various efforts. To do so would be to dissipate our strength. We seek unity, not through imposed control, but through *harmonious* initiative and lateral coordination.

Commander's Intent

We achieve this harmonious initiative in large part through the use of the commander's *intent*. There are two parts to a mission: the task to be accomplished and the reason, or intent.[13] The task describes the action to be taken while the intent describes the desired result of the action. Of the two, the intent is predominant. While a situation may change, making the task obsolete, the intent is more permanent and continues to guide our actions. Understanding our commander's intent allows us to exercise initiative in harmony with the commander's desires.

In order to maintain our focus on the enemy, we should try to express intent in terms of the enemy. The intent should answer the question: *What do I want to do to the enemy?* This may not be possible in all cases, but it is true in the vast majority. The intent should convey the commander's *vision*. It is not satisfactory for the intent to be 'to defeat the enemy.' To win is always our ultimate goal, so an intent like this conveys nothing.

From this discussion, it is obvious that a clear explanation and understanding of intent is absolutely essential to unity of effort. It should be a part of any mission. The burden of understanding falls on senior and subordinate alike. The senior must make perfectly clear the result he expects, but in such a way that does not inhibit initiative. Subordinates must have a clear understanding of what their commander is thinking. Further, they should understand the intent of the commander two levels up. In other words, a platoon commander should know the intent of his battalion commander, or a battalion commander the intent of his division commander.

Focus of Effort

Another tool for providing unity is through the *focus of effort*. Of all the efforts going on within our command, we recognize the focus of effort as the most critical to success. All other efforts must support it. In effect, we have decided: *This is how I will achieve a decision; everything else is secondary*.

We cannot take lightly the decision of where and when to focus our efforts. Since the focus of effort represents our bid for victory, we must direct it at that object which will cause the most decisive damage to the enemy and which holds the best opportunity of success. It involves a physical and moral commitment, although not an irretrievable one. It forces us to concentrate decisive combat power just as it forces us to accept risk. Thus, we focus our effort against *critical enemy vulnerability*, exercising strict economy elsewhere.

Normally, we designate the focus of effort by assigning one unit responsibility for accomplishing that effort. That unit becomes the representation of the focus of effort. It becomes clear to all other units in the command that they must support that unit in its efforts. Like the commander's intent, the focus of effort becomes a harmonizing force. Faced with a decision, we ask ourselves: 'How can I best support the focus of effort?'

Each commander should establish a focus of effort for each mission. As the situation changes, the commander may shift the focus of effort, redirecting the weight of his combat power in the direction that offers the greatest success. In this way he exploits success; he does not reinforce failure.

Surfaces and Gaps

Put simply, surfaces are hard spots – enemy strengths – and gaps are soft spots – enemy weaknesses. We avoid enemy strength and focus our efforts against enemy weakness, since pitting strength against weakness reduces casualties and is more likely to yield decisive results. Whenever possible, we exploit existing gaps. Failing that, we create gaps.

Gaps may in fact be physical gaps in the enemy's dispositions, but they may also be any weakness in time or space: a moment in time when the enemy is overexposed and vulnerable, a seam in an air defense umbrella, an infantry unit caught unprepared in open terrain, or a boundary between two units.

Similarly, a surface may be an actual strongpoint, or it may be any enemy strength: a moment when the enemy has just replenished and consolidated his position or an integrated air defense system.

An appreciation for surfaces and gaps requires a certain amount of judgment. What is a surface in one case may be a gap in another. For example, a forest which is a surface to an armored unit because it restricts vehicle movement can be a gap to an infantry unit which can infiltrate through it. Furthermore, we can expect the enemy to disguise his dispositions in order to lure us against a surface that appears to be a gap.[14]

Due to the fluid nature of war, gaps will rarely be permanent and will usually be fleeting. To exploit them demands flexibility and speed. We must actively seek out gaps by continuous and aggressive reconnaissance. Once we locate them, we must exploit them by funneling our forces through rapidly. For example, if our focus of effort has struck a surface but another unit has located a gap, we shift the focus of effort to the second unit and redirect our combat power in support of it. In this manner we 'pull' combat power through gaps from the front rather than 'pushing' it through from the rear.[15] Commanders must rely on the initiative of subordinates to locate the gaps and must have the flexibility to respond quickly to opportunities rather than following pre-determined schemes.

Combined Arms

In order to maximize combat power, we must use all the available resources to best advantage. To do so, we must follow a doctrine of combined arms. Combined arms is the full integration of arms in such a way that in order to counteract one, the enemy must make himself more vulnerable to another. We pose the enemy not just with a problem, but with a dilemma – a no-win situation.

We accomplish combined arms through the tactics and techniques we use at the lower levels and through task organization at higher levels. In so doing, we take advantage of the complementary characteristics of different types of units and enhance our mobility and firepower. We use each arm for missions that no other arm can perform as well; for example, we assign aviation a task that cannot be performed equally well by artillery. An example of the concept of combined arms at the very lowest level is the complementary use of the automatic weapon and grenade launcher within a fire team. We pin an enemy down with the high-volume, direct fire of the automatic weapon, making him a vulnerable target for the grenade launcher. If he moves to escape the impact of the grenades, we engage him with the automatic weapon.

We can expand the example to the MAGTF level: We use assault support to quickly concentrate superior ground forces for a breakthrough. We use artillery and close air support to support the infantry penetration, and we use deep air support to interdict enemy reinforcements. Targets which cannot be effectively suppressed by artillery are engaged by close air support. In order to defend against the infantry attack, the enemy must make himself vulnerable to the supporting arms. If he seeks cover from the supporting arms, our infantry can maneuver against him. In order to block our penetration, the enemy must reinforce quickly with his reserve. But in order to avoid our deep air support, he must stay off the roads, which means he can only move slowly. If he moves slowly, he cannot reinforce in time to prevent our breakthrough. We have put him in a dilemma.

Conclusion

We have discussed the aim and characteristics of maneuver warfare. We have discussed the philosophy of command necessary to support this style of warfare. And we have discussed some of the tactics of maneuver warfare. By this time it should be clear that maneuver warfare exists not so much in the specific methods used – we eschew formulas – but in the mind of the Marine. In this regard, maneuver warfare – like combined arms – applies equally to the Marine expeditionary force commander and the fire team leader. It applies regardless of the nature of the conflict, whether amphibious operations or sustained operations ashore, of low or high intensity, against guerrilla or mechanized foe, in desert or jungle.

Maneuver warfare is a way of thinking in and about war that should shape our every action. It is a state of mind born of a bold will, intellect, initiative, and ruthless opportunism. It is a state of mind bent on shattering the enemy morally and physically by paralyzing and confounding him, by avoiding his strength, by quickly and aggressively exploiting his vulnerabilities, and by striking him in the way that will hurt him most. In short, maneuver warfare is a philosophy for generating the greatest decisive effect against the enemy at the least possible cost to ourselves – a philosophy for 'fighting smart.'[16]

NOTES

1. Sun Tzu, *The Art of War*, p. 101.
2. *Ibid.*, p. 134.
3. Sir William Slim, *Defeat into Victory* (London: Cassell and Co. Ltd., 1956) pp. 550–551.
4. JCS Pub. 1-02: '**Maneuver** – (*DOD, NATO*) . . . 4. Employment of forces on the battlefield through movement in combination with fire, or fire potential, to achieve a position of advantage in respect to the enemy in order to accomplish the mission.'
5. Boyd introduces the idea of implicit communication as a command tool in his lecture, 'An Organic Design for Command and Control.'
6. *We must also put it into practice in 'operations other than war' or low intensity conflicts. H.T.H.*
7. *There is one more step in clearly establishing a commander's 'intent.' It is not only what we want to accomplish and why but it is also what we want to do after . . . Major General P.K. Van Riper put it best when he said that you state the commander's intent and add '. . . in order to:' It is not enough to just attack. The Confederates won the field on the first day of the Battle of Shiloh, but then they paused for lack of a field commander (General A.S. Johnson had died) and lost the campaign the following day. Again the Confederates won a great victory at Chickamauga but failed to follow-up and take Chattanooga. Marshal Ney and Marshal Grouchy lost the Battle of Waterloo for Napoleon before the Emperor ever confronted the Duke of Wellington on the field of Waterloo. H.T.H.*
8. Hence the terms *area of influence* and *area of interest*. JCS Pub. 1-02: '**Area of Influence** – (*DOD, NATO*) A geographical area wherein a commander is directly capable of influencing operations, by maneuver or fire support systems normally

under his command or control.' '**Area of Interest** – (*DOD, NATO, IADB*) That area of concern to the commander, including the area of influence, areas adjacent thereto, and extending into enemy territory to the objectives of current or planned operations. This area also includes areas occupied by enemy forces who could jeopardize the accomplishment of the mission.'

9. Much of the material in this section is adapted from John F. Schmitt's article, 'Observations on Decisionmaking in Battle,' *Marine Corps Gazette*, March 1988, pp. 18–20.

    Teaching a 'decision making process,' like the OODA Loop, is the first step in teaching 'decision making.' Some people make the same mistakes all their life and call it experience. It is not enough to 'have the courage to make tough decisions.' If you are caught unawares it does no good to say 'I made the best decision I could.' You have to learn a process that helps you make the best decision. There is seldom only one right decision. H.T.H.

10. Napoleon Bonaparte, 'Maxims of War,' *Napoleon and Modern War; His Military Maxims*, annotated C.H. Lanza (Harrisonburg, PA: Military Service Publishing Co., 1953) p. 19.

11. George S. Patton, Jr., *War As I Knew It* (New York: Houghton Mifflin, 1979) p. 354.

12. JCS Pub. 1-02: '**Mission Type Order** – (*DOD, IADB*) . . . 2. Order to a unit to perform a mission without specifying how it is to be accomplished.'

13. JCS Pub. 1-02: '**Mission** – (*DOD, IADB*) 1. The task, together with the purpose, which clearly indicates the action to be taken and the reason therefor.'

14. The well known Soviet *fire-sack* defense, for example.

15. Hence the terms *reconnaissance pull* and *command push* respectively. See William S. Lind's *Maneuver Warfare Handbook* (Boulder, CO: Westview Press, 1985) pp. 18–19.

16. *There are some men who will never be comfortable with maneuver warfare. Some people like a structured life. They learn it from birth. Maneuver warfare theory and doctrine will only be fully grasped by a certain personality – aggressive, independent, intuitive, curious, intellectual, and a man who knows that you go for the kill . . . it is not a game. The ancient Greek mothers had a caution for their sons before they left for battle: Come back carrying your shield high or come back on it (the dead were carried from the field on their shields). Today I do not think that western society breeds many such men. H.T.H.*

FMFM 1-1 Campaigning

Book Two reproduces, in a new setting, the complete and unabridged original text and notes of FMFM 1-1 *Campaigning*, first published January 1990 by the Department of the Navy, Headquarters United States Marine Corps, Washington D.C.

New, additional notes by Lt. Col. H.T. Hayden are set in italics.

As used in this book, the terms 'operations' and 'operational' refer specifically to the operational level of war and not to military actions in the general sense.

Foreword

Tactical success in combat is not enough, because tactical success of itself does not guarantee victory in war. History has proved this. What matters ultimately in war is success at the level of strategy, the level directly concerned with attaining the aims of policy. That these two levels of war are connected and that there is an art to the way tactical results are used to advance the strategic purpose are beyond doubt. With this thought as its point of departure, *this book discusses this intermediate operational level which links strategy and tactics, describing the military campaign as the primary tool of operational warfare.*

This book, *Campaigning*, thus establishes the authoritative doctrinal basis for military campaigning in the Marine Corps, particularly as it pertains to a Marine Air-Ground Task Force (MAGTF) conducting a campaign or contributing to a campaign by a higher authority. *Campaigning* is designed to be in consonance with FMFM 1, *Warfighting*, and presumes understanding of the philosophy described therein. In fact, *Campaigning* applies this warfighting philosophy specifically to the operational level of war. Like FMFM 1, this book is descriptive rather than prescriptive in nature; it requires judgment in application.

Chapter 1 provides a conceptual discussion of the campaign and the operational level of war, their relationship to strategy and tactics, and their relevance to the Marine Corps. In many situations, the MAGTF clearly has operational – vice merely tactical – capabilities; therefore it is essential that Marine leaders learn to think operationally. Chapter 2 describes the considerations and the mental process for developing a campaign. *This mental process, and the strategic vision it derives from, are essential to success at the operational level.* Chapter 3 discusses the operational considerations vital to conducting a campaign, examining in detail the differences between tactical and operational activities.

Central to this book is the idea that military action, at any level, must ultimately serve the demands of policy. Marine leaders at all levels must understand this point and must realize that tactical success does not exist for its own sake. The importance of this understanding is particularly evident in conflicts at the low end of the intensity spectrum – the revolutionary warfare environment – where military force is not the dominant characteristic of the struggle but is only one of several components of national power, all of which must be fully coordinated with one another. *In a campaign Marine leaders must therefore be able to integrate military operations with the other elements of national power in all types of conflict.*

This book makes frequent use of familiar historical examples to put its concepts into concrete terms. *But do not be deceived into thinking this is a history book with little relevance to the challenges facing today's Marine Corps.* These are classical examples intended to illustrate principles with enduring and universal application. Many future crises will be 'short-fuzed' and of limited duration and scale. *But make no mistake; no matter what the size and nature of the next mission — whether it be general war, crisis response, peacekeeping, nation building, counter-insurgency, counterterrorism, or counternarcotics operations — the concepts and the thought process described in this book will apply.*

This manual is designed primarily for MAGTF commanders and their staffs and for officers serving on joint and combined staffs. However, the method described here for devising and executing a progressive series of actions in pursuit of a distant objective in the face of hostile resistance and the broad vision that this demands apply equally to commanders at all levels. *Therefore, as with FMFM 1, I expect all officers to read and reread this book, understand its message, and apply it. Duty demands nothing less.*

A.M. GRAY
General, U.S. Marine Corps
Commandant of the Marine Corps

CHAPTER 1

The Campaign

'Battles have been stated by some writers to be the chief and deciding features of war. This assertion is not strictly true, as armies have been destroyed by strategic operations without the occurrence of pitched battles, by a succession of inconsiderable affairs.'[1]

— Baron Henri Jomini

'For even if a decisive battle be the goal, the aim of strategy must be to bring about this battle under the most advantageous circumstances. And the more advantageous the circumstances, the less, proportionately, will be the fighting. The perfection of strategy would be, therefore, to produce a decision without any serious fighting.'[2]

— B.H. Liddell Hart

'It is essential to relate what is strategically desirable to what is tactically possible with the forces at your disposal. To this end it is necessary to decide the development of operations before the initial blow is delivered.'[3]

— Field-Marshal Bernard Montgomery

This book is about military campaigning. A campaign is a series of related military actions undertaken over a period of time to achieve a specific objective within a given region. Campaigning reflects the operational level of war, at which the results of individual tactical actions are combined to fulfill the needs of strategy.

In this chapter we will describe how events at different levels of war interact, focusing on the operational level as the link between strategy and tactics. We will examine the campaign as the basic tool of commanders at the operational level, and we will discuss its relevance to the Marine Corps.

Strategy

Civil policy creates and directs war. Thus, Liddell Hart wrote, 'any study of the problem ought to begin and end with the question of policy.'[4] The activity that strives directly to attain the objectives of policy, in peace as in war, is strategy. At the highest level, the realm of grand strategy,[5] this involves applying and coordinating all the elements of national power — economic, diplomatic, psychological, technological, military. Military strategy is the applied or threatened use of military force to impose policy.[6] Military strategy must be subordinate to grand strategy and should be coordinated with the use of the other elements of national power, although historically neither has always been so. U.S. military strategy is applied regionally by the unified commanders in chief of the various theaters of war. Military strategy will likely be combined strategy, the product of a coalition with allies.

In war, military strategy involves the establishment of military strategic objectives, the allocation of resources, the imposition of conditions on the use of force, and the development of war plans. We can describe military strategy as the discipline of winning wars. The means of military strategy are the components of military power. Its ways are the strategic concepts[7] devised for the accomplishment of its end, the policy objective.

Military strategy is the province of national policymakers, their military advisors, and the nation's senior military leadership – seemingly far beyond the professional concern of most Marines.

Tactics

Marines are generally most familiar and comfortable with the tactical realm of war, which is concerned with defeating an enemy force at a specific time and place.[8] The tactical level of war is the world of combat. The means of tactics are the various components of combat power at our disposal. Its ways are the concepts by which we apply that combat power against our adversary. These are sometimes themselves called tactics – in our case, tactics founded on maneuver. Its end is victory: defeating the enemy force opposing us. In this respect, we can view tactics as the discipline of winning battles and engagements.

The tactical level of war includes the maneuver of forces in contact with the enemy to gain a fighting advantage, the application and coordination of fires, the sustainment of forces throughout combat, the immediate exploitation of success to seal the victory, the combination of different arms and weapons, the gathering and dissemination of pertinent combat information, and the technical application of combat power within a tactical action – all to cause the enemy's defeat. Although the events of combat form a continuous fabric of activity, each tactical action, large or small, can generally be seen as a distinct episode contested over a limited field of battle and span of time.

Tactical success of itself does not guarantee victory in war. In modern times, the result of a single battle is seldom sufficient to achieve strategic victory, as it often was in Napoleon's time. In fact, a single battle alone can rarely resolve the outcome of a campaign, much less an entire war. One example in which a single tactical victory did end a campaign ironically demonstrates that tactical victory does not necessarily even result in strategic advantage. Robert E. Lee's costly tactical victory at Antietam in 1862 was an operational defeat in that it compelled him to abort his offensive campaign into the North. Even a succession of tactical victories, taken together, often does not ensure strategic victory, the obvious example being the American experience in the war in Vietnam. Thus, we must recognize that *to defeat the enemy in combat cannot be an end in itself, but rather must be viewed as a means to a larger end.*

Operations

It follows that there exists a discipline of the military art above and distinct from the realm of tactics but subordinate to the lofty domain of strategy. This discipline is called operations (or the operational level of war), and it is the link between strategy and tactics.[9] The aim at this level is to give meaning to tactical actions in the context of some larger design, which itself ultimately is framed by strategy. Put another way, the aim is to get strategically meaningful results through tactics.

The operational level of war thus consists of the discipline of conceiving, focusing, and exploiting a variety of tactical actions to realize a strategic aim. In its essence, the operational level involves deciding when, where, for what purpose, and under what conditions to give battle – and to refuse battle as well – with reference to the strategic design. It governs the deployment of forces, their commitment to or withdrawal from combat, and the sequencing of successive tactical actions to achieve strategic objectives.[10]

The nature of these tasks implies that the commander has a certain amount of latitude in the conception and execution of plans. 'The basic concept of a campaign plan should be born in the mind of the man who has to direct that campaign.'[11] If execution is prescribed by higher authority, he is merely the tactical executant, as in the case of Air Force and Navy forces conducting the 1986 air strike against Libya.

The basic tool by which the operational commander translates tactical actions into strategic results is the campaign. Thus as strategy is the discipline of making war, and tactics is the discipline of fighting and winning in combat, we can describe the operational level of war as the discipline of campaigning. Its means are tactical results – be they victories, losses, or draws. Its end is the accomplishment of the established strategic aim. Its ways are the schemes by which we combine and sequence the tactical means to reach the strategic end.

Strategic-Operational Connection

Strategy must be clearly understood to determine the conduct of all military actions. But we must understand as well that the strategy-operations connection is a two-way interface. Just as strategy shapes the design of the campaign, so must strategy adapt to operational circumstances. Failure to adapt results in a strategy that is ignorant of operational reality, such as Napoleon's ill-fated war of 1812 against Russia, in which 'the problems of space, time and distance proved too great for even one of the greatest military minds that has ever existed.'[12]

Strategy guides operations in three basic ways: it establishes aims, allocates resources, and imposes conditions on military action.[13] Together with the enemy and the geography of the theater or area, strategic guidance defines the parameters of operations.[14]

First, strategy translates policy objectives into military terms by establishing military strategic aims. It is important to keep in mind that these aims will likely be but one component of a broader grand strategy. The overriding criterion for the conduct of a campaign is the reference, direct or derivative, to the strategic aim. The operational commander's principal task is to determine and pursue the sequence of actions that will most directly serve that aim.[15]

Strategists must be prepared to modify aims as they reevaluate costs, capabilities, and expectations. When strategic aims are unreasonable, the operational commander must so state. When they are unclear, he must seek clarification. While required to pursue the established aim, he is obliged to communicate the associated risks.[16]

Second, strategy provides resources, both tangible resources such as material and personnel and intangible resources such as political and public support for military operations.[17] When resources are insufficient, the operational commander must seek additional resources or request modification of the aims.[18]

Third, strategy, because it is influenced by political and social concerns, places conditions on the conduct of military operations. These conditions take the form of restraints and constraints. Restraints prohibit or restrict certain military actions, such as the prohibition imposed on MacArthur in Korea against bombing targets north of the Yalu River in 1950 or Hitler's order (arguably in the hope of gaining a favorable negotiated peace with Great Britain) putting a temporary halt on the overrunning of France in 1940. Restraints may be constant, as the laws of warfare, or situational, as rules of engagement. Constraints, on the other hand, obligate the commander to certain military courses of action – such as Hitler's insistence that Stalingrad be held, which resulted in the loss of the Sixth German Army in 1943, or the political demand for a symbol of American resolve which necessitated the defense of Khe Sanh by the 26th Marines in 1968, although the position was of questionable military significance.[19] Similarly, strategy may constrain the commander to operations which gain rapid victory, such as Germany's need to defeat Poland quickly in 1939 so to be able to turn to face the western Allies or Abraham Lincoln's perceived need to end the American Civil War quickly lest Northern popular resolve falter.

When limitations imposed by strategy are so severe as to prevent the attainment of the established aim, the commander must request relaxation of either the aims or the limitations. But we should not be automatically critical of conditions imposed on operations by higher authority, since 'policy is the guiding intelligence'[20] for the use of military force. However, no senior commander can use the conditions imposed by higher authority as an excuse for military failure.[21]

Tactical-Operational Connection

Stemming from strategic guidance, operations assist tactics by establishing focus and goals. In that manner, operations provide the context for tactical decision making. Without this operational coherence, warfare at this level is reduced to a series of disconnected and unfocused tactical actions with relative attrition the only measure of success or failure.[22]

Just as operations must serve strategy by combining tactical actions in such a way as to most effectively and economically achieve the aim, they must also serve tactics by creating the most advantageous conditions for our tactical actions. In other words, we try to shape the situation so that the outcome is merely a matter of course. 'Therefore,' Sun Tzu said, 'a skilled commander seeks victory from the situation and does not demand it of his subordinates.'[23] And just as we must continually interface with strategy to gain our direction, we must also maintain the flexibility to adapt to tactical circumstances as they develop, for tactical results will impact on the conduct of the campaign. As the campaign forms the framework for combat, so do tactical results shape the conduct of the campaign. In this regard, the task is to exploit tactical victories to strategic advantage and to minimize, nullify, or even reverse the strategic effect of tactical losses.

Operations imply broader dimensions of time and space than do tactics, because the strategic orientation at this level forces the commander to broaden his perspective beyond the limits of immediate combat.[24] While the tactician fights the battle, the operational commander must look beyond the battle. In advance he seeks to shape events to create the most favorable conditions possible for those combat actions he chooses to fight. Likewise he seeks to anticipate the results of combat and to be prepared to exploit them to the greatest strategic advantage.

The operational level of war is sometimes described as the command of large military units. Indeed, at its upper limits, it is the province of theater commanders. However, it is erroneous to define the operational level according to echelon of command. Large is a relative term; in general, the larger the scale and complexity of a war, the higher the echelons of command performing at the operational level. For example, in a conventional conflict in central Europe, the corps commander may very well be the lowest-level operational commander. However, in a small war the operational conduct of war will take place at a much lower echelon. 'Regardless of size, if military force is being used to achieve a strategic objective, then it is being employed at the operational level.'[25]

Interaction of the Levels

The levels of war form a definite hierarchy. The technical application of combat power is subordinate to the needs of tactical combat, just as tactical actions merely compose the parts of a campaign, which is itself but one phase of a strategic design for gaining the objectives of policy. While there exists a clear hierarchy, there are no sharp boundaries between the levels, which tend rather to merge together. As all the levels share the same purpose of serving the ends set down by policy, the difference is one of scale rather than principle.

Consequently, a particular echelon of command is not necessarily concerned with only one level of war. A theater commander's concerns are clearly both strategic and operational. A MAGTF commander's responsibilities will be operational in some situations and largely tactical in others and may actually span the transition from tactics to operations in still others. A commander's responsibilities within the hierarchy depend on the scale and nature of the war and may shift up and down as the war develops.

Actions at one level can often influence the situation at others. Edward Luttwak calls this the interpenetration[26] of levels, in which results at one level can, in part or whole, dictate results at another. Harmony among the various levels tends to reinforce success, while disharmony tends to negate success. Failure at one level tends naturally to lessen success at the next higher level. This is fairly obvious.

Less obvious is the phenomenon that the manner of success at one level may also negate success at higher levels – as British reprisals in the Carolinas in 1780 fanned the dying embers of revolution into open flame; many of the patriotic troops at the battles of King's Mountain and Cowpens were local militia not imbued with any particular revolutionary fervor but fighting only to protect their homes against the depredations of British forces. Or, imagine a government whose strategy is to quell a growing insurgency by isolating the insurgents from the population but whose military tactics cause extensive collateral death and damage. The government's tactics alienate the population and make the insurgent's cause more appealing, strengthening the insurgent strategically.[27]

Brilliance at one level may to some extent overcome shortcomings at another, but rarely can it overcome incompetence. Operational competence can rarely overcome the tactical inability to perform, just as strategic incompetence can squander what operational success has gained.

The natural flow of influence in the hierarchy is from the top down; that is, it is much easier for strategic incompetence to squander operational and tactical success than it is for tactical and operational brilliance to completely overcome strategic incompetence or disadvantage. The Germans are generally considered to have been tactically and operationally supreme in two world wars, but the obstacle of strategic incompetence proved insurmountable. Conversely, outgunned and overmatched tactically, the Vietnamese Communists nonetheless prevailed strategically.

But the flow can work in reverse as well; brilliance at one level can overcome, at least in part, shortcomings at a higher level. In this way the tactical and operational abilities of the Confederate military leaders held off the overwhelming strategic advantage of the North for a time – until Lincoln found a commander who would press that strategic advantage. Similarly, Erwin Rommel's tactical and operational flair in North Africa in 1941–42 transcended for a time Britain's strategic advantage. Interestingly, this operational flair was coupled with a strategic shortsightedness in another example of interaction among the levels. Rommel's ambitious campaigning in a theater that was clearly of subsidiary importance had the ultimate effect of drawing German attention and resources from more important theaters.[28]

What matters finally is success at the level of strategy, for it is the concerns of policy which are the motives for war in the first place and which determine success or failure. The important lesson is not to be able to discern at what level a certain activity takes place or where the transition occurs between levels, but to ensure that from top to bottom and bottom to top all activities in war are coordinated and focused. Further, we should never view the tactical realm of war in isolation, for the results of combat become relevant only in the larger context of the campaign. The campaign, in turn, only gains meaning in the context of strategy.

A Comparative Case Study: Grant Versus Lee

A comparative examination of the strategic, operational, and tactical methods of Generals Ulysses S. Grant and Robert E. Lee during the American Civil War offers an interesting illustration of the interaction of the levels.[29] Popular history regards Grant as a butcher and Lee a military genius. But a study of their understanding of the needs of policy and the consistency of their strategic, operational, and tactical methods casts the issue in a different light.[30]

Policy

The North faced a demanding and complex political problem, namely 'to reassert its authority over a vast territorial empire, far too extensive to be completely occupied or thoroughly controlled.'[31] Furthermore, Abraham Lincoln, recognizing that Northern popular resolve might be limited, established rapid victory as a condition as well. Lincoln's original policy of conciliation having failed – as translated into a military strategy for limited war by General George McClellan – the President opted for the unconditional surrender of the South as the only acceptable aim. His search for a general who would devise a strategy to attain his aim ended with Grant in 1864. By comparison, the South's policy aim, Southern independence having already been declared, was simply to prevent the North from succeeding, to make the endeavor more costly than the North was willing to bear.

Military Strategy

Grant's strategy was directly supportive of the established policy objectives. He recognized immediately that his military strategic aim must be the destruction of Lee's army, and he devised a strategy of annihilation focused resolutely on that aim. General George Meade's Army of the Potomac was to lock horns with Lee's Army of Northern Virginia, battling relentlessly – 'Lee's army will be your objective point. Wherever he goes, there you will go also.'[32] Similarly, he gave his cavalry commander, General Philip Sheridan, 'instructions to put himself south of the enemy and follow him to the death. Wherever the enemy goes, let our troops go also.'[33] Meanwhile, General William Sherman was to sweep out of the west in a strategic envelopment into Lee's rear. Consistent with the policy objective of ending the war as rapidly as possible, Grant initiated offensive action simultaneously on all fronts to close the ring quickly around his opponent. His order shortly after assuming command terminating the common practice of prisoner exchanges, which was a vital source of manpower for the Confederates, demonstrated a keen appreciation for the larger situation. Satisfied that he had finally found a commander who could translate policy into a successful military strategy, Lincoln wrote Grant in August 1864: 'The particulars of your plans I neither know nor seek to know.... I wish not to obtrude any restraints or constraints upon you.'[34]

The South's policy objectives would seem to indicate a military strategy of attrition based on prolonging the war as a means to breaking Northern resolve – as had been George Washington's strategy in the Revolution. In fact, this was the strategy preferred by Confederate President Jefferson Davis. Such a strategy would involve Lee's dispersal of his army into the greatest possible expanse of territory. Lee, however, chose to concentrate his army in Virginia.[35] This was due in part to a perspective much narrower than Grant's and the fact that he was constrained to defend Richmond. But it was due also to Lee's insistence on offensive strategy – not merely an offensive-defensive as in the early stages of the war, but eventually an ambitious offensive strategy in 1862 and '63 aimed at invading the North as a means to breaking Northern will. Given the South's relative weakness, Lee's strategy was questionable at best[36] – both as a viable means of attaining the South's policy aims and also in regard to operational practicability, particularly the South's logistical ability to sustain offensive campaigns.

Operations

Consistent with his strategy of grinding Lee down as quickly as possible and recognizing his ability to pay the numerical cost, Grant aggressively sought to force Lee frequently into pitched battle, which he accomplished by moving against Richmond in such a way as to compel Lee to block him. Even so, it is unfair to discount Grant as nothing more than an unskilled butcher. 'He showed himself free from the common fixation of his contemporaries upon the Napoleonic battle as the hinge upon which warfare must turn. Instead, he developed a highly uncommon ability to rise above the fortunes of a single battle and to master the flow of a long series of events, almost to the point of making any outcome of a single battle, victory, draw, or even defeat, serve his eventual purpose equally well.'[37]

Lee, on the other hand, had stated that, being the weaker force, his desire was to avoid a general engagement.[38] But in practice, he seemed unable to resist the temptation of a climactic battle of Napoleonic proportions whenever the enemy was within reach. By comparison, General Joseph Johnston in the west seemed to better appreciate the need for a protracted conflict. 'He fought a war of defensive maneuver, seeking opportunities to fall upon enemy detachments which might expose themselves and inviting the enemy to provide him with such openings, meanwhile moving from one strong defensive position to another in order to invite the enemy to squander his resources in frontal attacks, but never remaining stationary long enough to risk being out-flanked or entrapped.'[39] Between Chattanooga and Atlanta, while suffering minimal casualties, Johnston had held Sherman to an average advance of a mile a day. Of Johnston's campaign, Grant himself had written: 'For my own part, I think that Johnston's tactics were right. Anything that could have prolonged the war a year beyond the time that it did finally close, would probably have exhausted the North to such an extent that they might have abandoned the contest and agreed to a separation.'[40]

Tactics

Lee's dramatic tactical successes in battles such as Second Manassas, Chancellorsville, and Antietam speak for themselves. But neither Lee nor Grant can be described tactically as particularly innovative. In fact, both were largely ignorant of the technical impact of the rifled bore on the close-order tactics of the day, and both suffered high casualties as a result.[41] However, due to the relative strategic situations, Grant could better absorb the losses that resulted from this tactical ignorance than could Lee, whose army was being bled to death. In this way, Grant's strategic advantage carried down to the tactical level.

While Grant's activities at all levels seem to have been mutually supporting and focused on the objectives of policy, Lee's strategy and operations appear to have been, at least in part, incompatible with each other and with the requirements of policy and the realities of combat.[42] In the final analysis, Lee's tactical flair could not overcome operational and strategic shortcomings.[43]

CAMPAIGNS AT ODDS WITH STRATEGY: LEE, 1862–63

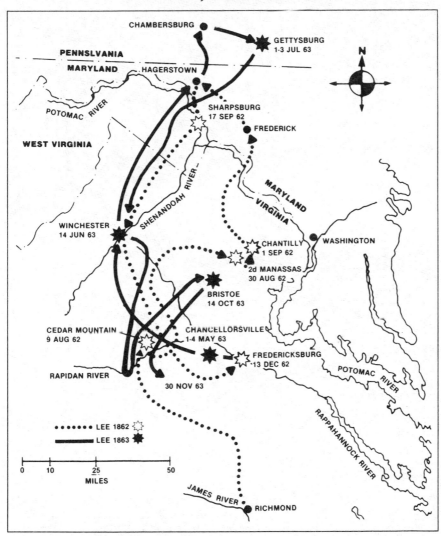

In spite of a Confederate policy of simple survival, Lee adopts an ambitious offensive strategy comprising two campaigns of invasion which fail in their strategic purpose.

CAMPAIGNS SUPPORTING STRATEGY:
GRANT, 1864–65

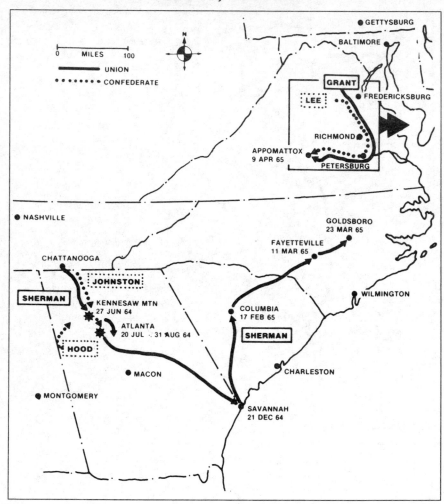

Compatible with the Federal aim of rapid unconditional victory, Grant devises an all-encompassing strategy of annihilation which includes the relentless attack of Lee and the loosing of Sherman into Lee's rear.

THE WILDERNESS TO APPOMATTOX: GRANT, 1864–65

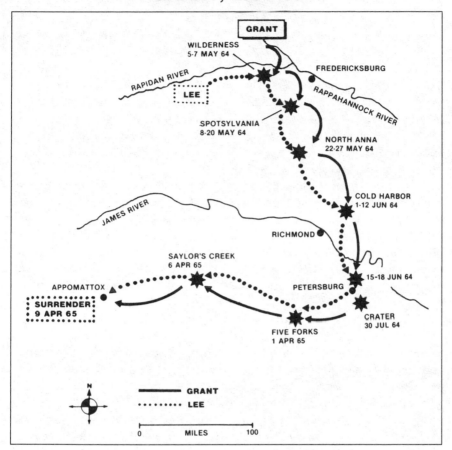

Grant clearly defines his aim: the destruction of Lee's army. He attacks relentlessly, maneuvering against Richmond to compel Lee to fight him. Grant's instructions to Meade: 'Lee's army will be your objective point. Wherever he goes, there you will go also.'

In fact, it proved irrelevant; even tactical victories such as Antietam became operational defeats.

Campaigns

As we have seen, the principal tool by which the operational commander pursues the military conditions that will achieve the strategic goal is the campaign. Campaigns tend to take place over the course of weeks or months, but they may encompass years. They may vary drastically in scale, from large campaigns conceived and controlled at the theater or even National Command Authority level to smaller campaigns conducted by task forces within a larger command. Generally, each campaign has a single strategic objective. If there is more than one strategic objective in a theater, campaigns are waged sequentially or simultaneously.

In that way, minor campaigns may exist within larger ones. For example, the Allied Pacific campaign during the Second World War comprised subordinate campaigns by General Douglas MacArthur in the southwest Pacific, Admiral William Halsey in the south Pacific, and Admiral Chester Nimitz in the central Pacific. Halsey's campaign in the south Pacific itself included a smaller campaign in the Solomon Islands which lasted five months and comprised operations from Guadalcanal to Bougainville.

Battles and Engagements

A battle is an extensive tactical fight between sizable combat forces. Battles generally last days, sometimes weeks. They occur when adversaries commit to fight to a decision at a particular time and place for a significant objective. Consequently, battles are usually of operational significance, if not necessarily operationally decisive. But this is not always the case; the Battle of the Somme in 1916, which was actually a series of inconclusive battles over the span of four and a half months, had the net effect of moving the front some eight miles while exacting over 600,000 casualties on each side.

An engagement is a combat between opposing forces on a scale of magnitude less than that of a battle. Several engagements may compose a battle. Engagements may or may not be operationally significant, although the object, of course, is to turn the result to operational advantage.

Battles and engagements are the physical clashes that make up the hard points[44] of a campaign. They generally provide the campaign its shape; at the same time the campaign gives them meaning. This is not to say that campaigns are merely a succession of tactical clashes, nor even that these clashes are the chief and deciding features of a campaign. A campaign may be characterized as much by the lack of battle; for example, General Nathanael Greene versus Lord Cornwallis in North Carolina in 1781. For six weeks Greene led the battle-thirsty Cornwallis on a wearying chase through the North Carolina countryside.

Only after the British force had been 'worn to a frazzle,'[45] did Greene agree to battle. The Revolutionaries were driven from the field, but the Britsh were so exhausted after the chase that in spite of the tactical victory they were forced to withdraw to the coast.

We have mentioned before, but it bears repeating, that to defeat the enemy in battle is not an end in itself, but a means to an end – unless the operational concept is simply to gain the strategic end by attrition, as was the U.S. strategy in Vietnam.[46] The true object is to accomplish the aim of strategy with the minimal amount of necessary combat, reducing 'fighting to the slenderest possible proportions.'[47]

We do not mean to say that we can, or should, avoid all fighting. How much fighting we do will vary with the strength, skill, and intentions of the opponent as well as our own. War being a violent enterprise, clashes will occur. The ideal is to give battle only where we want and when we must – when we are at an advantage and have something important to gain we cannot gain without fighting.[48] But, understanding that we are opposed by a hostile will with ideas of his own, we recognize that we will not always have this option. Sometimes we must fight at a disadvantage: when faced with an unfavorable meeting engagement, when ambushed, when simply forced to by a skilled enemy, or when strategic obligations constrain us (such as an inability to give ground – NATO's current plan for the forward defense of Germany, for example).

Strategic Actions

As we have seen, tactical actions gain strategic significance only when placed in the construct of a campaign. Strategic actions, on the other hand, by definition bear directly on strategic objectives, although their magnitude and duration are less than those of a campaign. Examples of strategic actions include the 1983 invasion of Grenada to restore order and evacuate U.S. medical students, the truck-bombing of the Marine headquarters by a single Shi'ite at the Beirut airport in the same year, and the 1986 punitive U.S. airstrike against Libya. Actions need not be of large scale to have strategic impact.[49]

Due to their very nature, strategic actions are normally conceived at the national level, at which they may also be planned and directed. However, planning and execution may also be delegated to the theater or even task force level. If such actions are controlled at senior levels, the operational commander tasked with execution will have little latitude in the manner of execution.

Strategic actions sometimes include special operations. As their name implies, special operations may require forces that are specially trained or equipped. But it is important to keep in mind that what makes these actions operations is not elite units or the specialized equipment they use. Rather, it is the effective employment of forces toward the achievement of specific objectives of strategic significance.

The Marine Corps and Campaigning

Having described the interaction of the levels of war and introduced the campaign, we must ask ourselves what its relevance is to the Marine Corps. We can answer this question from several angles. Organizationally, the MAGTF is uniquely equipped to perform a flexible variety of tactical actions, amphibious, air, and land, and to focus those actions into a united scheme. The MAGTF's organic aviation allows the commander to project power well in advance of close combat, to shape events in time and space. The headquarters organization, with separate headquarters for the tactical control of ground and air actions, can free the MAGTF command element to focus on the operational conduct of war.

From a conventional employment angle, a MAGTF may be the first American ground force at the scene of a crisis in an undeveloped theater of operations where no command structure is in place. In that case, the MAGTF commander's responsibilities will rest firmly in the operational realm – regardless of the size of the MAGTF. Even in a developed theater, a MAGTF may be required to conduct a campaign in pursuit of a strategic objective as part of a larger maritime campaign or as part of a larger land campaign by a Joint Task Force (JTF). In some cases, the MAGTF may itself be the JTF headquarters. Perhaps most important, a MAGTF commander must be prepared to articulate the most effective operational employment of his MAGTF in a joint or combined campaign. If he cannot, he will in effect depend on the other services to understand fully the capabilities of the MAGTF and employ it correctly, an assumption which is likely to prove unwarranted.

A less conventional perspective offers further reasons the operational level is important to Marines. The importance of strategic actions has led the Marine Corps to designate some units special operations-capable. As we have determined, to be special operations-capable, a unit must be able to function operationally. While lacking the scope and duration of a campaign, such operations share the campaign's strategic orientation.

Further, the changing nature of war resulting from the emergence of the electronic media offers another reason for understanding the operational level of war. Television by its range and influence on popular opinion can work operationally; that is, it can often elevate even minor tactical acts to higher importance. Consequently, all Marines must understand how tactical action impacts on strategy, which is the essence of war at the operational level.

Finally, regardless of the echelon of command or scale of activity, even if it rests firmly in the tactical realm, the methodology described here – devising and executing a progressive plan in pursuit of a distant goal and deciding when and where it is necessary to fight for that goal – applies.

NOTES

1. Henri Jomini, *The Art of War* (Westport, CT: Greenwood Press, 1971), p. 178. What Jomini describes as strategic would be classified as operational by today's construct.
2. B.H. Liddell Hart, *Strategy* (New York: Signet Books, 1967), p. 324.
3. *The Memoirs of Field-Marshal Montgomery* (New York: World Publishing Co., 1958), p. 197.
4. Liddell Hart, *Strategy*, p. 338.
5. JCS Pub. 1–02: '**National Strategy** – (DOD, IADB) The art and science of developing and using the political, economic, and psychological powers of a nation, together with its armed forces, during peace and war, to secure national objectives.' The term *national* strategy may be misleading to some since it often connotes a global perspective. Clearly, the need to coordinate all the elements of national power exists at the regional or theater level as well, and so the term *grand* strategy may be more useful.
6. JCS Pub. 1–02: '**Military Strategy** – (DOD, IADB) The art and science of employing the armed forces of a nation to secure the objectives of national policy by the application of force or the threat of force.' And: '**Strategic Level of War** – (DOD) The level of war at which a nation or group of nations determines national or alliance security objectives and develops and uses national resources to accomplish those objectives. Activities at this level establish national and alliance military objectives; sequence initiatives; define limits and assess risks for the use of military and other instruments of power; develop global or theater war plans to achieve these objectives; and provide armed forces and other capabilities in accordance with the strategic plan.'
7. JCS Pub. 1–02: '**Strategic Concept** – (DOD, NATO, IADB) The course of action accepted as the result of the estimate of the strategic situation. It is a statement of what is to be done in broad terms sufficiently flexible to permit its use in framing the military, diplomatic, economic, psychological and other measures which stem from it.' (Sometimes itself referred to as a 'strategy.')
8. JCS Pub. 1–02: '**Tactical Level of War** – (DOD) The level of war at which battles and engagements are planned and executed to accomplish military objectives assigned to tactical units or task forces. Activities at this level focus on the ordered arrangement and maneuver of combat elements in relation to each other and to the enemy to achieve combat objectives.'
9. JCS Pub. 1–02: '**Operational Level of War** – (DOD) The level of war at which campaigns and major operations are planned, conducted, and sustained to accomplish strategic objectives within theaters or areas of operations. Activities at this level link tactics and strategy by establishing operational objectives needed to accomplish the strategic objectives, sequencing events to achieve the operational objectives, initiating actions, and applying resources to bring about and sustain these events. These activities imply a broader dimension of time or space than do tactics; they ensure the logistic and administrative support of tactical forces, and provide the means by which tactical successes are exploited to achieve strategic objectives.'

10. FM 100–6 (Coordinating Draft), *Large Unit Operations* (Fort Leavenworth, KS: U.S. Army Command and General Staff College, 1987), p. vii.
11. Erich von Manstein, *Lost Victories* (Novato, CA: Presidio Press, 1982), p. 79.
12. David G. Chandler, *The Campaigns of Napoleon* (New York: MacMillan Publishing Co., 1966), p. 861.
13. FM 100–6, p. 1–3.
14. *Ibid.*, p. 1–5.
15. David Jablonsky, 'Strategy and the Operational Level of War,' *The Operational Art of Warfare Across the Spectrum of Conflict* (Carlisle, PA: U.S. Army War College, 1987), p. 5.
16. FM 100–6, p. 1–3.
17. *Ibid.*, p. 1–4.
18. *Ibid.*
19. *For Gen Vo Nguyen Giap, NVA, to commit six NVA divisions and for Intelligence reports to suggest that Giap wanted another Dien Bien Phu is to misunderstand his grand strategy. In maneuver warfare the enemy is the 'focus of effort' not cities or terrain features. However, Khe Sanh would have been of major military significance if we had lost it. H.T.H.*
20. Carl von Clausewitz, *On War*, trans. and ed. M. Howard and P. Paret (Princeton University Press, 1984), p. 607. 'No other possibility exists, then, than to subordinate the military point of view to the political.'
21. Manstein: 'There are admittedly cases where a senior commander cannot reconcile it with his responsibilities to carry out an order he has been given. Then, like Seydlitz at the Battle of Zorndorf, he has to say, 'After the battle the king may dispose of my head as he will, but during the battle he will kindly allow me to make use of it.' No general can vindicate his loss of a battle by claiming that he was compelled – against his better judgment – to execute an order that led to defeat. In this case the only course open to him is that of disobedience, for which he is answerable with his head. Success will usually decide whether he was right or not.' *Lost Victories*, pp. 361–2. *Lebanon. 23 Oct 1983: 241 Marines killed? H.T.H.*
22. FM 100–6, p. vii.
23. Sun Tzu, *The Art of War*, trans. Samuel B. Griffith (New York: Oxford University Press, 1971), p. 93.
24. Jablonsky, p. 11.
25. John F. Meehan III, 'The Operational Trilogy,' *Parameters*, vol. XVI, no. 3 (September 1986), p. 13.
     This quotation is fundamental to the understanding of special operation forces. Their aggregate utility for operational or tactical missions makes them a very valuable asset to any commander. The problem arises in the 'chain of command relationships' for the daily assignments. H.T.H.
26. See Edward N. Luttwak, *Strategy: The Logic of War and Peace* (Cambridge, MA: Harvard University Press, 1987), pp. 69–71, 208–230.
27. *This is not always the case. The U.S. Cavalry counterinsurgency campaign against the American Indians often caused 'collateral damage.' The harsh counterinsurgency campaign*

in Guatemala caused extensive collateral damage. Collateral damage was never a reason for any Vietnamese to join the VC. In these and many other cases the population accepted the facts of life. H.T.H.

28. By comparison, consider the equally successful German, Gen. Paul von Lettow-Vorbeck, in the First World War in German East Africa, who wrote in his memoirs: 'Owing to the position of German East Africa and the weakness of the existing forces – the peace establishment was but little more than two thousand – we could only play a subsidiary part. I knew that the fate of the colonies, as of all other German possessions, would be decided only on the battlefields of Europe. The question was whether it was possible for us in our subsidiary theatre of war to exercise any influence on the great decision at home. Could we, with our small forces, prevent considerable numbers of the enemy from intervening in Europe, or in other more important theatres, or inflict on our enemies any loss of personnel or war material worth mentioning?' *East African Campaigns* (New York: Robert Speller & Sons, 1957), p. 1.

29. *This is not a fair comparison. General Lee commanded only the Army of Northern Virginia. General Grant commanded all Union armies in the field: Meade, Sherman, and Sheridan. President Jefferson Davis fancied himself as a great military leader and controlled the three major Confederate armies from Richmond. H.T.H.*

30. See J.F.C. Fuller, *Grant and Lee: A Study in Personality and Generalship* (Bloomington, IN: Indiana University Press, 1982). Particularly pp. 242–283.

31. Russell F. Weigley, *The American Way of War* (Bloomington, IN: Indiana University Press, 1973), p. 92.

32. Ulysses S. Grant, *Personal Memoirs* (New York: Da Capo Press, 1982), p. 369.

33. *Ibid.*, p. 469.

34. Fuller, pp. 79–80.

35. *Lee did not choose to concentrate his army in northern Virginia. He only commanded the Army of Northern Virginia. General Joseph E. Johnson commanded the army against Sherman. Lee wrote to Johnson late in the war and 'asked' Johnson if he would join forces with Lee so that they might concentrate on one Union army at a time. Lee did not control the grand strategy of the Confederacy. In 1865, only weeks before the end at Appomattox, Jefferson finally appointed Lee commander of all Confederate armies, but by then it was too late. H.T.H.*

36. Weigley, p. 118. Fuller, p. 253.

37. Weigley, p. 139.
Grant became an 'attrition warfare' practitioner when he came to the conclusion at the Battle of the Wilderness that he could not win a war of maneuver against Lee. He had the manpower and the resources and Lee did not. Grant lost more men from the Union in his 1864–65 campaign than had been lost in the entire war until that time. Nevertheless, Grant's Black River Campaign and his investiture of Vicksburg has been seen by many as the best military campaign ever fought on American soil. H.T.H.

38. Weigley, p. 108.

39. *Ibid.*, p. 123.

40. Grant, p. 384.

41. Fuller, p. 268. 'In this respect there is no difference between Grant and Lee;

neither understood the full powers of the rifle or the rifled gun; neither introduced a single tactical innovation of importance, and though the rifle tactics of
the South were superior to those of the North, whilst the artillery tactics of the
North were superior to those of the South, these differences were due to circumstances outside generalship.'

42. *Lee was an operational genius. He left tactics to his great lieutenants. Southern 'strategy'
came from Jefferson Davis. Lee's first invasion of the north into Maryland was well under
way before he wrote to Jefferson Davis to tell him what he was going to do. He knew that
Davis would not approve. But Lee needed to give the farmers of Northern Virginia a
breathing spell while he fed and clothed his Confederates with Yankee resources. With what
Jackson captured at Harpers Ferry and what Longstreet took from Maryland, the Army of
Northern Virginia could fight again. H.T.H.*

43. *Lee never thought he could defeat the northern army. His entire strategy was to make the
war so costly that the Yankees would tire of the bloodshed and sue for peace. In 1863
President Lincoln even sent a letter to his cabinet thinking that his party would not win
reelection in 1864 and they had better prepare for it. Gettysburg changed all that.
H.T.H.*

44. L.D. Holder, 'Operational Art in the US Army: A New Vigor,' *Essays on
Strategy*, vol. III (Washington: National Defense University Press, 1986),
p. 129.

45. Weigley, p. 32. 'Cornwallis arrived at the Dan worn to a frazzle, 500 men of
2,500 having dropped out since Ramsour's Mills, haversacks empty, and the
Carolina partisans stripping away provisions from the countryside in their
rear.'

46. Contrary to Clausewitz, who describes the battle as 'primarily an end in itself.'
He writes: 'But since the essence of war is fighting, and since the battle is the
fight of the main force, the battle must always be considered as the true center
of gravity of the war. All in all, therefore, its distinguishing feature is that, more
than any other type of action, battle exists for its own sake alone.' *On War*,
p. 248.

47. Liddell Hart, *Strategy*, p. 324.

48. *If you wait until you have an advantage or something important to gain, you may miss a
number of opportunities to inflict major damage on an unsuspecting enemy. Napoleon was
often outnumbered by his enemies; however, he knew when and where to apply a small force
against an equivalent number and by routing that force usually caused such a disorder in
the whole line, particularly if quickly repeated, that inferior numbers defeated the larger.
H.T.H.*

49. In fact, they can be quite small; for example, the killing of Haitian guerrilla
leader Charlemagne Peralte by two Marine noncommissioned officers in 1919.
During this period, U.S. Marines were involved in the occupation of Haiti.
Peralte had raised a rebel force of as many as five thousand in the northern part of
the country. From February through October, Marine forces pursued the rebels,
known as *cacos*, fighting 131 engagements but unable to suppress the rebel
activity. So, disguised as *cacos*, Sgt. Herman Hannekan and Cpl. William Button
infiltrated Peralte's camp, where Hannekan shot and killed the *caco* leader. The

rebellion in the north subsided. In this case, a special operation consisting of two Marines accomplished what seven months of combat could not.

CHAPTER 2

Designing the Campaign

'No plan survives contact with the enemy.'[1]
— Field Marshal Helmuth von Moltke ('The Elder')

'By looking on each engagement as part of a series, at least insofar as events are predictable, the commander is always on the high road to his goal.'[2]
— Carl von Clausewitz

'To be practical, any plan must take account of the enemy's ability to frustrate it; the best chance of overcoming such obstruction is to have a plan that can be easily varied to fit the circumstances met; to keep such adaptability, while still keeping the initiative, the best way is to operate along a line which offers alternative objectives.'[3]
— B.H. Liddell Hart

Having defined and described the operational level of war and its principal weapon, the campaign, we will now discuss the mental process and the considerations involved in designing a campaign. In this respect, the commander's key responsibility is to provide focus[4] – by his campaign design to fuse a variety of disparate tactical acts, extended over time and space, into a single, coalescent whole. It is important to note at the outset that due to the inherently uncertain and disordered nature of war, campaign design is of necessity a continuous and fluid process, as Moltke reminds us.

Strategic Aim, End State, and Operational Objectives

The design should focus all the various efforts of the campaign resolutely on the established theater strategic aim. Economy is an essential ingredient in campaign design. Any activity or operation which does not contribute, directly or derivatively, in some necessary way to this aim is unjustifiable. Of course, the aim may shift over time, for a variety of reasons – including the success, failure, or cost of the unfolding campaign itself – and we must continuously adjust our design appropriately. This focus on the military strategic aim is the single overriding element of campaign design.

This notion is reflected in U.S. Grant's strategy for the Civil War as described in his memoirs:

The armies were now all ready for the accomplishment of a single object. They were acting as a unit so far as such a thing was possible over such a vast field. Lee, with the capital of the Confederacy, was the main end to which all were working. Johnston, with Atlanta, was an important obstacle in the way of accomplishing the result aimed at, and was therefore almost an independent objective. It was of less importance only because the capture of Johnston and his army would not produce so immediate and decisive a result in closing the rebellion as would the possession of Richmond, Lee, and his army. All other troops were employed exclusively in support of these two movements.[5]

Given the strategic aim as our destination, our next step is to determine the desired end state, the military conditions we must realize in order to reach that destination, those necessary conditions which we expect by their existence will provide us our established aim. Grant envisioned these conditions to be the destruction of Lee's army and the capture of Richmond.[6] These conditions will vary with the nature of the conflict and need not always consist of the destruction of the enemy. In fact, the lethality of modern weapons may necessitate the adoption of limited aims, such as protecting a region, denying or capturing enemy war resources, curbing or limiting enemy influence, diverting enemy resources from more important theaters or areas, or deterring enemy aggression.

In the main, the more general the conflict, the more predominant are the military factors, and the easier it is to translate aims into military terms. The unconditional surrender of the enemy as a policy aim translates easily into the outright defeat of his military forces: 'You will enter the continent of Europe and, in conjunction with other Allied Nations, undertake operations aimed at the heart of Germany and the destruction of her Armed Forces.'[7] But the more limited the aims of conflict, the less predominantly military is the conduct of the war, and the more difficult it is to translate those aims into military conditions, as illustrated by the questionable military mission of Marine forces in Beruit 1982–84.

From the envisioned end state, we can develop the operational objectives which, taken in combination, will achieve those conditions. In Grant's concept, the defeat of Joseph Johnston and the capture of Atlanta were important operational objectives. It is important to note that as the strategic aim shifts, so must our determination of the conditions of success and operational objectives shift as well.

Identifying Critical Enemy Factors

We must anticipate that the enemy will do everything within his power to interfere with our attaining our aims. Therefore, we must plan to deal with the enemy in such a way that foils his ability to interfere. Our design must focus on critical enemy factors, and the ability to do this depends on an accurate estimate of the situation.

Economy demands that we focus our efforts toward some object or factor of decisive importance in order to achieve the greatest effect at the least cost. The most effective way to defeat our enemy is to destroy that which is most critical to his success in the theater. Clearly, we should focus our efforts against an object of strategic importance since this will have the greatest effect. Failing the ability to do that, we focus against objects of operational importance.[8] In other words, we should strike him where and when we can hurt him most, or, as Sun Tzu said, 'Seize something he cherishes and he will conform to your desires.'[9] Returning to the example of Grant in the Civil War, while his aim was the defeat of Lee, the critical factor on which this hinged was Sherman's campaign into the heart of the South. This is reflected in Grant's instructions to Sherman in April 1864: 'You I propose to move against Johnston's army, to break it up and to get into the interior of the enemy's country as far as you can, inflicting all the damage you can against their war resources.'[10]

We obviously stand a better chance of success by acting against enemy vulnerability rather than against strength. In some cases, these vulnerabilities may be of critical importance, such as the maldeployment of forces at the outset of a campaign, insufficient air defenses, or comparatively poor operational mobility. We should search for and exploit such critical vulnerabilities directly. By using multiple simultaneous thrusts or initiatives, we may identify these vulnerabilities more quickly.

Often, a factor is critical to the enemy because it represents a capability he cannot do without. It is a source of strategic or operational strength. Clearly, if we can destroy such a critical capability we can weaken our enemy severely. But we do not want to attack this capability directly, strength versus strength; rather, we prefer to attack it from an aspect of vulnerability or even to preempt it before it becomes a strength (such as to delay by air power the junction of enemy forces in order to defeat a superior foe piecemeal). Critical capabilities may be immediately vulnerable to attack; for example, by means of a choke point at which we can sever the enemy's line of operation. However, the enemy will likely recognize the importance of this capability and will take measures to protect it. Thus, a critical capability may not be directly vulnerable. We may have to create vulnerability: we may have to design a progressive sequence of actions to expose or isolate the critical capability, perhaps focusing on lesser capabilities and vulnerabilities en route, creating by our actions over time the opportunity to strike the decisive blow.

Just as we ruthlessly pursue our enemy's critical factors, we should expect him to attack ours, and we must take steps to protect them over the course of the campaign. This focus on critical factors as they bear at the operational level, from both our and the enemy's points of view, is central to campaign design.

The Concept

Having established, at least temporarily, the aim and having identified those critical factors which we believe will lead most effectively and economically to the enemy's downfall, we must develop a concept or scheme which focuses on these factors in pursuit of the aim. This is the truly creative aspect of campaign design and of the military art in general: conceiving an original overall scheme for success, attuned to the complex set of particulars which make each situation unique.[11]

The concept captures the essence of the design and provides the foundation from which spring the more mechanical aspects of campaign design. It encompasses our broad vision of what we plan to do and how we plan to do it. Our intent, clearly understood and explicitly stated, therefore must be an integral component of the concept. Our concept should also contain in general terms an idea of when, where, and under what conditions we intend to give and refuse battle.

The concept should demonstrate a certain boldness, which is in itself 'a genuinely creative force.'[12] It should demonstrate a ruthless focus on critical enemy factors. It should exhibit creativity and novelty; avoid discernible conventions and patterns; make use of artifice, ambiguity, and deception; and reflect, as Churchill wrote, 'an original and sinister touch, which leaves the enemy puzzled as well as beaten.'[13] It should create multiple options, so that we can adjust to changing events and so that the enemy cannot discern our true intent. And it should provide for speed in execution, which is a weapon in itself.

History is replete with examples at all levels of a superior idea as the basis for notable success: Hannibal's concept of a thin center and heavy wings, which enabled his rout of Varro at Cannae; Grant's plan for fixing Lee near Richmond and loosing Sherman through the heart of the South; the conceptual marriage of infiltration tactics with mechanization which became the blitzkrieg in 1940; the idea of bypassing Japanese strongholds which became the basis for the island-hopping campaigns in the Second World War in the Pacific; MacArthur's bold concept of a seaborne, operational envelopment to topple the North Korean advance, which became the Inchon landing in 1950; and the idea of eliminating the Viet Cong guerrillas' support base by pacifying the South Vietnamese villages, which was the basis for the generally successful but short-lived Combined Action Program.[14]

Conceptual, Functional, and Detailed Design

We can describe this conceiving of an overall scheme for accomplishing our goal as conceptual design. Conceptual design becomes the foundation for all subsequent design, which we can call functional design and detailed design.[15] These are the more mechanical and routine elements of campaign design which are concerned with translating the concept into a complete and practicable plan. Functional design is, just as the name implies, concerned with designing the functional components necessary to support the concept: the subordinate concepts for logistics, deployment, organization, command, intelligence, fire support, sequencing. Functional design provides for the general characteristics and conditions required by the concept. Detailed design encompasses the specific planning activities necessary to ensure that the plan is coordinated: movements, landing tables, deployment or resupply schedules, communications plans, reconnaissance plans, control measures, specific command relationships. Detailed design should not become so specific, however, that it inhibits flexibility. Mindful of Moltke's dictum, we must recognize that any plan, no matter how detailed, is simply a common basis for change.

It should be clear that no amount of subsequent planning can reduce the requirement for an overall concept. But while we must clearly recognize that conceptual design becomes the foundation for functional and detailed design, we must also recognize that the process works in the other direction as well. Our concept must be receptive to functional realities. Functional design in turn must be sensitive to details of execution. In this way, the realities of deployment schedules (a functional concern) can dictate employment schemes (a conceptual concern). Likewise, logistical requirements shape the concept of operations – logistics becomes the tail that wags the dog.[16] Campaign design thus becomes a continuous, two-way process aimed at harmonizing the various levels of design activity.

Sequencing

Given a strategic aim not attainable by a single tactical action at a single place and time, we design a campaign comprising several related phases sequenced over time to achieve that aim. Phases are a way of organizing the extended and dispersed activities of the campaign into more manageable parts which allow for flexibility in execution. 'These phases of a plan do not comprise rigid instructions, they are merely guideposts ... Rigidity inevitably defeats itself, and the analysts who point to a changed detail as evidence of a plan's weakness are completely unaware of the characteristics of the battlefield.'[17]

An excellent example is General Dwight Eisenhower's broad plan for the recapture of Europe in the Second World War, which described, in his words, 'successive moves with possible alternatives':

Land on the Normandy coast.

   Build up resources needed for a decisive battle in the Normandy-Brittany region and break out of the enemy's encircling positions. (Land operations in the first two phases were to be under the tactical direction of Montgomery.)

   Pursue on a broad front with two army groups, emphasizing the left to gain necessary ports and reach the boundaries of Germany and threaten the Ruhr. On

PHASES OF A CAMPAIGN:
EISENHOWER, 1944–45

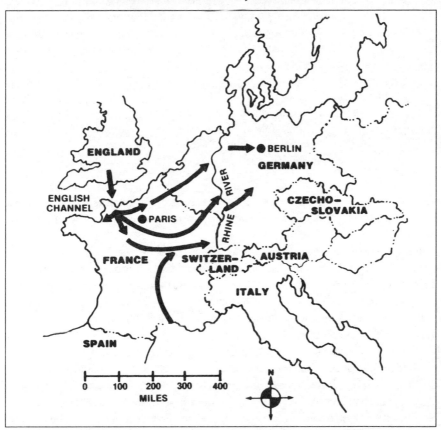

The phases of Eisenhower's broad design for the reconquest of Europe in the Second World War, as originally conceived. His directive from the Combined Chiefs of Staff: 'You will enter the continent of Europe, and, in conjunction with the other Allied Nations, undertake operations aimed at the heart of Germany and the destruction of her Armed Forces.'

our right we would link up with the forces that were to invade France from the south.

Build up our new base along the western border of Germany, by securing ports in Belgium and in Brittany as well as in the Mediterranean.

While building up our forces for the final battles, keep up an unrelenting offensive to the extent of our means, both to wear down the enemy and to gain advantages for the final fighting.

Complete the destruction of enemy forces west of the Rhine, in the meantime seeking bridgeheads across the river.

Launch the final attack as a double envelopment of the Ruhr, again emphasizing the left, and follow this up by an immediate thrust through Germany, with the specific direction to be determined at the time.

Clean out the remainder of Germany.[18]

Eisenhower remarked that 'this general plan, carefully outlined at staff meetings before D-Day, was never abandoned, even momentarily, throughout the campaign.'[19]

Phases may occur simultaneously as well as sequentially. Each phase may be a single operation or, in the case of large campaigns, a minor campaign in itself. The phases of a campaign are the parts which, taken in proper combination, compose the operational whole. Our task is to devise the operational combination of actions which most effectively and quickly achieves the strategic aim. This means far more than simply the accumulation of tactical victories, which we have already concluded is no guarantee of strategic success.

While each phase may be generally distinguishable from the others as a distinct episode, it is necessarily linked to the others and gains significance only in the larger context of the campaign. As demonstrated in the example above, the manner of distinction may be separation in time or space or a difference in aim or forces assigned. We should view each phase as an essential component in a connected string of events, related in cause and effect. Like a chess player, we must learn to think beyond the next move, looking ahead several moves and considering the long-term effects of those moves and how to exploit them. In this way, each phase has an envisioned sequel or potential sequels.[20] 'The higher commander must constantly plan, as each operation progresses, so to direct his formations that success finds his troops in proper position and condition to undertake successive steps without pause.'[21] And like a chess player, we cannot move without considering the enemy's reactions or anticipations, unlikely as well as likely.

As the example shows, each phase of the campaign is generally aimed at some intermediate goal necessary to the ultimate accomplishment of the larger aim of the campaign. And as the example also shows, each phase should have a clearly understood intent of its own which contributes to the overall intent of the campaign. While we may envision each phase lasting a certain duration, the phases of a campaign are event-oriented rather than time-oriented. Each phase should represent a natural subdivision of the campaign; we should not break the campaign down into numerous arbitrary parts which can lead to a plodding, incremental approach that sacrifices tempo.[22]

The further ahead we project, the less certain and detailed will be our designs. We may plan the initial phase of a campaign with some degree of certainty, but since the results of that phase will shape the phases that follow, subsequent plans will become increasingly general. The design for future phases may consist of no more than contingencies, options, and a general intent.

The process of developing a sequence of phases in a campaign operates in two directions, forward and backward, simultaneously. On the one hand, we begin with the current situation and plan ahead, envisioning succeeding progressive phases that build upon each other. Each phase lays the groundwork for its successor until, by this connected chain of tactical events, the stage is set for the eventual decisive action. But at the same time, we cannot devise any sequence of events without a clear vision of the final object. We must have the desired end state clearly in mind – even while recognizing its tentative nature – from which we envision a reasonable series of phases backward toward the present.

The idea of sequencing applies to resources as well as to actions. Sequencing allows us to allocate resources effectively over time. The thought of economy, or conservation, rises to the fore again: taking the long view, we must ensure that resources are available as needed in the later stages of the campaign. Effective sequencing must take into account the process of logistical culmination. If resources are insufficient to sustain the force through to the accomplishment of the strategic aim, logistics may demand that the campaign be organized into sequential phases which can be supported, each phase followed by a logistical buildup – as in the case of Eisenhower's operational pause at the Rhine. Moreover, logistical requirements may dictate the direction of operational plans. For example, one phase of Eisenhower's plan for the reconquest of Europe after the Normandy breakout was a northern thrust with Montgomery's Twenty-first Army Group to capture needed ports.

Resource availability depends in large part on time schedules, such as sustainment or deployment rates, rather than on the events of war. Therefore, as we develop our intended phases we must reconcile the time-oriented phasing of resources with the event-oriented phasing of operations.

Direction

The commander further focuses the campaign by providing an operational direction which unifies the various actions within the campaign. As a campaign generally has a single strategic aim – which establishes a strategic direction – so should it have a single operational direction which leads most directly toward that aim. We should recognize that what is strategically most direct may in fact be indirect operationally. The need to move in more than one operational direction generally warrants more than one campaign.[23]

In the classic sense, direction equates to a line of operations along which the force advances or falls back, maneuvers and fights, and sustains itself. But direction does not apply only in the spatial sense – particularly in unconventional conflicts in which the spatial dimension seems to be less significant. Direction establishes a purposeful current of connectivity between actions which advances resolutely toward the final aim. It may be a physical axis. Or it may be a guiding manner of operating which harmonizes the phases of a campaign in purpose and makes them mutually supporting.

Where possible, we should select a variable direction which offers multiple options, or branches,[24] thus providing flexibility and ambiguity to our actions. A comparison of General Sherman's Atlanta campaign and his campaigns thereafter offers interesting insight. In his Atlanta campaign, Sherman had been hampered by the existence of a single objective, which simplified 'the opponent's task in trying to parry his thrusts. This limitation Sherman now ingeniously planned to avoid by placing the opponent repeatedly "on the horns of a dilemma" – the phrase he used to express his aim. He took a line of advance which kept the Confederates in doubt, first, whether Macon or Augusta, and then whether Augusta or Savannah was his objective. And while Sherman had his preference, he was ready to take the alternative objective if conditions favored the change.'[25] Then, campaigning through the Carolinas, he opted again for a variable direction 'so that his opponents could not decide whether to cover Augusta or Charleston, and their forces became divided. Then, after he had ignored both points and swept between them to gain Columbia ... the Confederates were kept in uncertainty as to whether Sherman was aiming for Charlotte or Fayetteville. And when in turn he advanced from Fayetteville they could not tell whether Raleigh or Goldsborough was his next, and final, objective.'[26]

A single operational direction does not mean that we must concentrate our forces in a single direction tactically as well. In fact, multiple tactical thrusts that are mutually enhancing increase the speed and ambiguity of our operations. Consider the German blitzes into Poland and France in 1939 and '40 which were characterized by multiple, broadly dispersed thrusts but all of which shared a common direction and were thus unified by a single focus – shattering the depth and cohesion of the enemy defenses.

Campaign Plan

The campaign plan is a statement of the commander's design for prosecuting his portion of the war effort, from preparation through a sequence of related operations to a well-defined end state which guarantees the attainment of the

MANY THRUSTS – ONE DIRECTION: POLAND, 1939

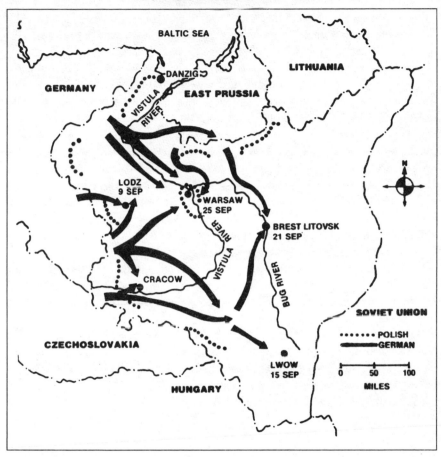

Multiple thrusts unified by a common theme: penetrating the Polish frontier to disrupt the cohesion of the defenses and converging on Warsaw and Brest Litovsk.

strategic aim.[27] The campaign plan is a mechanism for providing focus and direction to subordinates executing tactical missions.

The campaign plan must highlight the strategic aim. It should describe, to subordinates and seniors alike, the end state which will guarantee that aim, the overall concept and intent of the campaign, a tentative sequence of phases and operational objectives which will lead to success, and general concepts for key supporting functions, especially a logistical concept which will sustain the force throughout the campaign. The logistical concept is vital, since logistics, perhaps more than any other functional concern, can dictate what is operationally feasible.[28]

The plan may describe the initial phases of the campaign with some certainty. But the design for succeeding phases will become increasingly general as uncertainty grows and the situation becomes increasingly unpredictable. The campaign must remain at all times flexible. However, the final phase, the anticipated decisive action which will achieve final success and toward which the entire campaign builds, should be clearly envisioned and described.[29]

The campaign plan establishes tentative milestones and becomes a measure of progress, but, short of the dictates of strategy, is not a schedule in any final, immutable sense. Until the final aim is realized, we must continuously adapt our campaign plan to changing aims (ours and the enemy's), results, resources, and limiting factors. Like any plan, the campaign plan is only 'a datum plane from which [we] build as necessity directs and opportunity offers.'[30]

The campaign plan should be concise; General MacArthur's plan for his Southwest Pacific theater of operations was only four pages.[31] The campaign plan does not describe the execution of its phases in tactical detail. Rather, it provides guidance for developing the operations plans and orders which will in turn provide the tactical design for those phases.

NOTES

1. Attributed.
2. *On War*, p. 182.
3. *Strategy*, p. 330.
   Quotes 1–3 are some of the most important quotations in this manual. H.T.H.
4. Meehan, p. 15.
5. Grant, p. 374.
6. *It is important to note that Grant saw three parts to his 'single objective': Richmond (symbolic in those days as the fall of a capitol usually meant the end of the war), Lee, and Lee's army. One without the other two was meaningless. H.T.H.*
7. Dwight D. Eisenhower, *Crusade in Europe* (New York: Da Capo Press, Inc., 1979), p. 225.
8. William S. Lind, 'The Operational Art,' *Marine Corps Gazette* (April 1988), p. 45.
9. Sun Tzu, p. 134.

10. Grant, p. 366.

11. But as this gift for conceptual design is the truly creative aspect of the military art, it is precisely this skill which has often been lacking. At the present, the Marine Corps as an institution devotes more time and effort to training officers in the procedural aspects of command and staff action than to developing intuitive, creative commanders – an error that must be remedied. This creative ability is generally an innate gift which can be developed in an individual to some extent, but not created. Part of the solution may be to institutionalize a method whereby we identify and develop such individuals as commanders.

12. Clausewitz, p. 77.

13. Winston S. Churchill, *The World Crisis* (New York: Charles Scribner's Sons, 1923) vol. II, p. 5.

14. *The Combined Action Program was not to 'pacify' a South Vietnamese village. The CAP Marines joined a Popular Force Platoon in an already secure hamlet to provide continual security for that village or hamlet (so that the VC would not come back without a fight). 'Pacification,' better known as Revolutionary Development, took a lot of resources including provincial regional force companies to drive out the VC, RD Cadre Teams to reintroduce GVN services in the village, and USAID economic and political support to help rebuild the economy of the village. A counterinsurgency campaign involves 'denial measures' – keeping the VC out; and 'supporting measures' – keeping the faith with the villagers. H.T.H.*

15. Consider as an analogy the designing of an automobile. The conceptual design establishes the overall features of the car: for example, we decide that (within our appreciation for current technical capabilities) we want a small sportscar with a certain general shape, certain performance capabilities, evoking a certain image, and appealing to a certain market. This concept becomes the theme for all subsequent design. We proceed to functional design, by which we design the necessary functional components within the parameters established by the concept: the engine, the suspension system, the body, the interior, and so on. In the process, we may discover that in designing the engine we cannot achieve the desired horsepower given the size, weight, or shape of the car established in the concept. It becomes necessary to modify the concept by adjusting the required performance or the size or shape. Finally, within the parameters of the concept and functional requirements, detailed design provides the specifications to which the car is actually built; literally, the nuts and bolts that hold the car together.

16. *A wise Marine general (General Robert Barrow), commenting on all the battlefield talk in the officer's mess, said that 'amateurs talk about tactics and professionals talk about logistics.' H.T.H.*

17. Eisenhower, p. 256.

18. *Ibid.*, pp. 228–9.
    Now that's what I call a mission-type order. H.T.H.

19. *Ibid.*, p. 229.

20. Holder, p. 124.

21. Eisenhower, p. 176. Also: 'In committing troops to battle there are certain minimum objectives to be attained, else the operation is a failure. Beyond this lies

the realm of reasonable expectation, while still further beyond lies the realm of hope – all that might happen if fortune persistently smiles upon us.

'A battle plan normally attempts to provide guidance even into this final area, so that no opportunity for extensive exploitation may be lost . . .', p. 256.

22. *This works well in conventional warfare – it does not work as well, all the time, in unconventional warfare. H.T.H.*
23. *The best example of this was the counterinsurgency campaign against the VC guerrillas and the conventional campaign against the NVA forces. H.T.H.*
24. Holder, p. 123.
25. Liddell Hart, *Strategy*, p. 134.
26. *Ibid.*, pp. 134–5.
27. William W. Mendel and Floyd T. Banks, 'Campaign Planning: Getting It Straight,' *Parameters*, vol. XVIII, no. 3 (September 1988), p. 45. From JCS Pub. 1–02: '**Campaign Plan** – (DOD, IADB) A plan for a series of related military operations aimed to accomplish a common objective, normally within a given time and space.'
28. *Amen brother, amen! H.T.H.*
29. Mendel and Banks, p. 45.
30. George S. Patton, Jr., *War As I Knew It* (New York: Bantam Books, 1980), p. 374.
31. Meehan, p. 15.

CHAPTER 3

Conducting the Campaign

'For to win one hundred victories in one hundred battles is not the acme of skill. To subdue the enemy without fighting is the acme of skill.'[1]
— Sun Tzu

'We must make this campaign an exceedingly active one. Only thus can a weaker country cope with a stronger; it must make up in activity what it lacks in strength.'[2]
— Stonewall Jackson

'A prince or general can best demonstrate his genius by managing a campaign exactly to suit his objectives and his resources, doing neither too much nor too little.'[3]
— Carl von Clausewitz

Having discussed designing a campaign, we now turn to the actual conduct of the campaign. This is not to say that there is a point at which design ceases and execution begins: we have already concluded that campaign design is continuous. In fact, design and conduct are interdependent: just as our design shapes our execution, so do the results of execution cause us to modify our design even in the midst of execution. Only with this thought firmly in mind can we proceed to discuss campaign execution.

Reduced to its essence, the art of campaigning consists of deciding who, when, and where to fight for what purpose. Equally important, it involves deciding who, when, and where not to fight. It is, as Clausewitz described, 'the use of engagements for the object of the war.'[4]

Strategic Orientation

As in campaign design, the overriding consideration in conducting the campaign is an unwavering focus on the requirements of the theater strategy. The aims, resources, and limitations established by strategy become the filter through which we view all our actions, even if, as at the lower echelons of command, the connection with strategy is only derivative. Even task force commanders and below, who do not function immediately at the theater level, must see their tactical decisions as derivative of the theater strategy. Consequently, the requirements of strategy must be communicated clearly to even tactical commanders.

Use of Combat

Fighting, or combat, is central to war. But because tactical success of itself does not guarantee strategic success, there is an art to the way we put combat to use. We must view each envisioned action – battle, engagement, refusal to give battle, interdiction mission, feint – as an essential component of a larger whole rather than as an independent, self-contained event.

At the tactical level, clearly, the aim is to win in combat (within the parameters dictated by strategy). But the overriding influences of the strategic and operational levels may put these actions in a different context. In this way, tactical defeat can amount to strategic success, as for the North Vietnamese at Tet in 1986, while tactical victory can bring operational failure, as for Lee at Antietam.[5]

While combat is a necessary part of war, it is by nature costly. The fuel of war is human lives and material; as Eisenhower wrote, 'the word is synonymous with waste . . . The problem is to determine how, in time and space, to expend assets so as to achieve the maximum in results.'[6] Economy thus dictates that we use combat wisely.

We do this first by fighting when it is to our advantage to do so – when we are strong compared to the enemy or we have identified some exploitable vulnerability in our enemy – and avoiding battle when we are at a disadvantage. When at a disadvantage tactically, economy means refusing to engage in battle in that particular situation. When at a tactical disadvantage theater-wide, it means waging a campaign based on hit-and-run tactics and a general refusal to give pitched battle, except when local advantage exists. This can be seen in countless historical examples: Rome under Fabius versus Hannibal, the Viet Cong in Vietnam, Washington and Nathanael Greene in the Revolutionary War, and Lettow-Vorbeck in German East Africa in the First World War.[7] By the same token, given a theater-wide advantage, we might want to bring the enemy to battle at every opportunity: Rome under Varro versus Hannibal, the United States in Vietnam, Eisenhower in Europe, or Grant versus Lee. But such a strategy is generally costly and time-consuming, and success depends on three conditions: first, that popular support for this strategy will outlast the enemy's ability to absorb attrition; second, that the enemy is willing or can be compelled to accept battle on a large scale – as Lee and the Germans were, but the Viet Cong generally were not; and third, and most important, that there is something to be gained strategically by exploiting this tactical advantage.

It is not sufficient to give battle simply because it is tactically advantageous to do so. It is more important that it be strategically advantageous or strategically necessary; that is, there should be something to gain strategically by fighting or to lose by not fighting. Strategic gain or necessity can be sufficient reason even when the situation is tactically disadvantageous. It thus is conceivable to accept or even expect a tactical defeat which serves strategy. In that way, after running away from Cornwallis' British forces for six weeks in the Carolinas in 1781, Nathanael Greene could decide 'to give battle on the theory that he could hardly lose. If Cornwallis should win a tactical victory, he was already so far gone in exhaustion it would probably hurt him almost as much as a defeat.'[8]

As an example of failure in this regard, consider the German offensive of March 1918 – a dramatic tactical success by standards of the day – in which General Erich Ludendorff had attacked 'at those points where it was easiest to break through and not at those points where the announced aim of the offensive could be served.'[9] Of the March offensive, Martin van Creveld commented: 'Ludendorff started from the assumption that tactics were more important than strategy; it was a question above all of launching an offensive at a point where a tactical breakthrough was possible, not where a strategic one was desirable.'[10] Ludendorff's failure was not so much that he pursued tactical success, but that he did not exploit that success strategically. When at a strategic and operational disadvantage, as was Ludendorff's case, we may have to pursue the only advantage left, even if it is only tactical. The essential key, however, is to elevate the effects of tactical success to a higher level. This was Ludendorff's failure. Rather than reinforcing the Eighteenth Army, which was succeeding and might have effected an operational breakthrough, he reinforced the Seventeenth, which had been halted. So, while a tactical success, the offensive failed to achieve the desired operational penetration.

Ideally, the operational commander fights only when and where he wants to. His ability to do this is largely a function of his ability to maintain the initiative and shape the events of war to his purposes. 'In war it is all-important to gain and retain the initiative, to make the enemy conform to your action, to dance to your tune.'[11] And initiative in turn is largely the product of maintaining a higher operational tempo. But we must realize that we may not always be able to fight on our own terms; we may be compelled to fight by a skillful enemy who wants to fight or by strategic constraints. In such cases, we have no choice but to give battle in a way that serves strategy as much as possible and to exploit the results of combat to the greatest advantage. It is in this light that a tactical defeat may amount to a strategic victory, as for the North Vietnamese in the 1968 Tet offensive, which, although repulsed, struck a serious blow against American resolve.[12]

The conduct of the battle, once joined, is principally a tactical problem, but even then the tactician should keep larger aims in mind as he fights. As an example, consider Guderian at the battle of Sedan, May 1940. Guderian's XIXth Panzer corps was attacking generally south 'to win a bridgehead over the Meuse at Sedan and thus to help the infantry divisions that would be following to cross that river. No instructions were given as to what was to be done in the event of a surprise success.'[13] By 13 May, Guderian had forced a small bridgehead. By the 14th, he had expanded the bridgehead to the south and west, but had not broken through the French defenses. Contemplating the tactical decision of how to continue the battle, without higher guidance, Guderian opted to attack west in concert with the strategic aim of the campaign. '1st and 2d Panzer Divisions received orders immediately to change direction with all their forces, to cross the Ardennes Canal, and to head west with the objective of breaking clear through the French defenses.'[14]

Perspective

The operational level of war is largely a matter of perspective. The campaign demands a markedly different perspective than the battle. It requires us to *think big*, as Slim put it, seeing beyond the parameters of immediate combat to the requirements of the theater strategy as the basis for deciding when, where, and who to fight. We should view no tactical action in isolation, but always in light of the design for the theater as a whole.

While the tactician looks at the immediate tactical problem and the conditions directly preceding and following, the operational commander must take a broader view. He must not become so involved in tactical activities that he loses his proper perspective. This broader perspective implies broader dimensions of time and space over which to apply the military art. The actual dimensions of the operational canvas vary with the nature of the war, the size and capabilities of available forces, and the geographical characteristics of the theater. But the commander must use all the time and space within his influence to create the conditions of success. In 1809, Napoleon carried with him maps of the entire continent of Europe, thus enabling consideration of operations wherever they suited his purposes.[15] Similarly, when after five years Rome had been unable to drive Hannibal out of Italy by direct confrontation, Scipio in 204 B.C. compelled the Carthaginian to abandon Italy without a fight by opening a new front in Africa.

Given this broader perspective, the MAGTF commander can use the inherent reach of his organic aviation to see and shape the course of the campaign in time and space well in advance of the close combat of ground forces. This reach applies not only to the direct application of aviation combat power, but also to the range it provides ground forces as well. Such activities include attempting to ascertain the enemy's operational intentions; delaying enemy reinforcements by interdiction; degrading critical enemy functions or capabilities such as command and control, offensive air support, or logistics; and manipulating the enemy's perceptions.

Based on this larger perspective, the operational commander views military geography on a different scale as well. He should not be concerned with the details of terrain that are of critical importance to the tactician in combat, such as hillocks, draws, fingers, clearings or small woods, creeks, or broken trails.

TACTICS SUPPORTING OPERATIONS: GUDERIAN, 1940

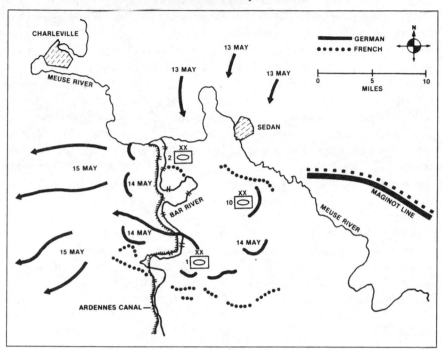

Guderian's tactical conduct of the battle of the Sedan bridgehead reflected an appreciation for the operational and strategic situations. In the midst of the battle he changed his direction of attack in keeping with the aim of the campaign: '1st and 2d Panzer Divisions received orders immediately to change direction with all their forces, to cross the Ardennes Canal, and to head west with the objective of breaking clear through the French defenses.'

Rather, his concern is with major geographical features which can bear on the campaign: rivers, roads, railways, mountain ridges, towns, airfields, ports, and natural resource areas. Although by this time the German army had introduced tactical maps with contour lines showing terrain relief, for his 1866 and 1870 campaigns Moltke used railroad maps of Europe[16] – his concern was with the movement of large forces. Similarly, Patton believed that 'in the higher echelons, a layered map of the whole theater to a reasonable scale, showing roads, railways, streams, and towns is more useful than a large-scale map cluttered up with ground forms and a multiplicity of nonessential information.'[17]

The difference among the levels of war being one of degree, many activities in war apply universally but manifest themselves differently at the different levels. The simplest way to understand these distinctions is to use the construct we established in chapter 1 which describes activities at the strategic level as bearing directly on the war overall, at the operational level as bearing on the campaign, and at the tactical level as bearing on combat; that is, the battle or engagement. Since a higher level in the hierarchy outweighs a lower, we should seek to give our actions impact at the highest possible level. Thus, as we mentioned, in designing our campaign we seek to attack those critical enemy factors of strategic vice operational or tactical importance.[18] In the same way, as we will see, operational maneuver carries a greater decisive effect than tactical maneuver.

LEVEL	FUNCTION/CAPABILITY							ARENA
STRATEGY	MANEUVER	MOBILITY	TEMPO	INTELLIGENCE	SURPRISE	LOGISTICS	LEADERSHIP	WAR
OPERATIONS								CAMPAIGN/ THEATER
TACTICS								ENGAGEMENT/ BATTLE

Maneuver

Maneuver is the employment of forces to secure an advantage – or leverage – over the enemy to accomplish the mission. Tactical maneuver aims to gain an advantage in combat. Operational maneuver, on the other hand, impacts beyond the realm of combat. In fact, it aims to reduce the amount of fighting necessary to accomplish the mission. By operational maneuver, we seek to gain an advantage which bears directly on the outcome of the campaign or in the theater as a whole. A classic example is MacArthur's landing of the 1st Marine

Division at Inchon in 1950, by which he collapsed the overextended North Korean army surrounding Pusan. Another is Sherman's Atlanta campaign in 1864 in which he repeatedly refused battle, instead turning the Confederate flank successively at Dalton, Resaca, Cassville, Allatoona, Marietta (but here only after his attempted assault had failed at Kennesaw Mountain), and the Chatahoochie River.[19] His opponent Joseph Johnston's response was to try to halt the Union advance by defending from strong battle positions (which he had had the entire winter to prepare) along the route of advance, falling back to subsequent prepared positions when necessary. By ignoring Johnston's attempts to bring him to battle, Sherman nullified the strength of Johnston's tactical defense; instead he maneuvered directly against the objective of the campaign, Atlanta.[20]

Typically, we think of maneuver as a function of relational movement and fire on a grand scale, but this is not necessarily the case. The Combined Action Program, begun by III Marine Amphibious Force under General Lewis Walt in 1965 during the Vietnam War, is an example of unconventional maneuver at the operational level.[21] The program sought to make the Viet Cong guerrillas' position untenable by attacking their essential base of popular support through the pacification of South Vietnamese villages.

If tactical maneuver takes place during and within battle, operational maneuver takes place before, after, and beyond battle. The operational commander seeks to secure a decisive advantage before battle is joined – as Napoleon did at Ulm in 1805 by means of a turning movement so decisive that Mack surrendered his army of 30,000 after only one half-hearted attempt to break out. Equally, the operational commander seeks to exploit tactical success to achieve strategic results – as General Sir Edmund Allenby did in Palestine and Syria in 1918 after penetrating the right wing of the Turkish line at the Battle of Megiddo. The victory at Megiddo was not decisive in itself, but was a necessary precondition for strategic success. In 38 days, Allenby had advanced 360 miles, destroyed three Turkish armies, took 76,000 prisoners, and knocked Turkey out of the war.[22] The only tactical action of the campaign was the breakthrough, during which Allenby suffered most of his 5,000 casualties; the rest was an operational pursuit. Interestingly, Allenby's original plan reflected only a tactical ambition; it would certainly have resulted in the defeat of the Turkish Eighth Army (one of three Turkish armies manning the front) but would not have unhinged the entire Turkish defense or threatened the critical Hejaz railroad. With no additional forces, Allenby used the same basic concept but modified the scope to exploit to greater depth and collapse the entire defense.

A vivid example of failure to exploit tactical opportunity is the battle of Sidi Barrani in North Africa, December 1940. In a maneuver reminiscent of Allenby in Syria, General Sir Richard O'Connor's Western Desert Force of two divisions

OPERATIONAL MANEUVER: SHERMAN, 1864

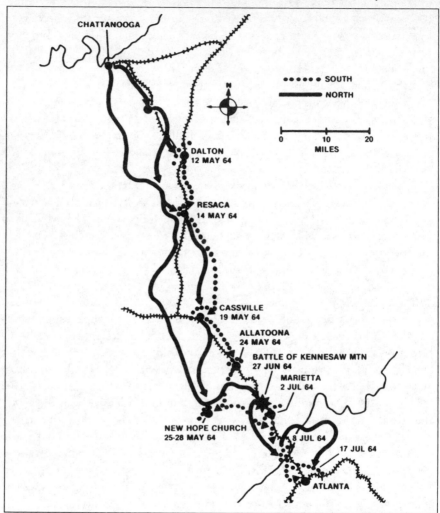

Advancing on Atlanta, Sherman refuses Johnston's repeated efforts to compel him to make frontal assaults against prepared defensive positions, instead turning the Confederate flank repeatedly.

EXPLOITING TACTICAL SUCCESS: ALLENBY, 1918

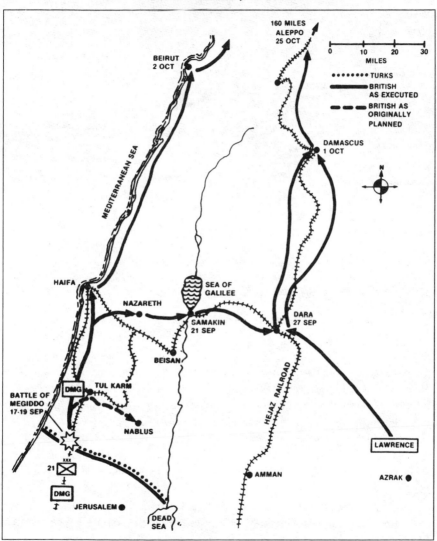

Exploiting the breakthrough at the second battle of Megiddo, Allenby's Desert Mounted Group (DMG) pours into the enemy rear; the Turkish armies collapse.

FAILING TO EXPLOIT TACTICAL SUCCESS: WAVELL, 1940

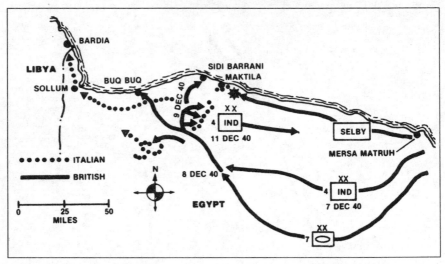

Failing to recognize the significance of the victory at Sidi Barrani, Wavell withdraws the 4th Indian Division rather than pursue.

penetrated and collapsed a much larger Italian force. The higher commander in Cairo, General Sir Archibald Wavell, who had never envisioned the attack as anything more than a raid, promptly withdrew the 4th Indian Division for an offensive in Eritrea, forfeiting the potential opportunity to end the war in North Africa and setting the stage for the arrival of Erwin Rommel and the legend of 'The Desert Fox.' Liddell Hart recounted: 'Thus on December 11, the third day of the battle, the routed Italians were running westwards in panic while half the victor's force was marching eastwards – back to back!'[23]

Closer to home, the Battle of the Crater at Petersburg in July 1864 illustrates the same sort of failure. Four tons of gunpowder detonated by Union forces in the Petersburg Mine tore a great gap in the Confederate defenses. Burnside's IXth Corps was to assault through the gap, but the operation was bungled, the Confederate forces rallied over time to seal the gap by fire, and 3,293 Union soldiers were lost in 'one of the great tragic fiascos of the war.'[24]

Carried to its perfect extreme, operational maneuver would, in Liddell Hart's words, 'produce a decision without any serious fighting'[25] – as for Napoleon at Ulm. 'For even if decisive battle be the goal, the aim of strategy must be to bring about this battle under the most advantageous circumstance. And the more advantageous the circumstance, the less, proportionately, will be the fighting.'[26] Therefore, the *'true aim is not so much to seek battle as to seek a strategic situation so advantageous that if it does not of itself produce the decision, its continuation by a battle is sure to achieve this.'*[27]

Mobility

If the classic application of maneuver is relational movement, then superior mobility – the capability to move from place to place while retaining the ability to perform the mission[28] – becomes a key ingredient. The object is to use mobility to develop leverage by creating superiority at the point of battle or to avoid altogether disadvantageous battle.

In maneuver at the operational level, naturally it is not tactical mobility that matters but operational mobility. The difference, if subtle, is significant. Tactical mobility is the ability to move in combat; that is, *within* the engagement or battle. Tactical mobility is a function of speed and acceleration over short distances, of protection, agility, and the ability to move cross-country. Operational mobility is the ability to move between engagements and battles within the context of the campaign or theater. Operational mobility is a function of range and sustained speed over distance.[29] If the essence of the operational level is deciding when and where to fight, operational mobility is the means by which we commit the necessary forces based on that decision. An advantage in operational mobility can have a significant impact. In the First World War, that advantage resided with the defender, who could shift forces laterally by rail faster than the attacker could advance on foot. By the Second World War, mechanization had reversed the advantage, as Germany's overrunning of France demonstrated.[30]

Tactics demand movement cross-country, but operational movement, for speed and volume, relies on existing road, rail, or river networks. Patton recognized this when he wrote: 'Use roads to march on; fields to fight on . . . When the roads are available for use, you save time and effort by staying on them until shot off.'[31]

Although we typically think of shipping as a component of strategic mobility, it may be employed to operational effect as well. In many cases, a MAGTF carried on amphibious shipping can enjoy greater operational mobility along a coastline than an enemy moving along the coast by roads – particularly when the amphibious force has the ability to interfere with the enemy's use of those roads. In this way, the MAGTF maneuvers by landing where the enemy is vulnerable.[32] If exploited, such an advantage in operational mobility can be decisive. Similarly, while we typically think of helicopters as a means of improving mobility tactically, we should not rule out their usefulness as a means of mobility in the operational sense as well.

Tempo

Tempo is a rate or rhythm of activity. Tempo is a significant weapon because it is through a faster tempo that we seize the initiative and dictate the terms of war. Tactical tempo is the rate of work within an engagement. Operational tempo is the rate of work between engagements. In other words, it is the ability to consistently shift quickly from one tactical action to another.

It is not in absolute terms that tempo matters, but in terms relative to the enemy. After his breakthrough at Megiddo, in what amounted to a rout Allenby averaged less than ten miles a day, but the tempo was more than the Turks could handle; they were never able to reconstitute their defense and return the action to the tactical level.

We create operational tempo in several ways. First, we gain tempo by multiple tactical actions undertaken simultaneously. Thus, the multiple tactical thrusts we discussed in chapter 2 as a means of creating flexibility and ambiguity also generate tempo.

Second, we gain tempo by anticipating tactical results and developing in advance *sequels* for exploiting those results without delay.

Third, we generate tempo by creating a command system based on decentralized decision-making within the framework of a unifying intent. Slim recalled of his experience in Burma in the Second World War: 'Commanders at all levels had to act more on their own; they were given greater latitude to work out their own plans to achieve what they knew was the Army Commander's intention. In time they developed to a marked degree a flexibility of mind and a firmness of decision that enabled them to act swiftly to take advantage of sudden information or changing circumstances without reference to their superiors.'[33]

And finally, we maintain tempo by avoiding unnecessary combat. Any battle or engagement, even if we destroy the enemy, takes time and thus saps our operational tempo. So we see another reason besides the desire for economy for fighting only when and where necessary. Conversely, by maintaining superior operational tempo we can lessen the need to resort to combat. The German blitz through France in 1940 was characterized more by the calculated avoidance of pitched battle after the breakthrough than by great tactical victories. By contrast, French doctrine called for deliberate, methodical battle. When denied this by the German tempo of operations, the defenders were overwhelmed; like the Turks versus Allenby, they were unable to reconstitute an organized resistance and force the Germans to fight for their gains.[34] Liddell Hart wrote of the 1940 campaign in France:

> The issue turned on the time-factor at stage after stage. French countermeasures were repeatedly thrown out of gear because their timing was too slow to catch up with the changing situations ... The French commanders, trained in the

slow-motion methods of 1918, were mentally unfitted to cope with the panzer pace, and it produced a spreading paralysis among them.[35]

Intelligence

The differences among the tactical, operational, and strategic levels of intelligence are principally ones of scope. Tactical intelligence provides information on the environment and enemy capabilities as they affect combat; that is, of an immediate or imminent impact. Operational intelligence provides information which impacts on the campaign; it must reflect the broader perspective of operations. Operational intelligence thus must take a wider view over area and a longer view over time. As the operational level of war is less a matter of actual fighting and more a matter of schemes and intentions, operational intelligence focuses less on current combat capabilities and more on forecasting future enemy capabilities, intentions, and options.

Because the operational level of war has as its aim the attainment of a strategic objective, operational intelligence must provide insight into the strategic situation and all factors, military and otherwise, that influence it. Most information-gathering assets organic to the MAGTF are principally tactical in scope, although by no means exclusively so. As a result, the MAGTF commander must often rely on assets external to the MAGTF for sources for much of his operational intelligence.

Surprise

Surprise is a state of disorientation which is the result of unexpected events and which degrades ability to react effectively. Surprise can be of decisive importance. Tactical surprise catches the enemy unprepared in such a way as to affect the outcome of combat; it is of a relatively immediate and local nature. Operational surprise catches the enemy unprepared in such a way as to impact on the campaign. To achieve operational surprise, we need not catch the enemy tactically unaware. For example, at the Inchon landing in 1950, the need for the early capture of Wolmi-do island, which dominated the inner approaches to Inchon harbor, compromised any hope of achieving tactical surprise with the main landings. But operational surprise was complete; although the assault on Wolmi-do was preceded by a five-day aerial bombardment, the North Korean army surrounding Pusan could not react in time. It was cut off and soon collapsed.[36] The subsequent entry of Communist China into the war achieved surprise of a strategic order, significantly altering the entire balance of the war.

Surprise may be the product of deception, by which we mislead the enemy into acting in a way prejudicial to his interests[37] – for example, the Normandy invasion in which an elaborate deception plan convinced the Germans the invasion would take place at Calais. Surprise may be the product of ambiguity, by which we leave the enemy confused as to our intentions through variable or multiple actions – for example, the Allied invasion of North Africa in 1942; Eisenhower's choice of a thousand miles of coastline from Casablanca to Tunis precluded the Axis forces from anticipating the actual landings. Or, surprise may simply be the product of a flair for the unexpected, such as MacArthur's stroke at Inchon.

Of the three, deception would seem to offer the greatest potential payoff because it deludes the enemy into a false move. But because it means actually convincing the enemy of a lie rather than simply leaving him confused or ignorant, deception is also the most difficult to execute. This is truer yet at the operational level than at the tactical. Due to the broader perspective of operations, operational deception must feed false information to a wider array of enemy intelligence collection means over a longer period of time. This increases the complexity of the deception effort, the need for consistency, and the risk of compromise.[38]

Allenby's Syrian campaign offers insight into the typical elaborateness of operational deception and the difference between tactical and operational surprise. For weeks before the beginning of the offensive, Allenby had put Colonel T.E. Lawrence, whose Arab force was operating far to the east, to work purchasing all the forage he could – enough for all Allenby's needs. Allenby had commandeered the largest hotel in Jerusalem, which was toward the eastern flank of his army, and had established a large mock headquarters there. Also, for weeks before the offensive, he had ordered large movements of forces behind his lines to simulate a concentration near the Dead Sea. The purpose of all this activity was to convince the Turks he meant to campaign in the east rather than the west. Finally, for tactical good measure to mislead the Turks as to the timing of the attack, he had scheduled and publicized widely a horse meet set for the same day. So convincing was the deception that, shortly before the offensive, an Indian defector who disclosed the plan to the Turks was dismissed by the Turks as an Allied ruse.

Logistics

At the operational level much more than at the tactical, logistics may determine what is possible and what is not; for 'a campaign plan that cannot be logistically supported is not a plan at all, but simply an expression of fanciful wishes.'[39]

Strategic logistics involves the development and stocking of war materials and their deployment from the United States to various theaters. At the opposite end of the spectrum, tactical logistics is concerned with sustaining forces in combat. It deals with the fueling, arming, and maintaining of troops and machines. Tactical logistics involves the actual performance of combat service support functions with resources immediately or imminently available – usually resident in the combat unit's trains. In order to perform these functions, the tactical commander must be provided the necessary resources. Providing these resources is the role of operational logistics.[40]

Operational logistics thus connects the logistical efforts at the tactical and strategic levels, taking the resources supplied by strategy and making them available in sufficient amounts to the tactical commander. Logistics at the operational level takes on three basic tasks. The first is to procure locally those necessary resources not provided by strategy. We may accomplish this through support agreements with a host nation or other Services, through the local economy, or by capturing resources from the enemy, as was sometimes a consideration for the German forces in North Africa during the Second World War.

The second task is to manage often limited resources as necessary to sustain the campaign. This involves both the apportioning of resources among tactical forces based on the operational plan and the rationing of resources to ensure sustainment throughout the duration of the campaign. Thus, at the operational level much more than the tactical, logistics demands an appreciation for the expenditure of resources and the timely anticipation of requirements. While failure to anticipate logistical requirements at the tactical level can result in delays of hours or days, the same failure at the operational level can result in delays of days or weeks.

The third task is to deliver resources in the necessary amounts to the tactical forces. This involves the creation of a logistical delivery system sufficient to sustain the force throughout the length of the campaign and the breadth of the theater or area of operations. This system requires sufficient ports of entry to receive the necessary volume of resources supplied by strategy, lines of communication (land, sea, or air) and facilities sufficient to support the movement of those resources, and a fleet of vehicles or craft to do the moving. Road networks are naturally of principal concern, but they are not the only means by which to sustain the force. Particularly in Third World areas where roads may be inadequate, commanders should consider the use of railways (which can move far greater volumes of supplies than vehicles can in the same amount of time), navigable waterways, and aircraft as well.

The logistical system organic to a MAGTF is primarily tactical in nature, designed to support the MAGTF within the confines of the beachhead. Thus, the MAGTF commander waging a campaign beyond the beachhead must construct a logistical apparatus primarily from external sources, such as through host nation support, inter-Service agreements, or local procurement. Furthermore, the advertised 60- and 30-day logistical capability of the MEF and MEB respectively will vary depending on the nature and scope of operations, particularly if the MAGTF launches an expeditionary campaign beyond the beachhead.

Historically, American strategy has often sought to obviate the first two tasks by providing operational commanders a superabundance of resources, making the distribution of these resources the only logistical concern at the operational level. However, in expeditionary warfare, this approach is infeasible without a large-scale commitment which may be politically unacceptable. Moreover, in expeditionary warfare, this approach may not even be desirable. A large logistical base to which the combat forces are tied becomes a vulnerability which must be protected and can also limit operational freedom. The concepts of seabasing and selective off-loading, in which limited resources are transferred ashore, can alleviate this problem. The real solution is to be able to operate without a cumbersome logistical tail. Forces able to operate on a shoestring are less vulnerable to attacks against their logistical tails, are less dependent on a continuous high-volume logistical flow, and can operate on lines which would not support a large logistical apparatus. Consider again the example of Sherman, having captured Atlanta and establishing a forward base there. Future offensive action was restricted by the need to protect his 400-mile line of communication to Nashville, which was being harassed continuously by Confederate cavalry. Sherman concluded that to try to track down the elusive Confederates would be counterproductive to Grant's strategy. His solution was to reduce the size of his force by returning the Army of the Cumberland to Nashville, abandon his line of communication, and continue the advance – his 'March to the Sea' – living off the countryside and making 'Georgia howl.'[41]

Inherent in the ability to operate this way is the willingness to sacrifice the level of luxury to which American forces have often become accustomed.

Leadership

Leadership is the personal ability to influence the performance of human beings in pursuit of a goal. The result of strong leadership is increased understanding and commitment from the members of the organization. At the higher levels of command, leadership is much less a matter of direct personal example and intervention than it is a matter of being able to energize and unify the efforts of large groups of people, sometimes dispersed over great distances. This is not to say that personal contact is unimportant at this level. Even at the highest levels, the commander must see and be seen by his Marines. As the supreme Allied commander in Europe, Eisenhower spent a great deal of time traveling throughout the theater being seen by his men. Nor does this imply that the higher commander does not intervene in the actions of his subordinates when necessary. But just as the operational level involves being able to decide when and where to fight, leadership at this level involves the ability to determine when and where personal influence is required. Since the higher commander cannot be in all places at once, he must pick his spots carefully. Finally, this is not to say that charisma and strength of personality are unimportant at this level. In fact, we might argue that because the operational commander must influence more people spread over greater distances, he should be correspondingly more charismatic and stronger of personality.

Leadership at the operational level requires clarity of vision, strength of will, and extreme moral courage – as demonstrated repeatedly by men such as MacArthur, Slim, and Manstein. Moreover, it requires the ability to communicate these traits clearly and powerfully through numerous layers of command, each of which exerts a certain friction on effective communication. As Slim said, the operational commander must possess 'the power to make his intentions clear right through the force.'[42] 'The will of Frederick and Napoleon,' Hans von Seekt wrote, 'was a living force in the humblest grenadier.'[43]

The operational commander must establish a climate of cohesion among the widely dispersed elements of his command and with adjacent and higher headquarters as well.[44] Because he cannot become overly involved in tactics, the operational commander must have confidence in his subordinate commanders with whom he must develop mutual trust and an implicit understanding.

The nature of theater operations places certain peculiar demands on leadership. These will be felt most keenly by the MAGTF commander, who must coordinate externally with other Services and nationalities. He must maintain effective relationships with external organizations – particularly when other cultures are involved.[45] He must have the ability to gain consensus for joint or combined concepts of operations.[46] And he must be able to represent the capabilities, limitations, and external support requirements of the MAGTF effectively to higher headquarters.

NOTES

1. Sun Tzu, *The Art of War*, p. 77.
2. In a letter, April 1863, as quoted in Robert D. Heinl, Jr., *Dictionary of Military and Naval Quotations* (Annapolis, MD: U.S. Naval Academy, 1978) p. 1.
3. Clausewitz, *On War*, p. 177.
4. *Ibid.*, p. 128.
5. *The defeat of the VC and NVA during the TET Offensive of 1968 was a tactical and operational success. The VC never again could mount anything larger than company size units. The NVA assumed the full burden for the war. The strategical defeat was in Washington, D.C. where a President and his closest advisors never attempted to win the allegiance of the people. The press only amplified the popular discontent and the disinformation was total. Only a few understood what a great operational victory had been won, but it was lost on the people and their elected representatives. H.T.H.*
6. Eisenhower, p. 119.
7. After a successful but costly tactical action, Lettow-Vorbeck concluded: 'Although the attack carried out at Jassini with nine companies had been completely successful, it showed that such heavy losses as we also had suffered could

only be borne in exceptional cases. We had to economize our forces in order to last out a long war ... The need to strike great blows only quite exceptionally, and to restrict myself principally to guerilla warfare, was evidently imperative.', pp. 56–57.

8. Weigley, p. 32.
9. Gordon A. Craig, 'Delbrueck: The Military Historian,' *Makers of Modern Strategy from Machiavelli to the Nuclear Age*, ed. Peter Paret (Princeton, NJ: Princeton University Press, 1986) p. 351. As quoted by William J. Bolt and David Jablonsky, 'Tactics and the Operational Level of War,' *The Operational Level of War Across the Spectrum of Conflict* (Carlisle, PA: U.S. Army War College, 1987), p. 38.
10. Martin van Creveld, *Command in War*, (Cambridge, MA: Harvard University Press, 1985), p. 172.
11. Sir William Slim, *Defeat Into Victory* (London: Cassell and Company, 1956), p. 292.
12. *It also struck a blow against American credibility. H.T.H.*
13. Heinz Guderian, *Panzer Leader* (Washington: Zenger Publishing, 1952), p. 97.
14. *Ibid.*, pp. 105–106.
15. van Creveld, p. 290.
16. Interview 1 Nov 89 with Bruce I. Gudmundsson, author of *Storm Troop Tactics* (New York: Praeger, 1989).
17. Patton, pp. 373–374. From this reasoning we might conclude that a 1:50,000 map, which clearly shows terrain in tactical detail and therefore promotes a tactical perspective, is in many cases inappropriate at the MAGTF level.
18. *In Iraq and Kuwait during the Gulf War air power attacked strategic targets daily, yet not one Iraqi division left Kuwait until operational targets were attacked by ground forces. H.T.H.*
19. *'Refused battle' is a wrong interpretation of the facts. In fact, Grant said that Johnston fought a grand rear guard action, thus delaying the end of the war much longer than anticipated. H.T.H.*
20. R. Ernest and Trevor N. Dupuy, *Encyclopedia of Military History*, 2d revised edition (New York: Harper & Row, 1986), pp. 898–900.
21. *This is partly right. See note 14, p. 113. H.T.H.*
22. *Ibid.*, p. 988.
23. B.H. Liddell Hart, *History of the Second World War* (New York: G.P. Putnam's Sons, 1970), p. 114. Ironically, Wavell, who had been with Allenby in the First World War, wrote shortly before the offensive: 'It is, however, possible that an opportunity may offer for converting the enemy's defeat into an outstanding victory.... I do wish to make certain that if a big opportunity occurs we are prepared morally, mentally and administratively to use it to the fullest.' Correlli Barnett, *The Desert Generals* (Bloomington, IN: Indiana University Press, 1986), p. 35.
24. Dupuy and Dupuy, p. 896. Grant, pp. 467–8.
The great tragedy of the battle was that a black Union regiment had trained for months in preparation for the Battle for the Crater. Unfortunately, Union generals changed the

regiment at the last moment and the men attacking in the crater were untrained for that maneuver and were slaughtered. H.T.H.

25. Liddell Hart, *Strategy*, p. 324.

26. *Ibid.* What Liddell Hart referred to as strategy in his two-part construct of strategy-tactics, we refer to today in the strategy-operations-tactics construct as the operational level.

27. Liddell Hart, *Strategy*, p. 326. Italics in the original.

28. JCS Pub. 1–02: '**Mobility** – (DOD, NATO, IADB) A quality or capability of military forces which permits them to move from place to place while retaining the ability to fulfill their primary mission.'

29. In this respect, the M1 tank, for example, with its speed, acceleration, armor, and agility has greater tactical mobility than the M60 in a tank-versus-tank comparison. But the M60 has superior operational mobility because it uses less fuel and has a greater cruising radius and because, being less complex, it demands less maintenance. Incidently, the M60 also has greater strategic mobility because, being lighter and smaller, it can be transported in greater numbers between theaters. The light armored vehicle has less tactical mobility than either tank in most environments but has operational and strategic mobility far superior to both. It can be transported in far greater numbers by strategic lift. Its comparatively simple automotive system, fuel efficiency, and wheels give it far greater operational range and speed.

30. Lind, p. 46.

31. Patton, pp. 380–381.

32. Lind, p. 46.

33. Slim, pp. 451–2.

34. See Robert A. Doughty, *The Seeds of Disaster: The Development of French Army Doctrine 1919–1939* (Hamden, CT: Archon Books, 1985), p. 4.

35. Liddell Hart, *History of the Second World War*, pp. 73–4.

36. In *Semper Fidelis: The History of the United States Marine Corps*, Allan R. Millett writes: 'Although hardly an artistic success, the Inchon landing caught the NKPA [North Korean People's Army] by surprise, and by early morning of September 16 there was no doubt that the 1st Division was ready to exploit the landing. With adequate tanks, artillery, and service units ashore and covered by carrier air, the 1st Division started down the highway for Seoul.

    'In five days of textbook campaigning, the 1st Marine Division closed on the approaches of Seoul by September 20.' (New York: Macmillan Publishing Co.), p. 488.

37. JCS Pub. 1–02: '**Deception** – (DOD, NATO, IADB) Those measures designed to mislead the enemy by manipulation, distortion, or falsification of evidence to induce him to act in a manner prejudicial to his interests.'

38. See FM 100–6, pp. 3–19 through 3–23.

39. Meehan, p. 16.

40. *Except in Saudi Arabia during the Gulf War, the Americans have often come close to losing campaigns due to poor operational logistical planning. General George S. Patton was stopped from his rapid advance into Europe because of this very factor. H.T.H.*

41. Dupuy and Dupuy, p. 900. Also, William T. Sherman, *Memoirs of General William T. Sherman* (New York: Da Capo Press, 1984), vol. II, p. 152.
42. Slim, p. 542.
43. Hans von Seekt, *Thoughts of a Soldier*, trans. G. Waterhouse (London: Ernest Benn Ltd., 1930), pp. 128–9.
44. FM 100–6, p. 3–23.
45. *Ibid.*, p. 3–24.
46. *Ibid.*

Conclusion

'Those who know when to fight and when not to fight are victorious. Those who discern when to use many or few troops are victorious. Those whose upper and lower ranks have the same desire are victorious. Those who face the unprepared with preparation are victorious. Those whose generals are able and are not constrained by their governments are victorious.'[1]

— Sun Tzu

At the risk of belaboring a point, we will repeat for the last time that tactical success of itself does not necessarily bring strategic success. 'It is possible to win all the battles and still lose the war. If the battles do not lead to the achievement of the strategic objective, then, successful or not, they are just so much wasted effort.'[2] Strategic success, which attains the objectives of policy, is the military object in war. Thus we recognize the need for a discipline of the military art which synthesizes tactical results to create the military conditions that induce strategic success. We have discussed the campaign as the principal vehicle by which we accomplish this synthesis.

Understandably perhaps, as tactics has long been a Marine Corps strength, we have tended to focus on the tactical aspects of war to the neglect of the operational aspects.[3] This neglect may be further caused by the often contradictory virtues of the two levels: the headlong tactical focus on winning in combat (and the spoiling-for-a-fight mentality it necessarily promotes) compared to the operational desire to use combat sparingly. But, as we have seen, actions at the higher levels tend to overpower actions at the lower levels in the hierarchy of war, and neglect of the operational level can prove disastrous even in the face of tactical competence. In the absence of an operational design which synthesizes tactical results into a coalescent whole, what passes for operations is simply the accumulation of tactical victories. Historically, this is not altogether uncommon.[4] As the Vietnam experience shows, even many tactical successes do not always lead to victory.

Tactical competence can rarely attain victory in the face of outright operational incompetence, while operational ignorance can squander what tactical hard work has gained. As the price of war is human loss, it is incumbent on every commander to attain his objective as economically as possible. This demands the judicious and effective use of combat, which in turn demands a skill for the conduct of war at the operational level.

NOTES

1. Sun Tzu, *The Art of War*, (abridged audio cassette), trans. by Thomas Cleary (Boston: Shambala Publications, 1989), side 1.
2. Meehan, p. 15.
3. *Not since WWII has a U.S. Marine Corps general been given independent command for a major conflict. Accordingly, it is not surprising that Marines study tactics more than the operational art. Had General Joseph P. Hoar, USMC, CinC CENTCOM following General Schwarzkopf (the Marine Corps and the Army rotate the CinC) been the CinC during the Gulf War . . . well who knows what might have happened. The CENTCOM headquarters certainly would have been a different place to work. H.T.H.*
4. Lind, p. 45.

BOOK THREE

FMFM 1-3 Tactics

Book Three reproduces, in a new setting, the complete and unabridged original text and notes of FMFM 1-3 *Tactics*, first published June 1991 by the Department of the Navy, Headquarters United States Marine Corps, Washington, D.C.

New, additional notes by Lt. Col. H.T. Hayden are set in italics.

Foreword

This book is about winning in combat. Winning in combat requires many things: excellence in techniques, understanding of the battlefield, an appreciation of the opponent, exemplary leadership, battlefield judgment, and combat power. Yet these factors by themselves are no indicator of probable success in battle. Our study of history unveils that many armies, both winners and losers, possessed many or all of these attributes. When we examine closely the differences between victor and vanquished, we draw one prevailing conclusion. This is that success went to the armies whose leaders, senior and junior, could best harmonize their efforts – their skills and their assets – toward a decisive end. Their success arose not from techniques, procedures, and material but from their leaders' abilities to uniquely and effectively combine them. What they share in common is an uncommon approach to combat. Then as now, winning in combat depends upon leaders – tactical leaders – who can think creatively and act decisively.

This manual is designed for all tactical leaders. Its content pertains equally to all Marine leaders, whether their duties entail combat service support, combat support, or combat arms. It applies to the MAGTF commander as well as the squadron commander and the fire team leader. Every Marine faces tactical decisions in battle regardless of his role.

The concepts and principles within this manual are battle-tested. During Operation Desert Storm, our success on the battlefield resulted directly from the military skill of our leaders at every level of command. Because of their tactical skill and battlefield judgment, our commanders shaped the battlefield and applied the available means of warfare, achieving the tactical and operational advantage at the decisive time and place. We must remember that, although our equipment was superior to that of our enemy, the professionalism of our leaders and warriors won our decisive victory.

Tactics is consonant with **FMFM 1**, *Warfighting*, and **FMFM 1-1** *Campaigning*. It presumes an understanding of the warfighting philosophy, applying it specifically to the tactical level. Like FMFM 1, it is not prescriptive but descriptive, providing guidance in the form of concepts and values. This manual illustrates a philosophy for waging and winning combat.

A.M. GRAY
General, U.S. Marine Corps
Commandant of the Marine Corps

Introduction

*There is only one principle of war and that's this. Hit the other fellow, as
quick as you can, and as hard as you can, where it hurts him the most, when
he ain't looking.'*[1]

What is Tactics?

All Marines know what tactics is. After all, we've heard people talking about
tactics since our first days in recruit training or Officer Candidates School. Most
of us probably recall encountering tactics even before becoming Marines.
People talk about chess tactics, tennis tactics, running tactics, tactics for
studying and for getting better grades, etc.

So what *is* tactics? This isn't just a rhetorical question. Think for a minute of
what tactics means to you. How would you define it? ...

Perhaps you just found that defining tactics isn't quite as simple as it appears.
A formal definition of tactics appears in Joint Pub 1–02. It says tactics is 'the
employment of units in combat ... the ordered arrangement and maneuver of
units in relation to each other and/or to the enemy in order to utilize their full
potentialities.' Although an official definition, it is merely a starting point. Our
inquiry should not stop there. Over the centuries even great military leaders
and thinkers have found it difficult to say exactly what tactics is. Each attempt
offers a somewhat different perspective:

> *'... proper means of organization and action to give unity to effort ...'*[2]
>
> – Du Picq
>
> *'... the changeable element in warfare.'*[3]
>
> – Palit
>
> *'... the art of leading troops in combat.'*[4]
>
> – Von der Goltz
>
> *'... the theory and use of military forces in combat.'*[5]
>
> – Clausewitz
>
> *'... the art of fighting.'*[6]
>
> – Montgomery

139

'... the art of executing the designs of strategy.'[7]

– Wheeler

'... the art and science of winning engagements and battles. It includes the use of firepower and maneuver, the integration of different arms, and the immediate exploitation of success to defeat the enemy ... the product of judgment and creativity ...'[8]

– FMFM 1

A Definition of Tactics

This last quotation is the Marine Corps' approach toward tactics. It is Marine Corps doctrine. What does it tell us?

First, it recognizes that tactics is neither purely art nor purely science, but rather the product of the two elements, each of which multiplies the other. We cannot simply add 'judgment and creativity' (art), to 'techniques and procedures' (science) and arrive at a sum which is tactics. Rather, we use each to increase manyfold the value of the others.

Second, it says that tactics is about 'winning engagements and battles.' Whereas the conduct of campaigns (operations) and wars (strategy) implies broad dimensions of time and space, engagements and battles involve fighting and defeating an enemy at more narrowly defined times and places.

Third, tactics relies upon the use of firepower, movement, and the integration of different arms, which is to say combined arms. Modern tactics is combined arms tactics.

Finally, a single tactical success is not an end in itself. Tactics must serve a greater purpose *beyond* winning the engagement or battle. Through 'immediate exploitation of success,' tactical actions yield operational gains.

Marine Tactics

This, then, is tactics. But is it all we can say on the subject that would be of use to Marines? As Marines, we have distinct characteristics. First, we may specialize in one of three basic areas – ground, aviation, or combat service support – which are three of the four basic components of every Marine Air-Ground Task Force (MAGTF). Second, regardless of that specialization, we all fight together as one single whole, as a MAGTF. So we need to think about tactics in ways that relate to each separate specialty (combat service support, ground, and aviation), but do so *in ways that relate each to the others* by showing what they share – their common tactical ground.

That is what this book attempts to do. It is not a book about fighter tactics, or infantry tactics, or tactics for emergency field repair of combat equipment. It is about tactics for all of these things and more.[9] It is a book of shared tactical concepts, common to all Marines in all our many skills and specialties.

Of course, you must apply these ideas according to the situation. With them, you can face any situation with a useful frame of reference common to all Marines. That brings us back to our definition of tactics from FMFM 1. As that definition notes, the purpose of tactics is winning. That is also the purpose of this book: to show all Marines some tactical concepts which can help us win.

NOTES

1. Sir William Slim, *Defeat into Victory* (London: Cassell and Co. Ltd., 1956), pp. 550–551.
2. Charles Jean Jacques Joseph Ardant du Picq, *Battle Studies* (New York: MacMillan, 1921), p. 47.
3. D.K. Palit, *The Essentials of Military Knowledge* (Aldershot, England: Gale and Polden, 1947), p. xviii.
4. Freiherr Colmar von der Goltz, *Conduct of War* (Kansas City, MO: Franklin Hudson, 1896; reprint, Carlisle Barracks, PA: U.S. Army War College, 1983), vol. 51, *Art of War Colloquium*, p. 25.
5. Karl von Clausewitz, *On War* (Princeton University Press, 1984), p. 86.
6. B.L. Montgomery of Alamein, *A History of Warfare* (Cleveland, OH: World Publishing, 1968), p. 14.
7. J.B. Wheeler, *Art and Science of War* (New York: Van Nostrand, 1889), p. 9.
8. FMFM 1, *Warfighting*, p. 47.
9. *This book is a 'philosophy' about winning. Winning in combat, or winning in a field training exercise, or winning a chess match, etc. It's about competition and that could be on the football field or in the business board room. H.T.H.*

CHAPTER 1

Achieving a Decision

'Combat situations cannot be solved by rule. The art of war has no traffic with rules, for the infinitely varied circumstances and conditions of combat never produce exactly the same situation twice. Mission, terrain, weather, dispositions, armament, morale, supply, and comparative strength are variables whose mutations always combine to form a new tactical pattern. Thus, in battle, each situation is unique and must be solved on its own merits.

'It follows, then, that the leader who would become a competent tactician must first close his mind to the alluring formulae that well-meaning people offer in the name of victory. To master his difficult art he must learn to cut to the heart of a situation, recognize its decisive elements and base his course of action on these.'[1]

The first basic concept in tactics is achieving a decision. This concept marks a major change from the customary American way of war. In the past, American forces have generally sought incremental gains: taking a hill here or a town there, pushing the FEBA[2] forward a few kilometers, or adding to the body count. This attitude was consistent with attrition warfare, which sees war as a slow, cumulative process. In contrast, tactics in maneuver warfare always aim at achieving a decision. What do we mean by achieving a decision?

Antietam

On September 17, 1862, General Robert E. Lee's Confederate Army of Northern Virginia fought the Union Army of the Potomac under Major General George B. McClellan in the vicinity of Antietam Creek, near Sharpsburg, Maryland. Lee's Maryland campaign had begun on September 4, when his army crossed the Potomac River, entered Maryland, and invaded Northern soil for the first time.

On September 16, both armies massed near Sharpsburg. McClellan initially enjoyed an almost 4:1 advantage in infantrymen but did not attack. By midday General T.J. 'Stonewall' Jackson's corps arrived from Harper's Ferry, but the Union still had an advantage of slightly over 2:1. Again, McClellan did not attack. Outnumbered, with his back to the Potomac, Lee constructed defensive works.[3]

At dawn on the 17th, General Joseph Hooker advanced his three Union divisions, with orders to assault the Confederate left. So began the savage fighting which remains the single bloodiest day in American military history — Antietam. Union and Confederate forces mauled one another in three essentially separate engagements. Twenty thousand Union infantrymen, over two divisions, were never committed. Combined casualties were nearly 4,000 dead, 17,000 wounded, and 2,000 missing. The Union suffered the lion's share.

The battle did not resume on the 18th, each force waiting for the other to move. That evening the Army of Northern Virginia recrossed the Potomac River into Virginia.[4] Although he retained a fully rested, combat-effective force of 20,000, McClellan did not pursue. The starving, exhausted, and ill-equipped Army of Northern Virginia was not defeated or destroyed. It withdrew to rebuild and fight Union forces on many other battlefields. Antietam was not decisive.[5]

What commentators mean when they call the combat at Antietam Creek *indecisive* is that it had *no result* beyond many dead and wounded American soldiers, Northern and Southern. It had no meaningful effect. Lincoln implored McClellan to 'not let him [the Confederates] get off without being hurt.' In reply, McClellan promised to 'send trophies'; however, all the commander in chief received was casualty lists and a prolonged war.

Some might argue that Antietam contributed to the ultimate Union victory because the Union could replace its losses more easily than the Confederacy. In a narrow sense, this is correct. Yet it reflects the attrition concept of incremental gains through *body counts*. Attrition warfare can lead to victory, but the cost is usually terrible — as the Civil War showed. The Marine Corps' doctrine of maneuver warfare is not satisfied to call an incremental gain a success. It demands a decision.

Cannae

On August 2, 216 B.C., the Carthaginian general Hannibal fought the Roman army under Varro near the city of Cannae.

As dawn broke, Hannibal drew up his force of 50,000 veterans with his left flank anchored on the River Aufidus, secured from envelopment by the more numerous Romans. His center contained only a thin line of infantry; his main force was concentrated on the flanks. His left and right wings each contained deep phalanxes of heavy infantry. Eight thousand cavalry tied the left of his line to the river. Two thousand cavalry protected his open right flank. Eight thousand men guarded his camp in the rear.

Varro and more than 80,000 Romans accepted the challenge. Seeing the well-protected Carthaginian flanks, Varro dismissed any attempt to envelop. He decided instead to crush his opponent by sheer weight of numbers. He placed 65,000 men in his center, 2,400 cavalry on his right, and 4,800 cavalry on his left and sent 11,000 men to attack the Carthaginian camp.

Following preliminary skirmishes, Hannibal moved his light center line forward into a salient against the Roman center. Then, his heavy cavalry on the left crushed the opposing Roman cavalry and swung completely around the Roman rear. The Roman cavalry fled the field.

The Carthaginian heavy cavalry next turned against the rear of the dense Roman infantry who were pressing Hannibal's thin center line. At the same time, Hannibal wheeled his right and left wings into the flanks of the Roman center. The Romans were boxed in, unable to maneuver or use their weapons effectively. Between 50,000 and 60,000 Romans died that day, and the Roman army was destroyed. At the tactical level, Hannibal's victory was decisive.

Understanding Decisiveness

What do these examples tell us about achieving a decision?

First, they tell us that achieving a decision is important. An indecisive battle wastes the lives of those who fight and die in it. It wastes the efforts of the living as well. All the wounds and pain, the sweat and striving, the equipment destroyed or used up, the supplies expended – all are for little. They bring no great result; they have no further meaning, except comparative attrition and perhaps an incremental gain.

Second, achieving a decision is not easy. History is littered with indecisive battles. Few of the commanders who fought them sought deliberately to avoid a decision. Sometimes the enemy kept them from achieving the decision they sought. In other cases, they were unable to think through how to make the battle decisive. In still other cases – far too many – the commanders had no concept of seeking a decisive result. They fought a battle because it was there to fight; they had no notion of a larger result.

That leads to the third lesson our examples point out. To be decisive, a battle or an engagement must lead to a result beyond itself. Within a battle, an action that is decisive must lead directly to winning the battle as a whole. For the battle as a whole to be decisive, it must lead directly to winning the campaign – to an operational success. Similarly, a decisive campaign must lead directly to strategic victory. A battle like that fought at Antietam was indecisive because it had no larger result. It had no meaning beyond the blood-soaked ground and the rows of dead.[6]

How to Achieve a Decision

Once you understand what is meant by the term *decisive* and why it is important always to seek a decision, a question naturally arises: How do you do it?

Conceptualizing the Battlefield

There is no easy answer to that question because each battle will have its own unique answer. As with so much in warfare, it depends on the situation. No formula or process or acronym can give you the answer.

Rather, the answer lies in military judgment, in the ability of the commander to conceptualize the battlefield and to act decisively. This is the first and greatest duty of a commander at any level: he must picture in his own mind how he intends to fight the battle. He must think through what he wants to do – what result he wants from his actions, and how he will get that result. Central to his thinking must be the question, 'In this situation, what result will be decisive?' He must ask himself this question not just once but constantly, as the battle progresses. As the situation changes, so will the answer and the actions that derive from it.

We can see a good example of conceptualizing the battle so that it leads to a decision in General Robert E. Lee's approach to the battle of Chancellorsville. Despite Union pontoon bridges thrown across the Rappahannock River at Fredericksburg, Virginia, General Lee foresaw that a battle at this location would merely be a Union holding action. Further, any Confederate attempt to stem a Union river crossing would mean fighting under Union artillery which dominated the town from the heights across the river. Thus, Fredericksburg itself was not a promising place for the Confederates to achieve a decision.[7]

General Lee predicted that the Union main effort would be against the center of the Confederate line, arrayed northwest of Fredericksburg. Leaving minimum forces in the city itself to protect his right flank, he reinforced his units already in the vicinity of Chancellorsville, contrary even to the counsel of his trusted 'Stonewall' Jackson.

After sending engineers forward to reconnoiter the Union center, General Lee confirmed his prediction: The Union positions at the center were too strong to assault. Having ruled out a Union attack to his right because of open terrain, and confirming no opening at his center, Lee considered what could be done on his left. Here, he determined to move a force around the Union right flank by way of concealed routes and to attack the Union rear. He put General Jackson to the task. Jackson's flanking march and attack at Chancellorsville unravelled the Union line and sent the Union forces reeling back across the Rapidan River. General Lee's ability to conceptualize the battlefield guided him in striking the Union forces at the decisive point.

Coup d'Oeil

At Chancellorsville, General Lee showed the quality which 18th century military pundits viewed as most important for any commander: *coup d'oeil* (pronounced koo dwee). It means literally 'strike of the eye.' *Coup d'oeil* is the ability to look at a military situation and immediately see its essence, especially the key enemy weakness or weaknesses which, if exploited, can lead to a decision.[8] We see this ability in history's great captains, in people like Alexander, Frederick the Great, and Napoleon. It is largely what made them great captains – what enabled them, in battle after battle, to achieve decisive results.

Napoleon demonstrated *coup d'oeil* in his recapture of Toulon in 1793. After just a quick look at the situation, he saw that the key to victory lay in isolating Toulon from the seaward as well as the landward side. That could be accomplished by placing artillery on a promontory that overlooked the harbor. The English held the promontory on which they had built a large, imposing earthwork known as Fort Mulgrave. Napoleon focused his effort, especially his artillery, on Fort Mulgrave with the result that it fell in the first hours of the French assault on December 17. By midday on the 18th, the French had a battery of ten guns on the promontory prepared to sweep the harbor. The British fleet was forced to evacuate.[9]

Coup d'oeil is the inspiration – the hunch – upon which a leader begins to conceptualize the battle. How does he translate that vision into action?

The Focus of Effort

The first and most important answer reflects one of the central concepts of maneuver warfare: You achieve a decision by focusing your efforts. The focus of effort is the *commander's bid to achieve a decision*. As he thinks about the battle, he determines, as best he can tell beforehand, what action will be decisive. Then, he designates a unit to perform that action. This is his focus of effort.

The focus of effort is the concept that makes maneuver warfare decisive. Maneuver means much more than forces rapidly moving around the battlefield with no intention of bringing force to bear on the enemy. Maneuver is the combination of movement and fire to gain an advantage on the enemy. The focus of effort ties together all the maneuvering and points it at the enemy so that Marines will win. Without a focus of effort, combat would quickly break down into a multitude of unrelated actions, each divergent from the others. With a focus of effort, you have a multitude of independent but related actions, each convergent with the others. Along with the commander's intent and the mission, the focus of effort is the glue that holds maneuver warfare together. And it does more than that: It hurls those many maneuvering elements against the enemy's key weakness.

The focus of effort is the commander's bid to achieve a decision; he works to ensure all his forces and assets support it. Sometimes, he may use them to support it directly. For example, he may give it all his air support, even all his artillery support. He may concentrate his reserve in echelon behind it. He may give it all his antitank or antiair weapons. Often, he will have to take substantial risks elsewhere in order to give his focus of effort the greatest possible punch.

In other situations, some actions may support the focus of effort indirectly. For example, a commander may use his aviation in an attempt to deceive, to lead the enemy to think his focus is other than where it really is. Aviation is particularly useful for this because it can concentrate to support the real focus more quickly than ground forces.

The Germans used their aviation this way at the beginning of their French campaign in 1940. On May 10, 'by scattering their bombing across a broad area, they hoped to conceal their intentions to make their main attack across eastern Belgium and toward Sedan and to make the French think the main effort was taking place in northern and central Belgium.' Yet, just three days later, on May 13, they had 310 medium bombers, 200 dive bombers, and 200 fighters over Sedan. They used the ability of aviation to drop its deception role quickly and focus its effort at the decisive point.[10]

While a commander always has a focus of effort, he may alter it during the course of a battle as events unfold. The enemy is unpredictable, and few battles flow exactly as the commander had originally conceived. He must adjust, and one way to do so is by changing the focus of effort. For example, if, in an attack by a Marine Expeditionary Force, 2d Marines were designated the focus of effort but ran into heavy enemy resistance while the adjacent 7th Marines made a breakthrough, the ground combat element commander would probably redesignate 7th Marines as the focus of effort. This new designation must not, however, be merely nominal. It means that all the combat power which was originally directed to support 2d Marines now goes to 7th Marines.

Central to the ability to defeat enemies more numerous than oneself, focus of effort enables you to have greater combat power at the decisive point.[11] That decision – deciding what unit would be the focus and why, then making it real by ruthlessly concentrating combat power in support of it – is a test of a commander's character. Field Marshal Paul von Hindenburg said that an operation without a focus is like a man without character.[12]

The focus of effort is the main and most important answer to the question, 'How do you achieve a decision?' However, it is an answer that immediately raises another question: 'How do I focus my effort?'

Intent and Mission

From the commander's concept of how he will fight and win the battle comes not only his focus of effort, but also his intent and the missions he assigns his subordinates.

The commander's intent describes the result he wants to get from the battle and his general concept of how he will get it. It gives his subordinates a clear understanding of what is in his mind – his mental picture of the battle. The result is especially important because the battle will often develop in ways he could not anticipate. His concept of how he will get the result he wants may therefore change. But as long as his subordinates clearly understand the end result he wants, they can adapt to changing circumstances on their own without risking a diffusion of effort.[13]

The commander's intent seems to be a simple concept. Yet, in practice, many people have difficulty with it. Often the difficulty stems from the fact that the commander does not have a clear mental picture of either the result he wants or how, in general terms, he thinks he can get it. Consequently, the commander's intent is either empty of content, like 'Defeat the enemy,' or focuses inward on process, like 'Use initiative and boldness,' rather than outward on the enemy and the situation.

Remember, the commander's intent tells you what is in the commander's mind. A commander's intent that is empty or procedural is of no value to subordinates in terms of how to fight and win the battle.

Once the commander has a clear concept of the battle in his mind, he then has a responsibility to convey it clearly to his subordinates. In doing this, the form of the order is unimportant. It may be oral or written; it may be short and to the point with little or no adherence to any set format. Again, it is the result that is important: the subordinates' understanding of what is in the commander's mind. The means should be flexible so that they can be adapted to the situation and to the people involved. The words needed to convey the intent clearly to one subordinate may be different from the words needed with another subordinate. Generally, clarity is easiest to achieve in face-to-face meetings.

From the commander's intent comes the subordinate unit's mission. The mission is in effect a slice of the overall intent, the result the commander wants from that particular unit. The subordinate needs to know both the mission and the intent so that he understands how the result he is to obtain fits into the result wanted from the battle. Again, that understanding is of key importance in allowing the subordinate to adapt to changing circumstances while keeping his effort focused and ensuring it supports and complements the efforts of other friendly units.

Once the commander has made certain his subordinates understand his intent, their missions, and the focus of effort, he should generally give them maximum latitude in deciding how to accomplish their mission and get the result their superior desires. If the how is dictated to them in detail, they will be unable to adapt to the rapid change that is characteristic of combat. They will miss taking advantage of fleeting opportunities, and they will be unable to respond to dangers that appear suddenly and unexpectedly. In short, they will be rigid and ineffective.

In many respects, the heart of maneuver warfare is telling the subordinate what result is needed, then leaving it up to him to obtain the result however he thinks best. That is why maneuver warfare is also called mission tactics.

Summary

As a leader, whether of a fire team or a Marine Expeditionary Force, you are responsible for results. In combat, the most important result is a decisive victory. To get it, you must work ceaselessly in peacetime to develop in yourself a talent for *coup d'oeil* and for thinking through how you are going to win whatever battle you face. You must learn how to translate that mental picture into a focus of effort, a statement of intent, and missions for your subordinates.

Finally, in all your relations with your subordinates, you must learn how to make crystal clear to them the results you want – the output – while leaving it to them to determine methods – the input. Only in this manner can you hope to have the speed and agility in your unit that maneuver warfare requires.

NOTES

1. *Infantry in Battle*, 2d ed. (Richmond, VA: Garrett & Massie, 1939), 1.
2. Joint Pub 1–02: 'forward edge of the battle area – (DOD, NATO) The foremost limits of a series of areas in which ground combat units are deployed, excluding the areas in which the covering or screening forces are operating, designated to coordinate fire support, the positioning of forces, or the maneuver units.'
3. *Lee had just won a great victory when Jackson took Harpers Ferry and fought a strong delaying action at South Mountain. McClellan knew Lee to be the master of the defense and was not sure how many men Lee had (the 'Lost Order' notwithstanding) at Antietam. H.T.H.*
4. *Lee had no fear of turning his back on McClellan, for he knew his opponent well. McClellan never marched more than 5 to 7 miles a day. Lee's army easily did 10 to 11 miles a day, on average, and could do 25 miles when required. Lee knew that once he started, McClellan would never catch him. H.T.H.*
5. For an authoritative account of the battle of Antietam and its consequences, see: James V. Murfin, *The Gleam of Bayonets* (Baton Rouge: Louisiana State University Press, 1965).
6. *How can Antietam be indecisive and Cannae be decisive? Each was a tactical victory, but for what strategic gain? After Hannibal's great victories at Trebia, Lake Trasimene and Cannae, Hannibal never destroyed the Roman army and never captured Rome. In each case Hannibal gained time to try to raise allies against Rome and he was only partially successful. Lee and the Roman army lived to fight again. Lee eventually capitulated but Rome later crushed Hannibal and destroyed Carthage. H.T.H.*
7. *This is a curious observation, particularly as on December 13, 1862, Lee had won a great battle defending Fredericksburg under similar conditions. Lee's cavalry reported major movements north in what was surely a flanking movement and Lee accurately predicted the river crossing that the Yankees would use. After the Union army crossed the river, General J.E.B. Stuart's CSA cavalry reported that the Union right flank was 'in the air,' – unprotected. Lee met with Jackson to discuss options. It was Jackson who recommended that they attack the enemy flank and when asked by Lee how many men he would need, Jackson said his whole corps. H.T.H.*
8. *Oxford English Dictionary* (U.K.: Oxford at the Clarendon Press, 1933), vol. II.
9. David G. Chandler, *The Campaigns of Napoleon* (New York: MacMillan, 1966), pp. 15–28.

10. Robert A. Doughty, *The Breaking Point: Sedan and the Fall of France, 1940* (Hamden, CT: Archon Books, 1990), 266–270.

11. *The very essence of Napoleon's maneuver warfare theory. H.T.H.*

12. Attributed.

13. *Maj. Gen. P.K. Van Riper said that the commander's intent must include 'in order to …' This will ensure that the full meaning of the commander's intent is fully understood. H.T.H.*

CHAPTER 2

Gaining Leverage

'I served over 31 years' active duty with the Marine Corps, saw combat in both Korea and Vietnam, and attended service schools from the Basic School to the National War College. Yet only toward the end of my military career did I realize how little I really understood the art of war. Even as a PFC in Korea, after being medevaced along with most of my platoon after a fruitless frontal assault against superior North Korean forces, it seemed to me there had to be a better way to wage war. Seventeen years later, commanding a battalion at Khe Sanh, I was resolved that none of my Marines would die for lack of superior combat power. But we were still relying on the concentration of superior firepower to win — essentially still practicing Grant's attrition warfare. And we were still doing frontal assaults!' [1]

Many Marines are poker players. When you play poker, you often try to control the expression on your face so as to mislead your opponents. We call that a poker face, and you often use it to bluff. You use it to gain a *decisive advantage*, one that does not come simply from the strength of the cards you hold. That is leverage.

Leverage

Many Marines study martial arts. A major principle of most martial arts is using the opponent's strength and momentum against him. Again, this gains a decisive advantage; it gives you more force than your muscles can provide. That is leverage.

Leverage through a decisive advantage is our next tactical concept. It runs through all tactics.

A light infantry force draws an enemy armored force into rugged, wooded terrain. Unable to see more than a couple hundred yards and restricted to moving on roads, the tanks are easy targets for infantrymen who remain invisible. The infantry destroys the armor by gaining a decisive advantage through terrain. [2]

An attack aircraft flies at treetop level, hugging the earth's contour. Recognizing the upcoming bluffs on his right as his reference point, the pilot pops the aircraft into a vertical climb to locate the enemy column at his 11 o'clock. He quickly rolls in to strafe and rocket the enemy vehicles. Despite enemy air defenses, the pilot destroys several vehicles and stalls the enemy convoy. By flying at an extremely low level and climbing quickly, the pilot evaded the enemy's air defenses. Neither radar nor shoulder-launched antiair weapons could acquire a target. The pilot attacked with a decisive advantage.

A Marine Air-Ground Task Force, using a mechanized force and deep air support, successfully penetrates the enemy's forward defenses and immediately exploits the breakthrough. As the force enters the enemy's support areas, it encounters extensive minefields. Few tanks and vehicles are destroyed, but many lose tracks and roadwheels, and the exploitation is threatened. As these mobility kills mount, momentum lessens. However, combat maintenance teams, traveling with the penetrating force, quickly repair the salvageable vehicles. The MAGTF recovers enough lost vehicles to restore its momentum and turns the exploitation into a pursuit, completely routing the enemy force. Marines gained a decisive advantage by being able to return vehicles to service as fast as the enemy could disable them.

Each of these cases illustrates leverage, or decisive advantage. Too often in history, people have thought of war as a jousting contest between medieval knights where rules put each knight on an equal basis. All they were allowed to do was charge head-on at each other. Like all sports, jousting was carefully designed to be fair.

In war, however, we shouldn't play at jousting. Victory goes to the side that fights smart. Creating and making use of decisive advantages is central to modern tactics. What are some ways you can gain leverage through decisive advantages?

Asymmetry

A common element in most cases of leverage is asymmetry. Think of a lever: its power comes from the fact that the fulcrum is not equidistant from the ends of the lever. The two arms of the lever are asymmetrical, and by putting force on the longer side, you get leverage.

The same is true of war. Considering a war in Europe, one Soviet specialist was questioned concerning the Soviet answer to the superiority of the U.S. Air Force's F-15 fighter. He replied that the answer was not another Soviet fighter; it was putting a T-72 tank on the U.S. Air Force's runway. That is asymmetry.

Fighting asymmetrically is not simply a matter of countering enemy forces with unlike forces: aircraft against tank or infantry against armor. Asymmetry also depends upon tactics that use the enemy's weaknesses as leverage. When an infantry force encounters an enemy infantry force entrenched in a linear defense, its leaders need not call tanks forward to apply asymmetry. Attacks by penetration and infiltration are asymmetrical tactics. Instead of attacking frontally, the infantry commander seeks to avoid the enemy's linear strength by either filtering forces through the defensive position for a follow-on attack (infiltration) or by concentrating his efforts on a very narrow front (penetration).

He gains leverage by avoiding the preponderance of enemy combat power dispersed across a wide front.

Ambush

Perhaps the most common tactical tool for gaining leverage and a decisive advantage is the ambush. All Marines are familiar with an ambush as a type of combat patrol. In maneuver warfare, ambush takes on a much broader meaning, and the *ambush mentality* runs through all tactics.

The ambush mentality is probably not new to you. You may know the ambush mentality from sports. In football, the trap block is an ambush. You pull an offensive lineman off the line, leaving a hole. When a defender comes through the hole, another lineman suddenly blocks him from the side, usually knocking him down. You blind-side him. That is the ambush mentality.

In basketball, setting up a pick is an ambush. As your teammate drives to the basket, you step into the defender's path from behind, blocking his path, stopping his defense, and momentarily clearing a new lane to the basket. Again, that is the ambush mentality.

The ambush mentality tries to turn every situation into an ambush. In this broader sense, an ambush has several distinct qualities.

First, in an ambush you try to *surprise the enemy*. Think of a patrol that you ambush. They are walking through the woods when suddenly, out of nowhere, they are under fire from every direction. Probably they are taking heavy casualties. In addition, their thinking may be paralyzed. The psychological effect of surprise has a quality all its own. To have an ambush mentality means that you always try to surprise the enemy, to do the unexpected. Surprise is the rule rather than the exception.

Second, you want to *draw your enemy unknowingly into a trap*. This will often involve deceiving him. You make one course of action appear inviting when, in fact, that is just where you want him to come because you are waiting for him.

Third, an ambush is *invisible*. If the ambush is not invisible, it ceases to be an ambush and becomes a target. On the modern battlefield, if you can be seen, you can be destroyed. Whether you are defending or attacking, the enemy must not see you until it is too late, until he is falling to your fires. Surprise often depends upon invisibility.

The reverse slope defense is an example of using invisibility to spring an ambush. The enemy does not know you are there until he comes over the crest of a hill and is hit by your fires. His vehicles are hit on their soft underbellies. His troops stand fully exposed to your weapons. Because he could not see you until the last moment, he could not plaster you with artillery fire. The reverse slope not only protects you from his fire; it protects you from his observation. That is the ambush mentality: *do not let yourself be seen*.

Fourth, in an ambush you want to *shock the enemy*. Instead of taking him under fire gradually with a few weapons at long range, you wait until he is within easy range of every weapon. You then open up suddenly, all at once, with everything you've got. He is paralyzed, at least for a time, by the shock. He cannot react. Everything was going fine, no enemy seemed to be anywhere around, and suddenly he is in a firestorm with people falling all around him. Often, he will panic, making his problem worse.

Finally, in the ambush mentality, you *always focus on the enemy*. The purpose of an ambush is not to hold a piece of terrain. It is to destroy the enemy. You use terrain to effect the ambush, but terrain is not what you are fighting for.

Maneuver

Gaining a decisive advantage is what maneuver is all about. Fighting by rules and checklists leads to linear defenses and frontal attacks. As you know, frontal attacks and linear defenses tend to be indecisive. To attain a decision, you need a decisive advantage, and you often get it by maneuvering.

What do we think of when we say 'maneuver'? The classical view of maneuver is movement in combination with fire to gain advantage over the enemy.[3] It conjures visions of a base of fire that keeps the enemy's head down while a maneuver element moves around the enemy's flank to assault from behind. Most of us recognize this maneuver as an envelopment.

An envelopment represents one general type of maneuver: maneuver in space. We can identify at least one other general type as well: maneuver in time. We can perhaps see each of these best by looking at air-to-air combat.

Classic air-to-air combat, as in a World War I dogfight, illustrates maneuver in space. Through turns, climbs, dives, and other moves, each aircraft seeks to gain an advantage in position – usually trying to get behind the enemy, in his six o'clock. Aircraft that can make tighter turns or climb faster or pull out of a dive better than their opponents have an advantage because they can better maneuver in space to get into an advantageous position.

Maneuver in time is shown in air-to-air combat by varying speed or use of energy. Here, in addition to classic dogfight moves, the pilot also varies the speed of his aircraft, trying to combine turns, climbs, and dives with acceleration and deceleration. The pilot wants to run his opponent out of energy – to lead him into going slow at a moment when he will need speed. While the opponent needs to accelerate, which takes time, the pilot uses that time to get into an advantageous position to shoot him down.

We see the same tactics in ground warfare. As noted, an envelopment is maneuver in space; you come around the enemy's flank. When we operate at a faster tempo than the enemy, e.g., if we can attack into his depth faster than he can shift reserves laterally to block us, we maneuver in time. Each type of maneuver gives us leverage; when we can combine them, we get still more leverage.

Building on Advantage

Once you have used one or another of these tools to create a decisive advantage and gain leverage, you must exploit it. FMFM 1 emphasizes exploiting opportunities to 'create in increasing numbers more opportunities for exploitation.'[4] In tactics, you exploit by seizing and maintaining the initiative to create decisive advantages faster than the enemy can cope with them. That means you must think ahead to your next move and the one beyond it: How are you going to use this decisive advantage to create yet another one? For example, in an attack by infiltration, once you have created one decisive advantage by bypassing the enemy's strength and getting into his rear, you create another by pouring forces through the gap you have found or created, generating the 'expanding torrent' Liddell-Hart wrote about.[5]

Rommel recounts in *Attacks* how during World War I exploiting each advantage in the battle for Kuk in the Carpathian mountains led to yet another opportunity. As his detachment exploited each opportunity and moved farther behind the enemy's lines, it generated more surprise and consequent leverage. It was during this action that Rommel's detachment captured thousands of enemy soldiers with very little fighting, due largely to his unwillingness to lose momentum. One success led directly to another opportunity which he immediately seized.[6]

Summary

As we said, leverage is about fighting smart. It is about using judo against an opponent who thinks he is in a fistfight. It is about overrunning his position with infantry as he prepares his antiarmor defenses. It is about not letting him know you are at his six o'clock with your F-18 until your cannon shells are ripping off his wing. It is about doing an impossible maneuver because you have cut loose from your supply line, knowing your logisticians can take another route and meet you before you run out of supplies.

We often see Marines fight this way in field exercises. Often, their role is that of the opposition forces. They fight smart because they are greatly outnumbered. They are generally effective far beyond their numbers because they fight smart. They infiltrate your lines. They capture your command post. They interdict your supply. They ambush you. In short, they fight only when they have a decisive advantage.

The lesson is: to fight smart, gain leverage. However, to be effective, tactics must go beyond merely gaining the upper hand.

NOTES

1. Col. John C. Studt, USMC (Ret), 'Foreword' in *Maneuver Warfare Handbook*, William S. Lind (Boulder, Colorado: Westview Press, 1985), p. xi.

2. *A very poor example . . . what commander would be stupid enough to use tanks in a confined area without infantry support?* H.T.H.

3. Joint Pub 1–02: '**Maneuver** – (DOD, NATO) . . . 4. Employment of forces on the battlefield through movement in combination with fire, or fire potential, to achieve a position of advantage in respect to the enemy in order to accomplish the mission.'

4. FMFM 1, *Warfighting*, p. 37.

5. Capt. B.H. Liddell-Hart, 'The "Man-in-the-Dark" Theory of Infantry Tactics and the "Expanding Torrent" System of Attack,' *Journal of the R.U.S.I.*, (February 1921), p. 13.

6. Erwin Rommel, *Attacks* (Vienna, VA: Athena Press, 1979), pp. 235–250.

CHAPTER 3

Trapping the Enemy

'In war the power to use two fists is an inestimable asset. To feint with one fist and strike with the other yields an advantage, but still greater advantage lies in being able to interchange them – to convert the feint into the real blow if the opponent uncovers himself.'[1]

If you read a history of, say, the Civil War, you may get the impression that most battles are glorified shoving matches. One side, the attacker, seeks to push the enemy off a piece of ground. If the attacker succeeds, the defender tries to push him back out again.

World War I often looked like this. After the initial battles, the Allies and the Germans secured their flanks on the English Channel and the Swiss border, creating a continuous front. For nearly three years, attacks consisted of one of these armies rushing across no man's land under murderous fires, attempting to push the opponent out of his earthworks. If the attack proved successful (and few did), the evicted forces would counterattack the same way, attempting to regain their lost terrain. These deadly shoving matches produced no decisive results. The war merely dragged on. The Korean War by 1952, long after the brilliance of Inchon, evolved into much the same thing with forces retaking the same ground time and again, producing only casualties.

The frustration with this kind of carnage was well expressed by F. Scott Fitzgerald's character in *Tender Is the Night*, who revisited the Somme years after the war. 'See that little stream – we could walk to it . . . a whole empire walking very slowly, dying in front and pushing forward behind. And another empire walked very slowly backward a few inches a day, leaving the dead like a million bloody rugs.'[2]

A New Order

Modern tactics is different. It is based not on pushing the enemy, but on trapping him. In early 1917, the Germans realized that they could not hope to sustain the staggering casualties of trench warfare much longer. They would run out of soldiers long before the Allied powers did. Their solution to this problem was to employ a defense in depth, consisting of many strong points rather than lines, all supported by a strong counterattack force. The idea was to allow the Allies to deeply penetrate and then cut off the penetrating forces. This trapping tactic proved very successful. It allowed the Germans to fight through 1917 and into late 1918.[3]

Why do we want to trap the enemy instead of just push him? Because a pushing contest is seldom decisive. The side that is pushed out comes back the next day, still full of fight. You have to fight him again and again and again. In Vietnam, most of our battles were pushing battles. We were always able to push the enemy off the ground he held and to inflict casualties on him. However, he just withdrew to regroup, replaced his losses, and came back to fight us again. The result was an endless war.[4]

However, if you can trap your enemy, you can win decisively. One prime example from Vietnam of trapping the enemy is Operation Dewey Canyon.

During early January 1969, North Vietnamese activity along the Laotian-South Vietnamese border increased dramatically. Large convoys, including armored vehicles, regularly traveled from Laos into South Vietnam. Colonel Robert H. Barrow and his 9th Marines responded with Operation Dewey Canyon.

The three battalions of the regiment crossed the Da Krong River on February 11th and 12th. The Third and First Battalions moved south-southeast through the mountainous terrain toward Laos. Second Battalion, to the west, swung south-southwest, turning east astride the Vietnam-Laos border. The North Vietnamese forces moving along Route 922 from Laos into the A Shau Valley were trapped between the three battalions. They were mauled. For every Marine killed, the North Vietnamese lost a dozen. Their equipment losses were staggering. More importantly, Dewey Canyon destroyed a North Vietnamese base area and disrupted their logistics to the point of pre-empting their spring offensive in I Corps.[5]

Battles like this are decisive.[6] The enemy force engaged is gone, vanished; it cannot return to fight you again. Most of history's decisive battles have been trapping actions, from Marathon to Stalingrad. Therefore, your goal in tactics is always to put the enemy in a trap. What are some ways you can do this?

Pincers

One way is to trap the enemy in pincers. You are familiar with pincers in the form of a nutcracker. Alone, each arm of the nutcracker can only push, but when the two arms are joined, they become a trap. The nut, which is damaged not at all by being pushed around, is crushed between the arms of a nutcracker.

Consider the case of an enemy rifleman shooting at you from behind a tree. If you fire at him only from the front, he is protected by the tree. If you go around him and start firing from his rear, he can simply go to the other side of the tree and still have the same degree of protection. However, if there are two of you and one fires at the enemy rifleman from the front while the other fires at him from the rear, you have put him in a pincer. If he faces toward the front, he exposes his unprotected back. If he faces toward the rear, he exposes his back to your buddy. He remains vulnerable no matter what he does. The arms of the nutcracker, equal in strength, have him.

Good tactics work like a nutcracker. They crush the enemy between two or more different actions that become your pincers. For example, you can use fire and movement; the fire causes the enemy to seek cover, but while covered he cannot respond effectively to your movement. Or, you can put pressure on the enemy's front while attacking into one or both of his flanks; he cannot respond to all your actions at once. You may seek to cut off your enemy and encircle him; this adds psychological to physical pressure. Many of history's decisive battles illustrate some form of pincer tactics. Leuctra is a good example.

In 371 B.C., two opposing Greek forces assembled near the city of Thebes at Leuctra. Ten thousand Spartans under King Cleombrotus I were organized into a phalanx – a mass of troops eight ranks deep. In phalanx tactics, two phalanxes advanced on and collided with one another. Usually, not much happened; battles were normally indecisive.

At the opposite end of the field, 6,000 Thebans under Epaminondas prepared for battle. Greatly outnumbered, Epaminondas realized the futility of throwing his small force against the Spartan phalanx. Contrary to the rules of his day, Epaminondas organized his forces unevenly, placing the bulk of his heavy infantry on his left, 48 ranks deep. His remaining forces formed thin ranks to his right and center. These were echeloned to his right rear.

Epaminondas initiated the attack by immediately charging with his weighted left while his center and right advanced slowly. Aside from being hopelessly confused by this original tactic, the eight-rank Spartan phalanx could not withstand the massed Theban attack on their right. The Spartan right collapsed. Epaminondas then wheeled against the exposed Spartan flank just as his center and right joined the battle. Facing Thebans on their flank and front (a pincer), the Spartans fled, leaving 2,000 dead on the field.

A good modern small-unit example comes from the experience of a French company in the opening days of World War I. As the Frenchmen moved up a small draw, groups of German riflemen infiltrated among the trees above them on either side. The Germans formed a horseshoe around the advancing Frenchmen and opened fire. The French lieutenant forced his men into a skirmish line and attacked into the ambushers; however, the farther they advanced, the more they exposed themselves to German crossfire. Although the French soldiers bravely returned fire, the crossfire proved overwhelming and their ranks broke. The attack became a rout. In this case, the fire from two directions provided the pincers, the arms of the nutcracker.[7]

Pincer tactics also play in aviation. It is a common technique in air-to-air combat. Upon detecting enemy aircraft, a flight of fighters splits into two or more elements beyond air-to-air missile range. The idea is to approach the enemy aircraft from as many directions as possible, not only from the flanks but at varying altitudes. No matter how he moves – dives, climbs, turns, or twists in a combination of moves – he is exposed.

The pincer is one way of trapping the enemy, but the nutcracker concept can be carried further. It has been one of the central concepts of modern tactics: combined arms.

Combined Arms

Modern tactics are combined arms tactics; on that, virtually every modern military is in agreement. What is meant by combined arms?

The Marine Corps is the only truly integrated air-ground-logistic team in the world. The MAGTF is often called a combined arms team. From the Marine Corps' standpoint, a combined arms team means one that has all the elements necessary for sustained combat and noncombat operations: combat, combat support, and combat service support. Combined arms in this context means combining all these assets to fight on the battlefield.

There is, however, another definition of combined arms which is fundamental to maneuver warfare. It is the idea of posing the enemy not just with a problem, but with a *dilemma* – a no-win situation. You combine your supporting arms, organic fires, and maneuver in such a way that the action which the enemy takes to avoid one threat makes him more vulnerable to another.[8]

Suppose an enemy fired at you from a fighting hole. Firing at him from two directions might force him to take cover in the bottom of his hole where he would be safe. If, however, you drove him to ground with rifle fire and then dropped a hand grenade in the hole, you face him with a dilemma. He can either get out of his hole, run for safer lodgings, and face the rifle fire; or he can stay in his hole and face the grenade. Either way, he loses. That is what combined arms is all about: giving the enemy equally distasteful choices and trapping him 'between a rock and a hard place.'

An enemy mechanized column suddenly encounters a hasty minefield. If the enemy commander tries to run through the minefield, he will undoubtedly lose vehicles and men. If he dismounts his infantry to move them around it while the drivers traverse it with empty vehicles, we call in airburst artillery fire. If he waits too long to decide, our oncall aircraft and direct support artillery attack the column. That is combined arms.

Surprise

In tactics, not all trapping is based on pincers. If you think about trapping a mouse in your house, you will quickly see another way to trap an enemy: *surprise*. The mousetrap springs and catches the mouse before it can react to save itself. In military tactics, we do the same thing with an ambush. We pounce upon him with concentrated fires, devastating him before he can react. As discussed earlier, an ambush depends on surprise.

Again, as with pincers, the use of surprise runs all through tactics. Since air-to-air combat began in 1915, between 60 and 80 percent of all planes destroyed in air-to-air combat were shot down by someone they never saw.

Surprise is also possible in logistics. How? On more than one occasion, one side in a conflict launched an unexpected offensive based on a logistics surprise. Their opponent had calculated that an attack was impossible for logistics reasons; the enemy simply could not have enough supplies to launch an attack because its supply lines were being bombed or otherwise attacked or because of the weather or terrain. Nevertheless, the attacker had, with great secrecy, built up sufficient supplies. Its logisticians surprised the enemy.

One such instance of logistical surprise was at Dien Bien Phu, a French outpost in northwest Vietnam. Contrary to French expectations, the Viet Minh moved hundreds of artillery pieces into the surrounding mountains. The Vietnamese did the impossible by dismantling the field pieces and man-packing them through the jungle and up the mountains. The French were caught unawares. The Vietnamese quickly put all the French artillery out of commission and eventually overran the French garrison.

Whether used in ground combat, air combat, or logistical preparation for combat, traps often depend on surprise. Surprise takes the enemy unawares. This raises the question, How do you take the enemy unawares?

Uncertainty and Deception

There are two basic answers: uncertainty and deception. Both are central elements in modern tactics because both are central to the art of trapping the enemy.

Uncertainty is a central characteristic of war. FMFM 1, *Warfighting*, says of it:

All actions in war take place in an atmosphere of uncertainty – the fog of war. Uncertainty pervades battle in the form of unknowns about the enemy, about the environment, and even about the friendly situation.[9]

In tactics, the challenge is to use this uncertainty to trap the enemy.

A common way to use uncertainty in tactics is to lead the enemy to try to cover all the bases because he is uncertain where your attack will come. The result is that he is weak everywhere – including where you actually attack. Insurgent or hit-and-run tactics are a good example of this. By striking hard but randomly, a relatively small force can often tie up a much larger force. Such was the case with Confederate Colonel John Mosby and his raiders. By remaining amorphous and unpredictable, Mosby's raiders kept several divisions of Union troops out of battle.

Sometimes, you can generate useful uncertainty through secrecy. More often you create it through ambiguity. It is usually difficult to conceal all your movements from your enemy, but you can confuse him as to the meaning of what he sees. That, in turn, sets him up to be surprised. A good example was Iraq's invasion of Kuwait in August 1990. The Iraqi build-up along the border adjacent to Kuwait was observed and widely reported. Through diplomacy, the Iraqis kept its meaning ambiguous. Most observers thought it was intended to put pressure on Kuwait to yield in negotiations that were then taking place. When Iraq actually invaded, it achieved virtually total surprise. Kuwait's army was trapped in its garrisons.

Ambiguity was central to the tactics of the World War II German *blitzkrieg*. An attack in *blitzkrieg* involved multiple thrusts with reinforcements following whichever thrusts were most successful. The multitude of thrusts created paralyzing uncertainty in the opponent because he could not determine which constituted the real attack. (Of course, with flexible reinforcement of success, all of them were potentially real.) There was nothing secret about the German attack, but it was ambiguous on a massive scale.

Sometimes, secrecy or (more commonly) ambiguity goes beyond creating uncertainty and results in deception. A deceived enemy is not uncertain; he is certain, but wrong. The German attack on France in 1940 is a good example. The French were certain the main German attack would come through Holland and northern Belgium. When instead the Germans made their main effort through the Ardennes, the French could not react effectively. They had been certain, but wrong.[10]

In 1973, the Israelis were similarly deceived by the Egyptians who used ambiguity to generate deception. The Egyptians had repeatedly maneuvered in ways that suggested an attack. Egypt's President Anwar Sadat said over and over that he would attack and did not, to the point where it became something of a joke. When finally the Egyptians really meant it, the Israelis dismissed the warning signs as yet another maneuver or bluff. They were certain Egypt would not attack. They were wrong.[11]

Summary

Pincers, surprise, uncertainty, deception, integration of all assets to create combined arms – all have the same purpose in tactics: *trapping the enemy in such a way that he has no escape*. That is how you fight and win decisive engagements and battles. The success of Operation Desert Storm attests to the effectiveness of these principles. Just pushing the enemy around usually accomplishes little, and pushing tactics rightly belong largely to history. Marine Corps tactics – maneuver tactics – demand more than that. They demand that Marines, in every fight, strive to achieve a decision. Almost always, that means catching the enemy in some kind of trap.

NOTES

1. B.H. Liddell Hart, *Thoughts on War* (London: Faber & Faber, 1944), p. i.

2. F. Scott Fitzgerald, *Tender Is the Night* (New York: Charles Scribner, 1934), pp. 56–57; quoted in Col. David Jablonsky, USA, *Churchill: The Making of a Grand Strategist* (Carlisle Barracks, PA: U.S. Army War College, 1990), p. 3.

3. For a comprehensive discussion of German tactical innovation during WWI, see: B.I. Gudmundsson, *Stormtroop Tactics* (New York: Praeger, 1989).

4. *There were many 'clear and hold' actions in Vietnam – particularly around populated areas. There would have been no endless war if the US/GVN had fortified a Korean-style '38th parallel' from the DMZ to the Mekong river or had the US/GVN been authorized to invade North Vietnam. H.T.H.*

5. *The Marines In Vietnam* 1954–1973; *An Anthology and Annotated Bibliography* (Washington, D.C.: Government Printing Office, 1985), pp. 173–181.

6. *What was decisive about Dewey Canyon? The enemy was back in force one year later. H.T.H.*

7. Andre Laffargue, *Fantassin de Gascogne. De Mon Jardin a la Marne et au Danube* [Infantryman of Gascony. From my garden to the Marne and the Danube] (Paris: Flammarion, 1962), pp. 59–78.

    Mr Laffargue presents one of the few personal accounts of small-unit tactics of WWI.

8. FMFM 1, *Warfighting*, p. 75.
    The very essence of maneuver warfare: get inside the enemy's OODA Loop and present him with a dilemma where every action he takes is too little too late. H.T.H.

9. FMFM 1, *Warfighting*, p. 38.

10. For a better understanding of the German perspective on the Battle of France and the thinking that entered into the final decisions, see:
    Erich von Manstein, *Lost Victories* (Novato, CA: Presidio Press, 1982), ch. 5.
    For a battalion-level account of the battle, see:
    Hans von Luck, *Panzer Commander* (New York: Praeger, 1989), ch 7.

11. For further reading on the 1973 Arab-Israeli War, see:
    Edgar O'Ballance, *No Victor, No Vanquished* (San Rafael, CA: Presidio Press, 1978).

CHAPTER 4

Moving Faster

'Open warfare demands elastic tactics, quick decisions, and swift maneuvers. Mobility includes far more than mere rapidity of movement. From the leader it demands prompt decisions, clear, concise orders, anticipation of the probable course of action and some sure means for the rapid transmission of orders. From the troops it demands promptness in getting started, the ability to make long marches under the most adverse conditions of terrain and weather, skill in effecting rapid deployments and abrupt changes of formation without delay or confusion, facility in passing from the defensive to the offensive, or the reserve, and finally, a high morale. In brief, then, mobility implies both rapidity and flexibility.'[1]

Usually, when you think of your weapons, you think of your personal M-16 or pistol, your unit's machine guns, mortars, and AT-4s, or your aircraft's Sidewinders or bombs or rockets. If you are a logistician, you may realize your weapons are also your trucks. Some Marines over-look one of their most powerful weapons, a weapon that serves infantrymen, aviators, and logisticians equally. That weapon is speed.

Speed in Combat

How is speed a weapon? Think of sports: The breakaway in hockey uses speed as a weapon. By rapidly passing the puck down the ice, one team denies the other the chance to set up a defense. Speed circumvents their opponent's ability to respond in an organized manner. The fastbreak in basketball seeks the same result. In two or three passes, the ball is downcourt, the basket scored, and the team quickly reorganized for the defense, all before the opposition knows what is happening.

The results of speed often reach beyond the immediate goal. How many times have you seen a team score on a fastbreak, steal the ball as it comes inbounds, and immediately score again, and even a third time? Unable to regain their composure, the victims of the fastbreak become the victims of a rally. The rallying team again fastbreaks and scores yet again. The victims lose confidence. Passes go astray; signals become crossed; tempers flare; arguments ensue. The rally becomes a rout. The beleaguered players see certain defeat. They virtually give up while still on the field of play.

The same thing happens in combat. The battalion or fighter aircraft or logistics train that can consistently *move* and *act* faster than its enemy has a tremendous advantage.

In 1862, Stonewall Jackson moved his foot cavalry up and down the Shenandoah Valley against several larger Union forces.[2] His corps' ability to quickly move considerable distances, strike, delay, move, and strike again tied up three times his numbers in Union forces. His speed in movement and action convinced Union leaders that a significant Confederate invasion force stood ready to attack Washington, D.C. As a result, Jackson's actions denied reinforcements to the Union General McClellan in his peninsula campaign. Jackson's speed offered immense advantage with relatively little risk to his limited manpower.

The British aviators bested the Germans during the Battle of Britain of World War II in part because they could reconstitute and redistribute fighter squadrons faster than the Germans could sortie. After each German bombing raid, the British quickly assessed their casualties and transferred combat-effective units into the active areas. The ineffective squadrons rotated out of action to recover and refit. Thus, German fighter and bomber pilots constantly faced fresh British pilots in serviceable airplanes. Eventually, German aircraft and pilot losses forced the Germans to end daylight bombing and resort strictly to night bombing sorties.

The great captains repeatedly commented on the value of speed in combat. Napoleon said, 'I may lose a battle, but I will never lose a minute.'[3] Nathan Bedford Forrest told the secret of his many victories: '... get there first with the most men.'[4] General Heinz Guderian's nickname was *schneller* Heinz – fast Heinz. General Hermann Balck's motto for his staff was, 'Don't work hard – work fast!'[5] History's great captains differed in many ways, but one thing they shared was a sense of the importance of speed.

In Operation Urgent Fury in 1983, Battalion Landing Team 2/8, under Lieutenant Colonel Ray Smith, moved fast, as he had trained them to do. When they captured the operations officer of the Grenadian army, he said to them, 'You appeared so swiftly in so many places where we didn't expect you that it was clear that resistance was hopeless, so I recommended to my superiors that we lay down our arms and go into hiding.'[6] That is what speed used as a weapon can do for you.

What is Speed?

This question would seem to have a simple answer: Speed is going fast. It is speed as we think of it when driving a car – more miles per hour.

That is part of the answer in tactics as well. For example, when a Soviet tank battalion attacks, it goes over the ground as fast as it can – at as many meters per minute as it can. General Balck was asked whether the Russian tanks ever used terrain in their attacks against him in World War II. He replied that they had used terrain on occasion, but that they usually used speed. The questioner followed up: 'Which was harder to defend against?' Balck answered, 'Speed.'[7]

Physical speed, more meters per minute or miles per hour, is a powerful weapon in itself.[8] On your approach to the enemy, speed narrows his reaction time. When you are going through him or around him, it changes his situation faster than he can react. Once you are past him, it makes his reaction irrelevant. In all three cases, speed gets inside his mind, causing fear, indecision, helplessness.

Speed and Time

There is more to speed in a military sense than simply going fast. First, there is a sense of *time*, and there is also a sense of *timing*. Speed and time are closely related. In fact, speed is defined in terms of time: miles or kilometers per hour. In tactics, what this means is that time is always of the utmost importance.

Even when you are engaged with the enemy, you are not always moving fast. Some of the time, you are not moving at all. Nonetheless, every moment is still of the utmost importance even when you are sitting still. A brigade staff that takes a day to plan an action is slower than one that takes an hour. A tank battalion that takes three hours to refuel is slower than one that takes two hours, just as one that must refuel every hundred miles is slower than one that must refuel every two hundred. A company that sits down to eat once it has taken its objective is slower than one that immediately presses on into the enemy's depth. A fighter squadron that can fly only three sorties per aircraft per day is slower, in terms of effect on the enemy, than one that flies six. A maintenance repair team that takes two days to fix a damaged vehicle and get it back into action is slower, in terms of effect on the enemy, than one that can do it overnight.

Making maximum use of every hour and every minute is as important to speed in combat as simply going fast when you are moving. It is important to every member of a military force whether serving on staffs or in units – aviation, resupply and repair, ground combat, everything. A good tactician has within him a constant sense of urgency. He feels guilty if he is idle. He never wastes time, and he is never content with the pace at which events are happening. Like Guderian, he is always saying to himself and to others, 'Faster! Faster!' He knows that if speed is a weapon, so is time.

Timing

Time, and the need to make maximum use of it, is also related to timing. At first glance, the two may seem to be in contention. Maximizing the use of time would appear to require acting at the earliest opportunity. On the contrary, timing may require *deliberate delay*. For example, if you are on the defensive, you may want to let an enemy penetration develop itself so that your counterattack, when it comes, bags the largest possible enemy force. One of the most common errors when on the defensive is counterattacking too soon so that the enemy is merely pushed back rather than cut off, encircled, and destroyed. Timing, in other words, seems to require that you sometimes sacrifice speed by waiting.

Generally, the contradiction is more apparent than real. The reason is that the results of your timing – a greater defeat for the enemy – give you the opportunity for greater speed over the longer run. The most frequent source of delay is the enemy. The greater the defeat you inflict on him in one situation, the less he will be able to delay you subsequently. So timing, instead of being in tension with time and in conflict with a sense of urgency, is actually a more skillful use of time.

Relative Speed

Going fast and making maximum use of time are both parts of the answer to the question, 'What is speed?' However, there remains something else to be considered: the enemy. As with all things in war, speed is relative. *It is only meaningful militarily if you are acting faster than the enemy.* You can do that either by slowing the enemy or by hastening yourself.

In the battle for the Falkland Islands in 1982, the British Army moved slowly. The terrain was difficult, the weather was abominable, and much of the material had to be moved on men's backs, all of which slowed down the British. Nevertheless, the British still had the advantage in speed, because they moved faster than the Argentines who, once they had made their initial dispositions, essentially did not move at all. That superiority in relative speed gave the British the initiative throughout the campaign.

Continuous Speed

To be decisive, a *superiority in relative speed must be constant.* It is not enough to move faster than the enemy only now and then because when we are not moving faster, the advantage, the initiative, passes to him. This need to operate continually faster makes the challenge more difficult. Most forces can manage a burst of speed now and then, provided they can then halt for a considerable period to recover. During that halt, they are likely to lose the advantage in speed over time ... the consistent advantage.

Here the speediness of the logistics or combat service support element of the MAGTF becomes of critical importance. Although physical exhaustion is often a factor, halts usually are driven by logistics: ground or aviation units must stop to catch up on maintenance and supplies. Nonetheless, supporting forces can minimize loss of speed if they can move and operate fast. If they can deliver the supplies and perform the maintenance quickly, the combat units can move again before the enemy gains the initiative.[9]

Speed and Change

In order to act consistently faster than the enemy, it is necessary to do more than move fast in whatever you are doing. It is also necessary to make *rapid transitions* from one action to another. In the 18th century, the importance of fast transitions (sometimes called agility) was often seen in the need to shift from column formation into line. If an army was caught by an enemy while still in column and could not rapidly deploy in line, it was often beaten. Much drill practice was devoted to making this difficult transition so that it could be accomplished rapidly in combat. A modern example of the importance of fast transitions comes from aerial combat.

In the Korean War, American aviators achieved a high kill ratio of about 10:1 over their North Korean and Chinese opponents. At first glance, this is somewhat surprising. The main enemy fighter, the MiG-15, was superior to the American F-86 in a number of key respects. It could climb and accelerate faster, and it had a better sustained turn rate. The F-86, however, was superior to the MiG in two critical, though less obvious, respects. First, because it had high-powered hydraulic controls, the F-86 could shift from one maneuver to another faster than the MiG. Second, because of its bubble canopy, the F-86 pilot had better visibility. The F-86's better field of vision also contributed to fast transitions because it allowed its pilot to understand changing situations more quickly.

American pilots developed new tactics based on these dual superiorities When they engaged the MiGs, they sought to put them through a series of changing maneuvers. At each change, the F-86's faster transitions gave it a time advantage which the pilot transformed into a position advantage. Often, when the MiG pilots realized what was happening, they panicked – and thereby made the American pilot's job all the easier.

These tactics illustrate the way fast transitions relate to overall speed and to time. They also show the importance of time and speed in a broader sense which has been brought out in the work of Colonel John Boyd, USAF (Ret). Colonel Boyd studied a wide variety of historic battles, campaigns, and wars. He noted that where numerically inferior forces had defeated their opponents, they often did so by presenting the other side with a sudden, unexpected change or a series of changes. The superior forces fell victim because they could not adjust to the changes in a timely manner. Generally, the defeat came at relatively small cost to the victor.[10]

This research led to the Boyd theory which states that conflict may be viewed as time-competitive cycles of observation-orientation-decision-action. First, each party to a conflict enters the fray by observing himself, his surroundings, his enemy. Second, based upon his observations, he orients to the situation, that is, he produces a mental image of his situation. Next, based upon this orientation, he makes a decision. Last, he puts the decision into effect – he acts. On the assumption that his action has changed the situation, he again observes, beginning the cycle anew. Actions continue to follow Boyd's cycle, often called an OODA (observation, orientation, decision, action) loop.

The Boyd theory defines the word 'maneuver' in the term 'maneuver warfare.' It means being consistently faster than your opponent. As your enemy observes and orients on your action, you must be observing, orienting, deciding, and acting upon your second action. As you enact your third, fourth, and fifth move, your enemy falls behind in a panicked game of catch up. The time gap between your actions and his reactions increasingly widens. As he tries to respond to your penetration, you attack his reserves and his command and control. As he counterattacks with his mobile reserve, you by-pass with helicopterborne forces. Everything he does is too late.

Colonel Boyd's research showed that historically forces faced with these continuous changes panicked or became passive. In the first case, they generally retreated. In the second, they surrendered. In either case, victory resulted from speed.

Thus, you see that the military answer to the question 'What is speed?' is not simple. Nonetheless, it is central to every aspect of tactics, especially in the context of maneuver warfare doctrine. As General George Patton said, 'In small operations, as in large, speed is the essential element of success.'[11]

Becoming Faster

Now you see clearly the importance of speed in tactics and why it is one of the basic concepts that shape tactics for ground, air, and combat service support. You want to be fast. How do you do it?

You start by having a sense of the importance of time. We already noted this, but mention it again here because many of us must make a change.

We, as Marines and leaders of Marines, have a responsibility to make things happen fast. If some set process gets in the way of operating fast, change it or get rid of it. You are responsible for results, not method. Your sense of the importance of time, of urgency, must direct your actions. You must work to create and build that sense within yourself.

Once you have it, there are a number of things you can do to increase speed. First, you can *keep everything simple*. Simplicity promotes speed; complexity slows things down. Simplicity should be central to your plans, your staffs (large staffs are one of war's greatest consumers of time), your command and control, and to your own actions. Fast decisions on your part, in place of lengthy councils of war, are an important element in simplicity and thus speed.

Second, you go fast by *using mission orders*. Mission orders allow everyone to harmonize efforts by knowing what result they are collectively attempting to achieve. Each person can act quickly as the situation changes without having to delay to pass information up the chain of command and wait for orders to come back down.

By 1815, the Prussian Army was already well advanced in the use of mission orders. General Friedrich Müffling detailed as the Prussian liaison officer to Wellington's army, was with the British at Waterloo. There, at one point, Müffling saw Napoleon's Imperial Guard halt. He sensed this as a critical moment in the battle and urged two British brigade commanders to attack with their cavalry. Both commanders agreed on the excellence of the opportunity. However, both refused to take action because they had not received orders to do so.[12] Without orders from Wellington, they could not act. General Müffling was astounded, but the British commanders expressed no misgivings. Throughout the 19th century and well into the 20th, the British Army remained noted for the slowness of most of its actions, while the Prussians had precisely the opposite reputation.

Third, you can *rely heavily on implicit communications*. Implicit communications are mutual understandings that require little or no actual talking. The commanding officer of Charlie Company on your left flank is well-known to you. You think alike because your battalion commander has established SOPs and has schooled his officers in his approach to war.[13] Thus, you do not need to talk with the Charlie Company commander very often in action because you know how he is likely to react to many different situations. If you create an opportunity for him, you know he will take advantage of it. That is implicit communication. It is faster and more reliable than explicit communication (trying to pass words or messages back and forth over radios or other equipment).

Of course, if you intend to raise your speed by using implicit communications, that implies that you take some other actions. It implies keeping people together in their units and stable in their assignments. It implies keeping good teams together. It implies developing a band of brothers in your unit, as Admiral Horatio Nelson did. He spent many evenings with his captains gathered in the cabin of his flagship talking over tactics, ways they might fight different engagements, how they would defeat this or that opponent. From those evenings came a shared way of thinking so strong that, at Trafalgar, Nelson needed only to signal 'England expects every man will do his duty,' and 'close action.'[14] They needed no more instruction than that.

Fourth, speed is greatly increased by decentralization. Mission orders are key to decentralization, as you know. Another key is *lateral communication*. If all communication is up and down the chain of command, action will move slowly. But if commanders and leaders at every level communicate laterally – if you, as a leader, talk directly to other leaders – action moves much faster. Lateral communication is in fact a natural consequence of mission orders. It represents a letting go on the part of the higher commander that follows after he states his intent and gives his subordinates their missions.

A good example of lateral communication comes from aviation. In the air, a squadron of aircraft communicates laterally as a matter of course. If one pilot needs to talk to another, he does so. He does not go through the mission commander and then wait for him to talk to the other pilot. Events would quickly outpace communication if he did. The same should be true of ground combat and logistics units as well.

Fifth, you can speed things up by *putting the commander forward*, at the anticipated focus of effort. If he is in the rear, trying to command with maps and telephones, events will often move faster than he can. If he is forward, at the focus of effort, he can instantly make the adjustments necessary as the situation develops.

Throughout World War I and while in command of 7th Panzer Division in France during May through June of 1941, Erwin Rommel led his formations from the front. He achieved extraordinary success during both wars almost entirely as a result of this style of command. Even as a corps and later an army commander, Rommel led from the front. During his defeat of the British field army in Libya and the seizure of Tobruk, he accompanied the advanced elements of the combat forces which he sensed were at the crucial point in the battle. Amid the climate of danger, uncertainty, and confusion, Rommel reduced friction and grasped fleeting opportunities through his personal, physical presence with the forward elements of attacking forces.[15]

Sixth, *improvisation* is of critical importance to raising speed. Often, you will find yourself in a situation where your assets – weapons, vehicles, etc. – are not adequate to keep you moving fast. Some of them may even be hindrances in your particular situation. When that happens, improvise. If you don't have enough mines, make some. If you do not have enough vehicles to move all your men, get some from the local economy. In France in 1940, Guderian put some of his infantry in commandeered French buses. On Grenada, when Army Rangers needed vehicles, they took East German trucks belonging to the Grenadian army. Sound extreme? If the situation were not extreme, you would not be improvising!

War – successful war – is filled with improvisation. You should start to learn how to improvise now, in your training. Leaders should value this innovative thinking. Moreover, they should expect it from their subordinates because it offers new opportunities.

For improvisation to be effective, commanders must readily exploit the opportunities uncovered by subordinates. Commanders cannot remain tied to plans that blind them to fleeting opportunities. While making the best possible preparations, they must welcome the unforeseen.

Finally, *experience* breeds speed. This is why veteran units are usually much faster than green, untried units. If you are familiar with a situation, or at least know generally what to expect, you can think, act, and move faster. In peacetime, your Marines are not likely to be veterans. Still, you can give them experience through tactical decision games, sand table exercises, war games, and field exercises.

Summary

You may think of additional ways to be fast. That is to the good. When you find one that works, tell your fellow Marines about it so they can use it too. Anything that works to make you faster is good whether or not it is in the books.

NOTES

1. *Infantry in Battle*, 2d ed. (Richmond, VA: Garrett & Massie, 1939), p. 94.
2. *General 'Stonewall' Jackson used trains in his valley campaign also. H.T.H.*
3. Attributed.
4. Attributed.
5. Gen. Hermann Balck, interview by Wm. S. Lind, 6 June 1980, Washington, D.C.
6. Col. Ray Smith, USMC, telephone interview by Capt. S.R. Shoemaker, USMC, 12 March 1991, Washington, D.C.
7. Gen. Hermann Balck, interview by Wm. S. Lind, 6 June 1980, Washington, D.C.
8. *Planning fast is also a factor in 'speed.' The Marine Corps amphibious forces afloat are required to be able to launch aircraft (troop-carrying helos) or splash amphibious assault vehicles six hours after receiving a mission. H.T.H.*
9. *The U.S. Marine Corps does not stop for logistics/combat service support. We use unit distribution, not supply point distribution. We build Combat Service Support Elements to run in trace of our maneuver elements. CSSEs together with the battalion or regimental log trains mean that Marine units usually do not have to stop (a good example being Kuwait in the Gulf War). The Army units attacking into Iraq had to move up their invasion H-hour to cover the flanks of the Marines. H.T.H.*
10. Wm. S. Lind, *Maneuver Warfare Handbook* (Boulder, CO: Westview Press, 1985), pp. 5–6.
11. George S. Patton, Jr., *War As I Knew It* (Boston: Houghton Mifflin, 1947), 341.
12. Charles Edward White, *The Enlightened Soldier* (New York: Praeger, 1989), 176.
13. *Battalion and regimental Standing Operating Procedures (SOPs) establish a mind set for the unit so that with mission-type orders, each unit will generally know how the other will operate. SOPs must not become a formula on how the unit operates. They must only establish general principles of task organizations, communications, tactics, techniques and procedures, etc. H.T.H.*
14. Capt. A.T. Mahan, USN, *The Life of Nelson: The Embodiment of the Sea Power of Great Britain* (Boston: Little, Brown, and Co., 1899), 730.
15. *21.Pz.D., Ia, Anglage zum KTB Nr. 5, Gefechtsbericht III./Schuetz. Rgt. 104 (mot), 2.6.42*, U.S. Archives, German Records, Divisions, T-31.

CHAPTER 5

Cooperating

'Unity of effort is coordinated action toward a common goal; it is cooperation. It is the working together by all commanders toward the accomplishment of a common mission, which is imperative for complete and final success. Commanders must develop in their staffs and subordinates the desire to cooperate, not only among themselves but with other elements ...'[1]

Each of these principles of tactics – gaining a decisive advantage, moving faster than the enemy, trapping the enemy, and the goal of all of them, achieving a decisive result – presents something of a dilemma. Each requires different elements, different units, and different Marines to work effectively together. If efforts are not in harmony, results will be indecisive. If, for example, the actions of aviation are not integrated with the ground battle, they are unlikely to have a decisive effect. If artillery support is not well coordinated with an infantry attack, you will not have the force of combined arms, and the attack will likely fail.

Control in Combat?

At the same time, because war is characterized by disorder, uncertainty, and rapid change, control in combat quickly breaks down. It is probably a mistake to speak of *control* in combat. As anyone who has survived combat will undoubtedly testify, it is one of the hardest of all human endeavors to control. In fact, it is impossible to control if by that we mean one man carefully directing the actions of others.

The dilemma is sharpened by the fact that attempts to control men in combat easily undermine initiative. You are not likely to trap, or move faster, or gain leverage over a competent opponent without a great deal of initiative from Marines at every level, down through private. Yet efforts to control those Marines too often work against initiative, by teaching them not to act without orders. That kind of control undermines the initiative upon which our tactics depend.

The dilemma, then, is this: How do we achieve the goal of working together in harmony without some sort of centralized control?

Cooperation

The beginning of an answer lies in the word *cooperation*. Cooperation, rightly understood, is the opposite of control. Control works top down: someone up above determines what you will and what you will not do and makes you conform to his dictates. Cooperation, in contrast, works laterally and also bottom up. You take the initiative to help those around you accomplish your shared mission.

Cooperation is essential to modern tactics. The flight leader and wingman work on the basis of cooperation; the Cobra pilots and the infantry they support cooperate; two infantry units, fighting side by side, cooperate; a mobile combat service support detachment and a mechanized force cooperate. We all work together far more effectively when we communicate laterally than when we talk only through a higher headquarters and respond only to centralized direction.

The history of tactics is rife with examples where cooperation made the difference — and control could not have done so. One such involves the Reconnaissance Battalion of the 12th SS Panzer Division during operations east of the Russian city of Kharkov on September 3, 1942.

For several hours, Major Kurt Meyer had moved his battalion along a narrow trail in deep snow through heavily wooded terrain in hope of interdicting the main road north of Kharkov. Progress was very slow. Only the fact that he could not turn his vehicles and tanks around in the close terrain kept him moving forward.

As his main body entered a clearing, Major Meyer noticed that his vanguard company had left the trail to conceal themselves in the trees on the far side of the clearing. Halting the column, Meyer crawled forward. From the trees on the far side of the clearing, the terrain sloped down to a road and rose again on the other side of it. To his astonishment, the road held several thousand Russians moving west toward Belgorod, recently occupied by German forces. These were fresh troops, supported by vehicles, artillery, and tanks. Overwhelmingly outnumbered and outgunned, Meyer ordered his battalion to move off the trail and into the woods and to remain quiet, hoping to avoid detection.

About to conceal themselves, the Germans suddenly heard the drone of aircraft. Halting the battalion, Meyer recognized the aircraft as German Stuka dive-bombers. The bombers, upon seeing the dense column, circled to gain altitude and began bombing and strafing the Russians. Pandemonium followed. Meyer, seizing upon the confusion, immediately ordered his companies to attack. When the Panzers emerged from the trees, the aircraft signaled recognition.

As the Stukas worked up and down the column, Meyer's Panzers blocked the Russians fleeing up his slope toward the trees. The far slope was a barren snowfield that offered no cover. Hundreds of Russians were killed, and hundreds more surrendered. The action prevented an estimated corps-sized unit from attacking the German assembly area at Belgorod.[2]

The example shows what cooperation, unplanned and uncommunicated, can accomplish. The aircraft were unexpected. Meyer's Panzers were present by coincidence. The aircraft had no radios with which to contact the tank unit. The outnumbered Panzers could not have attacked the Russians single-handedly. Undoubtedly, an air strike alone would have damaged the Russian column, but without the immediate cooperation of Meyer's Panzers it would not have been decisive.

Discipline

Cooperation resolves the dilemma of finding a way to harmonize efforts, to get everyone working together without creating the centralized control that undermines initiative. It also raises another question: How do we get people to cooperate?

The answer is the foundation of effective tactics: *discipline.*[3] Discipline is one of the basic components of tactics. It underlies all the other components because without it, you will not be able to gain leverage, maintain superior relative speed, or trap the enemy – or attain a decision, for that matter, which is the purpose of the other three.

However, the discipline needed for cooperation is different from what some may think of when they consider military discipline. It is not imposed discipline, but self-discipline.

Imposed discipline is the discipline of the Prussian army of Frederick the Great, where the object was to make each soldier fear his NCOs and officers more than he feared the enemy. That kind of discipline is part of control, and, as such, it is not appropriate to modern tactics. It is rigid, paralyzing, and utterly destructive of initiative.

Self-discipline is different. It is a moral force. As FMFM 1 states, war is also fought on the moral level. Here, in the matter of discipline, tactics and the moral level intersect. Self-discipline *morally obligates* every Marine to cooperate with every other Marine to achieve the common goal – in battle, a decision. The obligation is *internal*, in each individual; it is something he feels, powerfully. He is pulled from within to do everything he can to support his fellow Marines.

Imposed discipline is useful, if at all, only in the earliest stages of training. For maneuver warfare to work, every Marine needs a potent self-discipline. Why? Because in maneuver warfare everyone must harmonize his efforts – cooperate – at a very high level of initiative.

We can see self-discipline at work in many cases where we also see effective cooperation. This is most evident in successful athletic teams. Team players constantly take it upon themselves to back up their teammates. In baseball, the first baseman immediately covers the catcher on a play at home plate. The shortstop routinely backs up a ground ball to the third baseman, and the outfielders cover each other on flyballs. In hockey, rarely does only one player rush the goal. In football, offensive linemen don't stand by idly on a pass play if no defensive player faces them. They block the first defender to show himself. This cooperation among teammates cannot be enforced by a coach. It depends upon the self-discipline of the individual players.

While Marines have long been noted for their military discipline, we must focus our thinking on the fact that military discipline is self-discipline. What else can we say about it?

First, we can say that it is a heavy responsibility, because it is a *personal responsibility*. No one can shirk it by blaming someone else. No one else can be at fault when each individual is responsible for his own discipline. A discipline failure – often, a failure to act – is a personal failure. It is automatically the full and sole responsibility of the individual who failed.

Second, as military discipline, it is *absolute*. There is no time off. If, in a given situation, someone else is in charge, that does not in the least absolve others from their responsibility to attain the objective, the common goal. It does not reduce to any degree their responsibility to ensure effective cooperation within the unit and beyond it. All share alike discipline's demand that they do everything in their power to gain a decision. No one can 'drop his pack,' even for a moment.

In this respect, Marines have an advantage. It has been traditional in our Corps for every Marine always to think of himself as a Marine, on duty or off. We see it whenever off-duty Marines take the initiative to help out at the scene of a traffic accident, or act as leaders in their community or church, or otherwise do more than their share. They do so because of something inward, not because they are being compelled through control. That something is self-discipline, and it is not limited to one aspect of life. It is a mind set, *a way of thinking and behaving*. It runs through everything. It is as much part of garrison life as of combat, of combat service support as of the infantry, of time off as of duty time. It is, ultimately, a way of life.

Summary

Modern tactics depends on cooperation, not control. Cooperation, in turn, depends on self-discipline. As a leader of Marines, you must create a climate in which self-discipline, with the high level of initiative it requires, can flourish.

That climate of demand for and support of self-discipline depends upon you. Words are easy; anyone can give an occasional pep talk on the merits of self-discipline. People judge your actions, not your words, in determining their own actions. If you create a climate where self-discipline is expected, you will get it. There will always be some who are incapable of disciplining themselves. We must recognize those individuals for what they are: people who are unfit to be United States Marines. Those who are fit to be Marines will respond to a climate of self-discipline.

NOTES

1. NAVMC 7386, *Tactical Principles* (Quantico, VA: Marine Corps Schools, 1955), 7.
2. Panzermeyer (Kurt Meyer), *Grenadiere* (Munich: Schild Verlag, 1956), 196–201. Mr. Paul Garteman of Barcroft Books, 3621 Columbia Pike, Arlington, Virginia, translated the passages.
3. *Napoleon is reported to have said that the two most important attributes of a soldier are discipline and courage. H.T.H.*

CHAPTER 6

Making It Happen

'Nine-tenths of tactics are certain and taught in books: but the irrational tenth is like the kingfisher flashing across the pool and that is the test of generals. It can only be ensured by instinct, sharpened by thought practicing the stroke so often that at the crisis it is as natural as a reflex.'[1]

A Marine leader makes it happen. That means we must apply in practical terms the concepts outlined in this book. Merely reading the book will yield no victories. The question remains, 'How do we get beyond reading about these concepts and begin applying them?'

Training

Good tactics depend upon sound technical skills. These are the techniques and procedures which enable us to shoot, move, and communicate. Competence at the technical level is achieved through training, the building of skills through repetition. This is called the science of war.

Training develops familiarity with and confidence in weapons and equipment and the specialized skills essential to survive and function in combat. The ultimate aim of training is speed. Whether Marines compute firing data, rearm and refuel aircraft, repair vehicles, stock or transport supplies, or communicate information, the speed of their actions determines the tempo of the overall force. Training develops the competence which enables this effective speed.

At the small-unit level, training involves developing and refining techniques and procedures such as immediate actions, battle drills, and unit SOPs. These apply to all types of forces whether they are a section of aircraft executing air combat maneuvers, a maintenance contact team repairing a vehicle under fire, an artillery gun team conducting a hip shoot, or a rifle squad breaching a position. We develop and refine these measures so units gain and maintain the speed essential for decisive action.

Staffs, as well as units, must train for speed. Staff training should not focus on set procedures or processes. Rather, a staff should train to support a commander's individual approach to tactics. A staff's procedures should reflect the unique tactical approach of the commander and the abilities of each staff member. Operating in this way, staffs avoid the time-consuming work associated with a rigid, formal staff process. Cohesiveness, which can only be achieved through personnel stability, is the key to fast, efficient staffs. Field Marshal Erwin Rommel emphasized that:

> A commander must accustom his staff to a high tempo from the outset, and continuously keep them up to it. If he once allows himself to be satisfied with norms, or anything less than an all out effort, he gives up the race from the starting post, and will sooner or later be taught a bitter lesson.[2]

Training should also prepare Marines for the uniquely physical nature of combat.[3] Living and caring for themselves in a spartan environment, confronting the natural elements, and experiencing the discomfort of being hungry, thirsty, and tired are as essential in preparing for combat duty as any skills training. The point is not training individuals to be miserable, but to adapt to limited resources and harsh conditions.

Likewise, training should establish the ability to act decisively in any environment. This includes operating during inclement weather and periods of limited visibility. To gain advantage and deliver decisive force at a place and time of our choosing demands that we make rain, snow, fog, and darkness our allies. We can neither simulate, anticipate, nor appreciate the inherent friction which these natural factors produce unless we experience them. History is replete with stories of victory gained by forces who maintained the ability to fight amid this natural adversity. Plentiful also are the histories of those forces who failed for lack of this same ability. Training should provide the confidence, hardiness, individual skills, and small-unit proficiency critical to decisive action.

Education

Success in combat also depends on our ability to combine all the various tools of combat to meet each unique situation. It requires sound decisions rapidly and resolutely executed. The heart of making sound decisions is conceptualizing the battle which was discussed earlier. This is the art of war. A good tactician develops his judgment to the point of having *coup d'oeil*. He does so through education.

While the battlefield affords the most instructive lessons on decision making, the tactical leader cannot wait for war to begin his education. Like the surgeon, we must be familiar and competent in our profession before entering the operating room. The lives of our men hang in the balance.

Our education in tactics must be focused toward developing three qualities within all tactical leaders. The first is *intuitive skill*, the essence of *coup d'oeil*. The tactician must be readily able to recognize and analyze the critical factors in any situation. The enemy's intentions, the weather, the terrain characteristics, the condition of our own forces, these and many other factors concern us as tacticians.

The second quality is *creative ability*. Tactical leaders must be encouraged to devise and pursue unique approaches to military problems. There exist no rules governing ingenuity. The line separating boldness from foolhardiness is drawn with the ink of practiced judgment.

The third quality is *battlefield judgment*. While Marines must act as members of larger organizations, they must also make individual decisions. All Marines must be able to cut to the heart of a situation, identify its important elements, and make clear, unequivocal decisions. Establishing the intent, the focus of effort, and missions; determining when to shift the focus of effort; deciding when to give and when to refuse battle; recognizing and exploiting opportunity; creating advantage; and maintaining tempo are among the critical elements of our tactical philosophy. Our educational approach should emphasize making decisions which incorporate these elements.

Marine leaders need to learn not only how to make good decisions, but also how to make decisions fast. A good decision taken too late is, in combat, a bad decision. Speed in decision making is a key element in speed overall. The confusion of combat can easily lead commanders to delay making a decision while waiting for perfect information. Marine education must lead commanders at all levels to make timely decisions with whatever information is available. General Patton's remark that 'A good plan violently executed *now* is better than a perfect plan next week' reinforces this point.[4]

There exists no single vehicle to develop our decision makers; however, any educational approach should be adaptable to all echelons and to all grades. The environment should be informal and conducive to free thinking; there should be no fear of the consequences of making a wrong decision. The following examples may provide some tools for developing tactical decision making in Marines.

SAND TABLE AND MAP EXERCISES

These exercises present students with a general situation, mission orders from higher headquarters, and minimum information on enemy and friendly forces. Sand table exercises are especially suited to novice tacticians since a sand table presents the terrain in three-dimensional array whereas a map requires interpretation. In both cases, students offer their vision of the battle, deliver their decisions, and issue orders to subordinates. Then those are discussed and criticized. The discussion should emphasize making a decision in the absence of perfect information or complete intelligence. There is no school solution – only sound or unsound judgment based upon reason.

TERRAIN WALKS

Terrain walks introduce the realities of terrain, vegetation, and weather. There are several ways to conduct terrain walks. The desired end results of all are, however, decisions.

The first method provides students with an area of operations, a general and enemy situation usually shown on a map, and a mission. As in sand table and map exercises students derive and support their view of the battle. Choosing one plan, the group then begins to walk the terrain according to the plan. The group not only encounters unanticipated terrain and obstacles, but the instructors introduce enemy actions into the play of the problem. In this way students must confront the uncertainty and disorder which terrain, vegetation, inaccurate maps, and the enemy bring to battle.

The second method involves historical battle studies. When opportunity permits, past battlefields should be traversed with an eye for both sides. Special note should be given to the commanders' decisions. We gain a special vantage on battle by walking the ground and seeing the battlefield from the commanders' perspective. We receive a new appreciation for the blunders of commanders that history has condemned as obvious. The art in decision making quickly becomes evident.

TEWTs

Tactical exercises without troops, or TEWTs, provide tactical leaders opportunities to exercise judgment. The general and enemy situations usually do not change during these exercises. There are two approaches to conducting them.

The first method provides a leader an opportunity to evaluate a subordinate's ability to perform in a given scenario. This method places students in an area of operations and provides a situation upon which to plan and execute a task; e.g., 'Establish a reverse slope defense.'

The second method also places students in an area of operations and provides a situation, but they are then provided general guidance in the form of a mission order; e.g., 'Prevent enemy movement north of Route 348.' After walking the ground, the students must first decide whether to defend or attack, supporting their conclusions with reasoning. The reasoning is then discussed and criticized. Preparations for the attack or the defense may follow. This approach encourages the students to put forth maximum ingenuity and initiative. They have free rein to achieve the desired results.

WARGAMING

Educating our Marines to think about battle, develop *coup d'oeil*, and acquire practical experience is not limited to map work and countryside jaunts. The playing of war games is essential for all Marines to understand the factors weighing upon the leader's decisions. Morale, the enemy and friendly situations, the higher commander's intentions, firepower, mobility, and terrain are only a few of the decision factors included in the play of war games. In all these simulations, from the sand table to the TACWAR board to the CAS trainer, predictability should be constantly under assault. The less predictable the environment, the more creativity the student must display.

Professional Reading and Historical Study

Critical to developing *coup d'oeil* is the study of military history. Through it, we see how successful commanders thought through the situations facing them. A few people – very few – can do it instinctively. They have what we might call the Nathan Bedford Forrest touch, the inherent ability to think militarily.[5] Most people are not that lucky. We have to work to develop *coup d'oeil*.

In our studies of historical battles, we find the clearest details and most readily available sources of information on our profession. The leadership considerations, the horrors of war, the sacrifices endured, the commitment involved, the resources required, and much more may all be found in a wealth of available books, unit histories, afteraction reports, films, and documentaries. Naval, air, and ground battles may all be addressed through this medium. Both individual study and group discussions expand our perspective on the decisions of leaders.

Exercises

While both training and education provide the essential ingredients of combat, tactical success evolves from their synthesis: *the creative application of technical skills based on original, sound judgment.* Exercises enable individuals, units, and staffs to use their skills while leaders at all echelons face decisions in a real-time scenario. Exercises also serve as proving grounds for immediate actions, battle drills, and combat SOPs. Any procedure or technique which does not stand up to the test should be replaced or improved.

An exercise should serve as an internal assessment of the quality of training and education. The conclusions should aim *not to penalize poor performance but to note short-falls* so as to address them through future instruction. A unit will never be fully trained. There will always be room for improvement.

Exercises also test the ability of units to sustain operating tempo for an extended period of time. Since decisive results are rarely the product of initial actions, the ability to operate and sustain combat effectiveness over time is critical. Exercises should not become 4- or 5- or 10-day waiting games. Knowing when hostilities will cease is a convenience spared the combat soldier. Equipment must be maintained, and people sustained with adequate rest, nourishment, and hygiene until they achieve their mission. The aim is to develop warriors whose only concern is the job ahead. Whenever possible, the duration of exercises should be tied to achieving specific aims.

Competition

Exercises should provide realism. The means to achieve tactical realism is free-play or force-on-force exercises. Whenever possible, unit training should be conducted in a free-play scenario. This approach can be used by all leaders to develop their subordinates. It affords both leaders and unit members the opportunity to apply their skills and knowledge against an active threat.

Free play is adaptable to all tactical scenarios and beneficial to all echelons. Whether it is fire teams scouting against fire teams, sections of aircraft dueling in the sky, or companies, battalions, squadrons and MAGTFs fighting one another, both leaders and individual Marines benefit. Leaders form and execute their decisions against an opposing force as individual Marines employ their skills against an active enemy. Through free play, Marines learn to fight as an organization.

Critiques

A key attribute of decision makers is their ability to justify decisions with *clear reasoning*. Critiques elicit this reasoning process. Any tactical decision game or tactical exercise should culminate with a critique.

The standard approach for conducting critiques should promote initiative. Since every tactical situation is unique, and since no training situation can encompass even a small fraction of the peculiarities of a real tactical situation, there can be no ideal or school solutions. Critiques should focus on the student's rationale for doing what he did. What factors did he consider, or not consider, in making his estimate of the situation? Were the actions taken consistent with this estimate? How well were orders communicated? Were the actions taken tactically sound? Did they have a reasonable chance of being successful? These questions among others should form the basis for critiques. The purpose is to broaden a leader's analytical powers, experience level, and base of knowledge, thereby enhancing his creative ability to devise sound, innovative solutions to difficult problems.

Critiques should be lenient and understanding, rather than bitter and harsh. Mistakes are essential to the learning process and should be cast in a positive light. The focus should not be on whether the leader did well or poorly, but on what progress he is making in his overall development as a leader. We must aim to provide the best climate to grow leaders. Damaging a leader's self-esteem, especially publicly, should be strictly avoided. A leader's self-confidence is the wellspring from which flows his willingness to assume responsibility and exercise initiative.

In that light, the greatest failing of a leader is a failure to act. A leader should assume great risk willingly. For him, two steadfast rules apply. First, in situations clearly requiring independent decisions, a leader has not only the latitude to make them, but the solemn duty to do so. This is an honorable effort to practice the art of warfighting. Second, inaction and omission – the antithesis of leadership – are much worse than judgmental error based on a sincere effort to act decisively. While errors in judgment might result in unsuccessful engagements, the broad exercise of initiative by all will likely carry the battle. Failure resulting from prudent risk taken by a thinking leader carries no disgrace since no single action guarantees success.

Summary

Waging maneuver-style warfare demands a professional body of officers and men schooled in its science and art. As Marshal Foch said,

> No study is possible on the battle-field; one does there simply what one can in order to apply what one knows. Therefore, in order to do even a little, one has already to know a great deal and know it well.[6]

Everything we do in peacetime should prepare us for combat. Our preparation for combat depends upon training and education which develop the action and thought essential to waging decisive battle.[7]

NOTES

1. T.E. Lawrence, 'The Science of Guerrilla Warfare,' intro. to 'Guerrilla Warfare,' *Encyclopedia Britannica*, 13th ed. (New York: Encyclopedia Britannica, 1926).
2. As attibuted to Erwin Rommel by Robert Debs Heinl, Jr., *Dictionary of Military and Naval Quotations*, (Annapolis, MD: United States Naval Institute, 1985), p. 60.
3. *Easier said than done. One letter to a Congressman that troops are 'experiencing discomfort' and there may be a change in the training plan – if not the commander. This is a major challenge for effective leadership. H.T.H.*
4. George S. Patton, Jr., *War As I Knew It* (Boston: Houghton Mifflin, 1947), 354.
5. *General Nathan Bedford Forrest never read a book on the study of military history. He could hardly read and write. He developed his coup d'oeil from frontier survival skills and keen common sense. He knew men and he knew nature. H.T.H.*
6. Ferdinand Foch, *The Principles of War*, trans. Hillaire Belloc (London: Chapman & Hall, 1920(?)), pp. 5–6.
7. *As we train in peacetime – so we will fight in war! H.T.H.*

EPILOGUE

The Future

Theory will have fulfilled its main task when it is used to analyze the constituent elements of war, to distinguish precisely what at first sight seems fused, to explain in full the properties of the means employed and to show their probable effects, to define clearly the nature of the ends of view, and to illuminate all phases of warfare in a thorough critical inquiry. Theory then becomes a guide to anyone who wants to learn about war from books.

Carl von Clausewitz, *On War*,
Book Two, Chap. 2, p. 141

The Navy Times (Marine Corps edition), in an article by Robert Holzer and Steven C. LeSueur, 'A revolution on war tactics,' June 13, 1994, stated that a Net Assessment Office for the Pentagon under Mr Andrew Marshall has established task forces to conduct a series of war games, 'to start Pentagon officials thinking about how to use new and planned advances in modern military technology ...' Andrew Marshall is a member of a Pentagon team established in January 1994, by Defense Secretary William Perry to launch the Revolution in Military Affairs initiative. According to Holzer and LeSueur: 'Pentagon officials are anticipating a military revolution that will change the nature of modern warfare as significantly as armored vehicles and aircraft carriers changed it more than 50 years ago.' The task forces are war gaming the following areas:

1. Combined arms maneuver in theater warfare
2. Deep strike and deep attack
3. Forward operations
4. Smaller-scale operations such as special operations and peacekeeping
5. Fostering innovation, which examines technological trends

There seems to be a misstatement or a misunderstanding about the real world from the scenarios outlined above. Small-scale operations do not have to be special operations or confined to peacekeeping/peacemaking. Small-scale operations, sometimes called small wars, low intensity conflict, or operations other than war, need to be the number one priority. With the prolifation of weapons of mass destruction and the current propensity for guerrilla warfare throughout the world, it would seem that the western military leaders need to

185

dust off lessons learned from Orde Windgate's Chindits and Marine Raider Battalion's, or Army Ranger Battalion's, operations in World War II and small unit operations in the Malaya Emergency and Vietnam War.

Most Pentagon and 'think tank' institutions seem to have an aversion to thinking about how to conduct combat operations below the Army or division level, the carrier battle group or USAF air wing level. I predict that warfare in 2015 may need more emphasis on developing and training Small Independent Action Forces (SIAF) than armies, divisions and air wings. Fortunately, the culture of maneuver warfare taught by the Marine Corps, at the battalion and regimental level, may be far more important than revolutionary military technology.

In 1939 the French Army was the best equipped and largest army on the European continent. They had the latest technology and their weapons systems, except aircraft, were reported to be superior to the Germans', in quality and quantity. The 'seeds of disaster' in the French defeat of 1940 were in their doctrine. Let not the western military leaders of the late 20th century make the same mistake. Doctrine, as well as advanced technology, needs to be reviewed year after year.

Napoleon is reported to have said that in all his battles and campaigns, he had learned nothing that he had not known from the start – referring to his intense study and schooling in the art of war.

The study of this book (the three FMFMs) is important to military officers and civilian defense officials. Because absence of doctrine, or adhering to a faulty doctrine, is a serious danger to any military force. General understanding and acceptance of common doctrine is necessary before concentrated action by a large force engaged in hostilities is even conceivable. 'It is an essential element of command, and an essential prelude to great success in war,' wrote Lieutenant Commander Dudley W. Knox, USN, in the *U.S. Naval Proceedings* (March–April 1915), commenting on doctrine.

However, in the same way that Major General J.F.C. Fuller discovered in 1929 that the British Army had forsaken professional study to memorizing his nine principles as if they were sacred gospel, so some see the three FMFMs as establishing a doctrine that does not grow. Colonel Mike Wyly, USMC (Ret) has been one among many to call for revision and updating of the three FMFMs. He wrote in the *Marine Corps Gazette*, January 1994, that the omnipresent danger of doctrine is that it will inhibit needed change: 'Every new structure begins the process of erosion and decay the moment it is formed.'

The weakest parts of the three FMFMs are in the area of low intensity conflict or military operations other than war. Very little of maneuver warfare doctrine could have been applied in Somalia or can be applied in humanitarian/peacekeeping or peacemaking missions. However, the culture of maneuver warfare is applicable, e.g. decentralization, mission-type orders, focus of effort, etc. Colonel Mike Wyly correctly criticizes the main excuse given for the death of 18 U.S. Army Rangers in Somalia ('we didn't have tanks'). Tanks were not the solution – better intelligence, better tactics, and no set patterns would have been worth far more than tanks. The three FMFMs need to be revised in order to move beyond Clausewitz and his era (1850–1945).

If a future potential enemy, with advanced technology weapons, reads this book, reads all the 'lessons learned' from Operation Desert Storm and then creates a 'doctrine' and capability to fight and defeat our strong points – we will have a fight. Additionally, when we fight the next war – and we will – the individual appointed Commander-in-Chief, the CinC, will have a major challenge to balance the realisms of his battlefield with the expectations at home. The Western populace has been TV brain-washed to expect all major warfare to be dominated by advanced technology weapons, precision-guided munitions, and stealth aircraft. If heavy casualties appear on tomorrow's killing fields, the dead and wounded will result from those who have not really understood what this book is trying to say and that Operation Desert Storm was an aberration not the norm.

Now to the future. While the 'evil empire' of the old USSR may be gone, Russian military doctrine, and that of its former client states, may not have changed much (with the exception of national policy which the Russians call 'doctrine' as explained in the Introduction – see p. 33). While most books and proponents of maneuver warfare theory concentrate on the German school of maneuver, serious military commanders cannot forget the former Soviet and now Russian school of maneuver.

Robert Leonhard's book *The Art of Maneuver* has an outstanding section in the chapter 'Evolution of Maneuver Theory,' where he compares and contrasts the German and the Soviet (Russian) schools of thought. Leonhard says that Russian developments in mechanized warfare were guided by men like Genghis Khan, and Marshal Mikhail Tukhachevskii and his colleagues in the 1930s.

The old Soviet school, and probably the current Russian school, differed from the German in that the practice of mission-type orders (*Auftragstaktik*) was not feasible given the political nature of the Soviet military. The Red Army has traditionally used control by detail (rather than directive) orders (*Befehlstaktik* in German), according to Leonhard. In other words, Russian subordinate leaders are given very little flexibility in deciding their own courses of action. However, the western military commander had better be aware of the principles of Russian maneuver warfare.

The Soviets before, and the Russian generals now, surely continue to give pre-eminence to the preparation of the battle long before the first shot is fired. The philosophy has always been manifested in the attention Russians pay to their 'correlation of forces.' These two characteristics – detailed control and preparation – mean that execution is everything. The Russians believe that their commanders will succeed if their execution is correct. The Russians practice *Befehlstaktik* (directive control) before the battle begins – they show their imagination, flexibility, and boldness, in planning the battle. The Russians see the operational art far more readily than their western counterparts. While western military leaders focus on the forthcoming battle, the Russian commander is focused on the operational rear and the strategic objectives, not the tactical front. The operational maneuver group is most unsuitable for tactical engagement. The Russian echelonment of attack expects to lose the first battle. It is their follow-on forces that exploit the expended energy of the western forces that have borne the brunt of the first assault. This is why smart NATO planners developed the 'follow-on forces attack' (FOFA) as their only way to keep a war in Central Europe from going nuclear.

There has been some recent discussion in Russian military journals that more 'decentralized control' and more initiative should be given to the operational commanders. It appears that the Russian schools of maneuver warfare thought are taking a broad look at the American doctrine.

Some critics who argue that maneuver warfare is a 'bunch of bunk,' would say that at the lowest level there are no flank attacks – they are all frontal assaults. Yes, but even in a frontal assault you have timing, focus of effort, speed, and a search for surface and gaps. In maneuver warfare you assault through the enemy and you do not pause when you have obtained an objective – he who pauses first will die.

FMFRP 2–12, *Marine Air–Ground Task Force: A Global Capability*, provides a thumbnail description of the global capabilities of the Marine Air–Ground Task Force (MAGTF) and provides a detailed description, with weapons systems and number of troops, of each of the three main MAGTFs. The Fleet Marine Force is a balanced force of combined arms including ground, air, and combat service support elements of the Marine Corps which provides operating forces to support the fleet, or special missions, through deployment and employment of MAGTFs. The MAGTFs include infantry, armor, artillery, engineer, reconnaissance, aviation, and logistics/combat service support components.

Each MAGTF consists of a headquarters element, a ground combat element, an aviation combat element, and a combat service support element. The smallest MAGTF ever deployed for contingency operations is generally a Marine Expeditionary Unit (MEU), which is designed around an infantry battalion landing team, a composite helicopter squadron and a combat service support unit. The next, The Marine Expeditionary Force (Forward) formerly called a Marine Expeditionary Brigade (MEB), with an infantry regimental landing team (as its ground combat element), an aircraft group (as its aviation combat element), and a brigade service support group (as its combat service support element), is tasked to be prepared to receive the follow on of the remainder of a Marine Expeditionary Force (MEF). The largest MAGTF is a MEF, consisting of one or two infantry divisions, an aircraft wing, and a force service support group. I Marine Expeditionary Force (I MEF) in the Gulf War, for example, consisted of the 1st and 2d Marine Divisions, the 3d Marine Aircraft Wing and the 1st Force Service Support Group.

Today's MAGTFs are credible, mobile, sustainable, and flexible forces with combined arms capabilities in a wide range of operations which include:

- Forcible entry onto a hostile shore
- Crisis response
- Presence
- Alliance support/reinforcement
- Stability operations
- Counternarcotics operations
- Security assistance
- Humanitarian assistance

Marines can be used as the spearpoint or the opening blow for other forces (as in the Gulf War):

- Forward deployed (sea based) or rapidly deployable (airlifted) with Maritime Preposition Forces
- Employable in combinations (helo assault, surface assault or seaborne assault)
- Self sustaining
- Special operations capable

The Marine Corps has now released a new publication called FMFM 3, *Command and Control*, which would seem on initial review to fly in the face of FMFM 1. How can you have decentralization of command and control and then have a doctrinal publication that advocates command and control? Alfred Thayer Mahan once said: 'Communications dominates war. It is the single most important element in strategy, political or military.' FMFM 3 needs to be read after fully understanding both this present book and Mahan's words.

High speed interactive computers, multichannel communications, and photo/electra intelligence satellites to support sustainability, mobility, and firepower issues are important instruments to a commander in modern man-euver warfare. The American commanders-in-chiefs today have at their individual simultaneous disposal a World-Wide Military Command and Control System (WWMCCS). WWMCCS is a global, interactive computer network that provides a multipath channel of secure communications to transmit strategic warning and intelligence information to the National Command

Authorities (NCA) and then transmit direction from the NCA to the Combatant Commanders (CinCs). All current contingency plans for the major hot spots of the world are on WWMCCS, as are the 'time-phased force deployment data' (TPFDD) to provide forces for the assigned commander.

While the Commanding General of the 7th Marine Amphibious Brigade, Major General John I. Hopkins, was trying to establish a credible combat force ashore in Saudi Arabia, during the first 30 days of our deployment in Operation Desert Shield, he had WWMCCS communications with higher headquarters demanding attention almost hourly, he had Maritime Prepositional Forces off loading critical combat essential equipment, he had host nation formalities, and he had the security and well being of 16,000 Marines to consider. Thirty days later it was 40,000 Marines and by the time of the initiation of hostilities there were over 70,000 Marines in the KTO under Lieutenant General Walter E. Boomer. The intelligence summaries (INTSUMs), situation reports (SITREPs), requests for information or assistance, etc., that came into the I Marine Expeditionary Force Headquarters, amounted to an estimate of over 10,000 a day. However, the Marines of the I MEF staff ably assisted the MEF commander to process the unbelievable number of reports and messages.

The brain, like a computer, becomes ineffective if it receives too much data. The commander must avoid information overload and focus on information that will convey his influence over his forces and the enemy. Each element of a MAGTF (the Command Element, the Ground Combat Element, the Aviation Combat Element, and the Combat Service Support Element) has a computer assisted mechanism to help the commander marshal his resources, determine his capabilities and limitations, and to make a decision.

For the Aviation Combat Element (ACE) the Marine air command and control system enables the ACE commander to plan, direct, coordinate, and control airspace and air operations within an assigned sector. The principal command and control facilities within the ACE are:

Afloat: Helicopter Direction Center (HDC)
Ashore: Tactical Air Command Center (TACC)
          Tactical Air Direction Center (TADC)
          Tactical Air Operations Center (TAOC)
          Direct Air Support Center (DASC)
          Marine Air Traffic Control Facility (MATCF)

Each of the above are full of computers and communications equipment to help the commander accomplish his mission.

For the Combat Service Support Element (CSSE) during initial amphibious operations the principal command and control facilities of the CSSE are:

Afloat: Tactical Logistical Group (TACLOG)
Ashore: Force Movement Control Center (FMCC)
          Combat Service Support Operations Center (CSSOC)

To help the CSSE Marines there is a set of computer logistics systems called MAGTF II/LOGAIS (Marine Air Ground Task Force II/Logistics Automated Information System) which has a Computer-Aided Embarkation Management System (CAEMS), Transportation Coordinators Automated Information for Movement System (TCAIMS) and MAGTF Deployment Support System II (MDSS II).

For the Ground Combat Element (GCE) the principal command and control facilities within the GCE are:

Afloat: Landing Force Operations Center (LFOC)
          Supporting Arms Coordination Center (SACC)
          Tactical Logistics Group (TACLOG)
Ashore: Combat Operations Center (COC)
          Fire Direction Center (FDC)
          Fire Support Coordination Center (FSCC)
          Intelligence Center (IC)

During the last century and much of this century, men marched towards the sounds of the guns. During the 21st century, a high-tech enemy like the Russians or the Chinese may have the capability for the manipulation of information or intelligence before a shot is fired. A battle, and even a war, may be won or lost, in response to strategic and/or tactical moves as a result of faulty intelligence.

Where judgment is needed you need people; where the rapid retrieval and manipulation of data is needed, you need computers. The U.S. Marine Corps' future challenge is to be able to conduct increasingly complex maneuver warfare executions in joint/combined operations, under any climatic condition, sometimes with highly sophisticated command and control systems and sometimes with all radios jammed and all computers down. The Iraqi Army did not test our metal. Operation Desert Storm was a live fire exercise with moving targets that sometimes shot back.

The future Marine Corps commanders who master maneuver warfare, and are confident and competent in their command and control systems, will be the successful great captains of tomorrow.

FMFM 3 does not add to the theory or doctrine of maneuver warfare, it does remind the warfighting Marines that command and control of a modern battlefield is as much a concern for the effective use of the electro-magnetic spectrum as the communications for the appropriate and timely use of men and weapons.

As the German army applied maneuver warfare in their WW II tactics, the 1st Marine Division used the basis of modern maneuver warfare in their defensive (Aug 1990 to Feb 1991) tactics (Operation Desert Shield) and their offensive (23–27 Feb 1991) tactics (Operation Desert Storm) in the Gulf War. In August through December 1990, the Marines had a defense in depth that combined positions on reverse slopes, ambushes, small units operating independently to locate and confuse the invader, with a powerful counterattack ready to cut off and encircle any penetration of Saudi national territory. When the attack order came on 23 February, the 1st and 2d Marine Divisions penetrated the Iraqi positions in multiple thrusts aimed at weak points, reinforced successes and exploited the pursuit without too much concern for flanks. The Marines used speed as their pre-eminent weapon, always seeking to gain the rear of enemy units through encirclement, which usually brought total collapse and surrender.

It is important to remember that maneuver warfare is above all a 'time-competitive cycle.' One becomes consistently faster through constant practice of the operational art. In maneuver warfare, the goal of tactics is not 'close with and destroy the enemy'; but 'bypass, cut off resupply and/or reinforcement and collapse the enemy.'

Colonel Mike Wyly is reported to have said that if someone wants principles of war for maneuver warfare, there are only two: speed and focus.

Colonel Harry Summers in his *On Strategy II: A Critical Analysis of the Gulf War*, sticks to the U.S. Army's 1921 nine principles of war, in his analysis of the Gulf War. He says: 'The interrelated principles of mass, economy of force and maneuver regulate military action' and thus play a major role in the fundamental decision of the commander's intent. Summers states that at the strategic level, maneuver – 'place the enemy in a position of disadvantage through the flexible application of combat power' – has mainly to do with strategic mobility, the means of getting there, a critical consideration in view of the geographic reality of the United States.

Summers is absolutely correct when he says that many of our potential adversaries, and some allies, took the U.S. military performance in the Korean and Vietnam war as evidence that the military did not understand maneuver warfare. Summers used a quote from General Crosbie E. Saint, the commander of the U.S. Army in Europe and the Seventh Army, when Saint noted in his reflections on the Gulf War: 'Looking back, we should have known from the outset that the Iraqis were probably a pretty good tactical army, but not playing in our league. After all, Saddam spent his time talking about "the Mother of all battles," clearly a tactical event, while we were talking about the campaign, an operational set of sequenced events. One of our greatest successes which deserves further publicity was the return on investment we got from educational changes made in our schools to stress the operational art and warfighting thought in general.'

Brigadier Richard Simpkin, in his book *Race to the Swift: Thoughts on Twenty-First Century Warfare*, viewed warfare in three levels and explained his theory in terms of three well established disciplines: (1) classical physics, providing a model for the physical aspects of war, (2) risk, chance, and surprise (applying statistics), and (3) the imposition of the commander's will and the clash of wills (psychology). Simpkin said that as full-scale war is unlikely to be an acceptable instrument of policy in the future, traditional military leaders must adjust their doctrine, tactics, and techniques to consider alternatives such as deterrence, pre-emption and containment. He felt that future conflict would be more likely to be conducted by 'small groups of "special forces" employing maneuver theory as well a clandestine elements,' e.g. camouflage, concealment, and deception.

There are at least eleven maxims, inherent in the culture of maneuver warfare, that I consider to be at the heart of understanding maneuver warfare:

1. Mission tactics (commander's intent and subordinates' mission). The commander's intent must be fully understood in case circumstances change which makes it obvious that the old mission may no longer be relevant. The ability to act independently will be enhanced with a full under-standing of the commander's intent. Decentralized control is vital.

2. The focus of effort (the *Schwerpunkt* and multiple thrust). After searching for surfaces and gaps, and finding a weakness, the commander will want to conduct multiple thrusts at the enemy, but he must already know where he wants his focus of effort. It may be the weakest point in the defense or the hinge that the whole defense is anchored to. However, the commander must be ready to instantly change his focus of effort if a better opportunity should present itself.

3. Speed and surprise (speed in staff action and speed in execution). A smaller force may gain great advantage over a larger force if in acting it swiftly surprises an enemy in such a way that the enemy cannot react in time or space. Surprise can come at the strategic, operational, or tactical level. All that matters is: can the enemy react in time and space?

4. Reconnaissance pull (reconnaissance units as part of the scheme of man-euver). The Commander reacting to information from his reconnaissance units rather than pushing his main units forward to bring on battle. Reconnaissance units leading the attack with main battle units in trace as opposed to main battle units sitting idle awaiting reconnaissance reports or reconnaissance in force in order to bring on battle.

5. Surface and gaps (enemy strengths and weaknesses). The enemy strengths and weaknesses may be identified in the vacillation of the enemy

commander, enemy combat power at a given point, logistics support and sustainability, doctrine and tactics, or the enemy's operational plan. Surfaces and gaps should be sought in addition to the weakest points of the defense.

6. Firepower (combined arms – not supporting arms). Combined arms attack means the simultaneous use of air, artillery, armor, mechanized infantry, etc., in one coordinated focus of effort. Little bullets – big sky ... do not hold back an airstrike while other munitions are being directed at a target.

7. Camouflage, concealment, and deception (camouflaging your positions and your actions). Deceiving the enemy as to your location, strength, intentions, etc., can do more to reveal enemy surfaces and gaps than mounting reconnaissance probes. Deception can be a weapon more powerful than any armament. Deception must be part of any battle plan.

8. The concept of the reserve (counterattack). Whether on the offensive or on the defense, a fully constituted reserve must be prepared for the unexpected or the exploitation of success. Even if all units are engaged in the attack, one unit must be designated to be prepared to assume the reserve. The reserve is usually the assault element in a counterattack.

9. Command and control systems (command, control, communication and intelligence – C3I). Communication can dominate a battle. If the commander does not know what is going on in the four dimensions of a battlefield (air, land, sea, and space), at all times, he is open to surprise and possible defeat. C3I will help defeat an enemy before a shot is fired.

10. Center of gravity (the real center of gravity – it may be the main army in the field and/or it may be the national will). Normally the commander seeks to destroy the enemy forces in the field. Napoleon at Borodino may have won a battle but this did not win the war. The American armed forces in Vietnam won all the battles yet lost the war. The French in Algeria, the British in Cyprus, etc., are but a few examples.

11. Combat service support (with logistics, this may determine the outcome of a battle before troops are on line). Combat service support cannot be viewed in isolation from the correlation of forces or the operations plan. Combat service support, like fire support, must be immediately available to the commander.

Today, the U.S. Army sees a two-element assault force: one element pins the enemy while the other gets into positions and destroys the enemy. This is consistent with Sun Tzu's ideas on the dichotomy of force: an advance force ('ordinary force'), is used to hold the enemy and occupy his attention long enough for the main attack to begin; and the main attack is made by the main force ('extraordinary force'), to attain a major decision by rapidly dislocating the enemy. I say, and most maneuver warfare theorists agree, that there are three elements in the assault: a suppression element, a penetration element and a large exploitation element. This is the essence of U.S. Marine Corps maneuver warfare.

The Napoleonic Wars and the American War Between the States offer a multitude of examples of how inferior numbers defeated a larger force. Many insurgencies/counterinsurgencies and guerrilla warfare operations offer additional lessons learned, for small forces engaging larger forces. Suggestions for reading, for students of maneuver warfare, can be found in the bibliography. I place great emphasis on the lessons learned from 'small wars,' insurgency/counterinsurgency and guerrilla warfare due to the following:

1. A guerrilla warfare opponent may have a basic doctrine or some general principles of combat; however, they more often do the unexpected, develop local doctrine to fit the local situation and are highly unpredictable.
2. The overall ratio of guerrilla fighters to government forces is generally in favor of the government force; however, the guerrilla fighters usually master the tactic of searching for surfaces and gaps, and concentrating mass and speed at the appropriate point out-number their opponent.
3. If one can master the lessons learned in insurgency/counterinsurgency or guerrilla warfare, these lessons are easily transferable to mechanized warfare – maneuver warfare.

Let us not forget the essentials that provide the groundwork of a potential great captain of military history. First, and foremost, is field craft – basic combat skills. Second, education and training – the appropriate level schools for a given rank and the study of warfighting throughout the history of the world. Third, field exercises – taking troops to the field and leading them in 'force-on-force' field exercises, under all climates and against all forms of an opponent (infantry, armor, air, etc.). Fourth, and most difficult, is actual combat experience – Americans learned very little about prolonged, individually brutal combat from the Gulf War. Most of the combat hardened veterans from Vietnam are retired today. In contrast, the Russian army probably has all its battalion and higher commanders with two tours of combat experience in Afghanistan.

The mission of western military schools has got to be more than military historical education. We must focus on the development of judgment, not just the transmission of knowledge. Quick, sound, decision making is a prerequisite for a maneuver warfare practitioner.

Major General P. K. Van Riper said that war is probabilistic, not deterministic, therefore, he maintains that in this new era of multiple, diffused and vague threats, we must advance our warfighting capabilities to contend with a broad spectrum of ambiguous and dynamic challenges. Studying and understanding the nature of war make clear the connection of national security policy goals and military strategy. Doctrine has got to be a lot more flexible and Marines will need a lot more training to prepare for the wider array of enemies and battlefields they may encounter in the future.

For the future, small wars, or general war, think of the U.S. Marine Corps definition of maneuver warfare: 'Maneuver warfare seeks to shatter the enemy's cohesion through a series of rapid, violent and unexpected actions which create a turbulent and rapidly deteriorating situation with which he cannot cope.'

Bibliography

Adams, Sam. *War of Numbers: An Intelligence Memoir*. South Royalton, VT: Steerforth Press, 1994.

Alexander, Bevin. *How Great Generals Win*. New York: Norton, 1993.

Asprey, Robert. *War in the Shadows*. Garden City, NY: Doubleday, 1975.

Atkinson, Rick. *Crusade: The Untold Story of the Persian Gulf War*. Boston: Houghton Mifflin, 1993.

A Study of Strategic Lessons Learned in Vietnam. 9 vols, including 'Omnibus Executive Summary', Vienna, VA: BDM Corporation BDM/W-78-128-TR, April 1980.

Barber, Noel. *War of the Running Dog*. New York: Bantam, 1987.

Bassford, Christopher. *Clausewitz in English: The Reception of Clausewitz in Britain and America, 1815–1945*. New York and Oxford: Oxford University Press, 1994.

Batchelor, Joseph Branch. *Infantry Fire: Its Use In Battle*. Leavenworth, KA: George A. Spooner, 1892.

Beckwith, Col. Charlie A. and Donald Knox. *Delta Force*. New York: Harcourt Brace Jovanovich, 1983; London, Arms and Armour Press, 1984.

Billièrc, de la, Gen. Sir Peter. *Storm Command: A Personal Account of the Gulf War*. London: HarperCollins, 1993.

Blaufarb, Douglas S. *The Counterinsurgency Era: United States Doctrine and Performance, 1950 to the Present*. New York: The Free Press, 1977.

Blumenson, Martin. *The Many Faces of George Patton*. Colorado Springs, CO: USAFA, 1972.

—— *Patton: The Man Behind The Legend, 1885–1945*. New York: Berkley Books, 1985.

—— *The Patton Papers: 1885–1940*. Vol I & II. Boston: Houghton Mifflin, 1972.

Board on Army Science and Technology, Commission on Engineering and Technical Systems, National Research Council. *Star 21: Strategic Technologies for the Army of the Twenty-First Century*. Washington, D.C.: National Academy Press, 1992.

Boyd, John, Col. 'A Discourse on Winning and Losing.' (Lecture Handout.) Quantico, VA: Marine Corps Command & Staff College, August 1987.

Brown, Ben and Davis Shukman. *All Necessary Means: Inside the Gulf War*. London: BBC Books, 1991.

Caesar. *The Conquest of Gaul*. Trans. by S.A. Handford. Revised with new Intro. by Jane F. Gardner. London: Penguin, 1951; New York: Penguin, 1982.

Caesar's War Commentaries (De Bello Gallico and De Bello Civili). Ed. and Trans. by John Warrington. Letchworth, Herts: Aldine Press, 1915; London: J.M. Dent, 1953; New York: E.P. Dutton, 1953.

Callwell, C.E. *Small Wars: A Tactical Textbook for Imperial Soldiers*. London: Greenhill, 1990. (*Small Wars: Their Principles and Practice* was first published in 1896 by HMSO.)

Cao Van Vien, Gen. *The Final Collapse*. Washington, D. C.: Center of Military History, U.S. Army, 1983.

Chaliand, Gerard. (Ed.) *Guerrilla Strategies: An Historical Anthology from the Long March to Afghanistan*. Berkeley, CA: University of California Press, 1982.

—— *Revolution in the Third World*. Baltimore, MD: Penguin, 1978.

Chambers, James. *The Devil's Horseman*. New York: Athenaum, 1975.

Chandler, David G. *The Campaigns of Napoleon*. New York: Macmillan; London: Weidenfeld & Nicolson, 1966.

—— *The Illustrated Napoleon*. New York: Henry Holt; London: Greenhill, 1990.

—— *The Military Maxims of Napoleon*. (New Intro & Commentary by David Chandler). London: Greenhill, 1987.

—— *On the Napoleonic Wars: Collected Essays by David Chandler*. London: Greenhill, 1994.

Clarke, Jeffery J. *United States Army in Vietnam: Advice and Support – The Final Years, 1965–1973*. Washington D.C.: U.S. Army Center of Military History, 1989.

Clausewitz, Carl von. *On War*. Trans. by Col. J.J. Graham. London: N. Trubner, 1873.

—— *On War*. New & Rev. Ed. Trans. by Col. J.J. Grahan and Ed. by Col. F.N. Maude. London: K. Paul, Trench, Trubner, 1908.

—— *On War*. Trans. by O.J. Matthijs Jolles. New York: Random House, 1943; Washington, D.C.: Infantry Journal Press, 1950.

—— *On War*. Ed. with Intro. by Anatol Rapoport. New York: Penguin, 1968.

—— *On War*. Ed. by Michael Howard and Peter Paret. Princeton, NJ: Princeton University Press, 1976.

—— *Principles of War*. Trans. and Ed. with Intro. by Hans W. Gatzke. Harrisburg, PA: Military Service Publishing, 1942; Harrisburg, PA: Stackpole, 1987.

Collins, John M. *Grand Strategy: Principles and Practices*. Annapolis: Naval Institute Press, 1973.

Committee on Armed Services. *Defense For A New Era: Lessons of the Persian Gulf War*. U.S. House of Representatives, Washington, D.C.: U.S. Government Printing Office, Washington, D.C., 1992.

Cooper, Chester L. *The Lost Crusade*. New York: Dodd, Mead, 1970.

Corum, James S. *The Roots of Blitzkrieg. Hans Von Seeckt and German Military Reform*. Kansas: United Press of Kansas, 1992.

Creveld, Martin Van. *Supplying War. Logistics from Wallenstein to Patton*. Cambridge, UK: Cambridge University Press, 1977.

—— *The Transformation of War*. New York: The Free Press, 1991.

Dalton, John, Adm J.M. Boorda, and Gen C.E. Mundy, Jr. '*Forward . . . From The Sea: The Strategic Concepts for the Employment of Naval Forces*'. Washington, D.C.: The Department of the Navy, September 7 1944.

Davis, Burke. *Jeb Stuart: The Last Cavalier*. New York: Bonanza Books, 1957.

Daly, LtCol. Ron Reid, as told to Peter Stiff. *Selous Scouts: Top Secret War*. South Africa: Galago, 1982.

Department of Defense. *Conduct of the Persian Gulf War: Final Report to Congress*. Washington, D.C.: Department of Defense, April 1992.

Dewar, Michael. *Brush Fire Wars: Minor Campaigns of the British Army since 1945*. London: Robert Hale, 1990.

Dodge, Theodore Ayrault. *Alexander*. London: Greenhill, 1994.

—— *Hannibal*. London: Greenhill, 1994.

Doughty, Robert Allan. *The Seeds of Disaster: the Development of French Army Doctrine 1919–1939*. Hamden, CN: Archon, 1985.

Duffy, Christopher. *The Army of Frederick the Great*. New York: Hippocrene, 1974.

Dupuy, R. Ernest and Trevor N. Dupuy. *The Encyclopedia of Military History*. London and New York: Harper & Row, 1970, and subsequent editions.

Dupuy, Col. T.N. *A Genius For War: The German Army and General Staff, 1807–1945*. Englewood Cliffs, NJ: Prentice-Hall, 1977.

Engels, Donald W. *Alexander the Great and the Logistics of the Macedonian Army*. Berkeley: University of California Press, 1978.

Essame, H. *Patton: A Study in Command*. London: Batsford; New York: Scribner's, 1974.

Fall, Bernard. *Hell Is a Very Small Place*. Philadelphia: J.B. Lippincott, 1966.

—— *Last Reflection on a War*. New York: Doubleday, 1967.

—— *Street Without Joy: Insurgency in Indochina, 1946–63*. New York: Schocken Books, 1972, Mechanicsburg, Stackpole, 1994.

—— *The Two Viet-Nams*. New York: Praeger, 1963.

—— *Viet-Nam Witness*. New York: Praeger, 1966.

Farago, Ladislas. *The Last Days of Patton*. New York: McGraw Hill, 1981.

—— *Patton: Ordeal and Triumph*. New York: Obolensky, 1964.

Friedman, Norman. *Desert Victory: The War For Kuwait*. Annapolis, MD: Naval Institute Press, 1991.

Fuller, MGen. J.F.C. *Armoured Warfare*. London: Eyre and Spottiswoode; Harrisburg, PA: Military Service Publishing, 1943.

—— *Generalship, Its Diseases and Their Cure: A Study of the Personal Factor in Command*. London, Faber & Faber, 1933; Harrisburg, PA: Military Service Publishing, 1936.

Galula, David P. *Counterinsurgency Warfare*. New York: Praeger, 1964.

Gorman, LtGen. Paul F. 'Low Intensity Conflict: Not Fulda, Not Kola'. Student Text 100–39, *Low Intensity Conflict*. Ft. Leavenworth, KS: USACGSC, December 1985.

Grant, Michael. *Julius Caesar*. New York: M. Evans, 1992.

Grant, Ulysses S. *Ulysses S. Grant: Personal Memoirs of U.S. Grant (Selected Letters 1839–1865)*. New York: The Library of America, 1990.

Grivas, George. *General Grivas on Guerrilla Warfare*. New York: Praeger, 1965.

Guderian, Heinz. *Panzer Leader*. London: Joseph; New York: Dutton, 1952.

Guevara, Che. *On Guerrilla Warfare*. New York: Praeger, 1962.

—— *Reminiscences of the Cuban Revolutionary War*. New York: Grover Press, 1970.

Guidebook For Marines. Marine Corps Association. Quantico, VA: Marine Corps Association (Approved by HQMC.), July 1990.

Hackworth, David H. and Julie Sherman. *About Face*. New York: Simon and Schuster, 1989.

Hallion, Richard P. *Storm over Iraq: Air Power and the Gulf War*. Washington, D.C.: Smithsonian Institution Press, 1992.

Heinl, Col. Robert Debs. *Handbook for Marine NCOs*. Rev. by LtCol. Kenneth W. Estes. Annapolis, MD: Naval Institute Press, 1988.

—— *Soldiers of the Sea: The United States Marine Corps. 1775–1962*. Annapolis, MD: U.S. Naval Institute, 1962; Baltimore, MD: Nautical & Aviation Publishing, 1991.

—— *The Marine Corps Officer's Guide*. Annapolis, MD: Naval Institute Press, 1977. *The Marine Officer's Guide* by LtCol. Kenneth W. Estes. Annapolis, MD: Naval Institute Press, 1985.

Heiser, Gen. Joesph M. *Vietnam Studies – Logistics Support*. Washington, D.C.: Deparment of the Army, 1974.

Henderson, LtCol. G.F.R. *Stonewall Jackson and the American Civil War*. New York: William S. Konecky, 1911; Secaucus, NJ: The Blue Grey Press, 1989.

Hooker, Richard D. (Ed.) *Maneuver Warfare, An Anthology*. Novato, CA: Presidio, 1993.

Horne, Alistair. *To Lose A Battle: France 1940*. London: Macmillan, 1969.

Ikle, Fred Charles. *Every War Must End*. New York: Columbia University Press, 1971.

Indar, Jit Rikhye. *The Theory and Practice of Peacekeeping*. New York: St. Martins, 1984.

Johnson, Lyndon Baines. *The Vantage Point: Perspectives of the Presidency 1963–1969*. New York: Holt, Rinehart and Winston, 1974.

Joint Chiefs of Staff. JCS PUB 3-02, *Joint Doctrine for Amphibious Operations*. With Change 5. Washington, D.C.: The Joint Chiefs of Staff, November 1986 (Chg 5: Sept 1988).

—— JCS PUB 3-07, *Joint Doctrine for Military Operations other than War*. (JCS PUB 3-07 Series.) Washington, D.C.: The Joint Chiefs of Staff, February 1995.

Jomini, Baron de, General. *The Art of War*. London: Greenhill, 1992.

Jones, Archer. *Civil War Command & Strategy: The Process of Victory and Defeat*. New York: The Free Press, 1992.

Jones, Virgil Carrington. *Ranger Mosby*. McLean, VA: EPM Publications, 1987.

Kelso, F.B. Adm., and Gen. C.E. Mundy, Jr. Naval Doctrine Publication 1, *Naval Warfare*. Washington, D.C.: OCNO and HQMC, 28 March 1994.

Kepinevich, Andrew F., Jr. *The Army and Vietnam*. Baltimore: Johns Hopkins University Press, 1986.

Kissinger, Henry A. *The White House Years*. Boston: Little, Brown, 1979.

—— *Years of Upheaval*. Boston: Little, Brown, 1982.

Kitson, Frank. *Gangs and Counter-gangs*. London: Barrie & Rockliff, 1960.

—— *Low-Intensity Operations*. London: Faber & Faber, 1971.

—— *Bunch of Five*. London: Faber & Faber, 1977.

Komer, Robert W. *Bureaucracy At War: US Performance in the Vietnam Conflict*. Boulder, CO: Westview, 1986.

—— *Maritime Strategy or Coalition Defence?* Cambridge, Mass: ABT Books, 1984.

Lanza, C.H. (Ed.) *Napoleon and Modern War: His Military Maxims*. Harrisburg, PA: Military Service Publishing, 1949.

Laqueur, Walter. (Ed.) *The Guerrilla Reader*. New York: New American Library, 1977.

Larson, Jay L. and George A. Pelletiere. *Earth Data and New Weapons*. Washington, D.C.: National Defense University, 1989

Lawrence, T.E. 'Science of Guerrilla Warfare,' Vol 10. *Encyclopaedia Britannica*. London and New York, 1929.

—— *Seven Pillars of Wisdom*. Printed privately, 1926; London: Jonathan Cape, 1935; New York Doubleday, 1935.

Leonhard, Robert. *The Art of Maneuver: Maneuver-Warfare Theory and AirLand Battle*. Novato, CA: Presidio, 1991.

Liddell Hart, B.H. *Great Captains Unveiled*. London: William Blackwood, 1927; London: Greenhill, 1989

—— *A Greater than Napoleon: Scipio Africanus*. London: William Blackwood, 1926; London: Greenhill, 1992

—— (Ed.) *The Rommel Papers*. Trans. by Paul Findlay with asst. by Lucie-Maria Rommel, Manfred Rommel and General Fritz Bayerlein. London: Collins, 1953.

—— *Strategy*. London: Faber & Faber, 1954; New York: Frederick Praeger, 1954; New York: Dutton, 1991.

Lind, William S. *Maneuver Warfare Handbook*. Boulder, CO: Westview, 1985.

Lloyd Mark. *Tactics of Modern Warfare: Rapid Deployment in the 20th Century*. New York: Mallard Press, 1991.

Macksey, Kenneth. *Guderian: Panzer General*. London: Greenhill, 1992.

Mahan, Alfred Thayer. *Influence of Sea Power Upon History: 1660–1783*. London: S. Low, Marston, 1890.

Mahan, Dennis Hart. *Advance Guard, Out-post, and Detachment Service of Troops with the Essential Principles of Strategy and Grand Tactics For Use of Officers of Militia and Volunteers*. New Ed. New York: John Wiley, 1864.

Manstein, Field Marshal Erich von. *Lost Victories*. London: Methuen, 1958; Novato, CA: Presidio; London: Greenhill, 1994.

Mao Tse-tung. *Selected Works*. Peking: Foreign Language Press, 1961–65.

—— *Quotations from Chairman Mao Tse-tung*. [The Little Red Book] Peking: Foreign Language Press, 1966.

Marighella, Carlos. *Manual of the Urban Guerrilla*. Chaple Hill, NC: Documentary Publications, 1985.

Marine Corps Schools. *Tentative Landing Operations Manual*. Quantico, VA: Marine Corps Schools, 1934.

Marine Corps Schools. *Text for Landing Operations*. Quantico, VA: Marine Corps Schools, 30 June 1931.

Marshall, Col. S.L.A. *The Soldier's Load and the Mobility of a Nation*. Quantico, VA: Marine Corps Association, 1980.

Mayne, Charles Blair. *Infantry Fire Tactics*. Chatham, England: Gale and Polden, Brompton Works, 1885.

Moore, Lt. Gen. Harold G. and Joseph L. Galloway. *We Were Soldiers Once ... and Young*. New York: Random House, 1989.

Moore, Molly. *A Woman at War*. New York: Macmillan, 1993.

Morris, Roy, Jr. *Sheridan: The Life and Wars of General Phil Sheridan*. New York: Crown Publishers, 1992

National Security Strategy of the United States. Washington, D.C.: The White House, January 1987; January 1988.

National Security Strategy of Engagement and Enlargement. Washington, D.C.: The White House, July, 1994.

Nguyen Cao Ky. *How We Lost the War*. New York: Scarborough Books, 1978.

Nixon, Richard M. *The Memoirs of Richard Nixon*. New York: Grosset & Dunlop, 1978.

Nye, Roger H. *The Patton Mind*. Garden City, NY: Avery, 1993.

Pagonis, Lt. Gen. William with Jeffery L. Cruikshank. *Moving Mountains: Lessons in Leadership and Logistics from the Gulf War*. Boston: Harvard Business School Press, 1992.

Patton, General George S., Jr. *War as I Knew It*. Boston: Houghton Mifflin, 1947.

Pearce, Nigel. *The Shield and the Sabre: the Desert Rats in the Gulf, 1990–1991*. London: HMSO, 1992.

Pimlott, John and Stephen Badsey. (Ed.) *The Gulf War Assessed*. London: Arms & Armour Press, 1992.

Roberts, Kenneth. *The Battle of Cowpens: The Great Moral-Builder*. Garden City, NY: Doubleday, 1958.

Rommel, Field Marshal Erwin. *Infantry Attacks*. London: Greenhill, 1990.

Ross, Steven T. *Napoleon and Maneuver Warfare*. (The Harmon Memorial Lectures in Military History No 28.) Colorado: USAFA, 1985.

Ryan, Paul B. *The Iranian Rescue Misson*. Annapolis, MD: Naval Institute Press, 1985.

Schell, Capt. Adolf von. *Battle Leadership*. Fort Benning: The Benning Herald. 1933; Quantico, VA: Marine Corps Association, 1982.

Schemmer, Benjamin F. *The Raid*. New York: Harper & Row, 1976.

Schofield, Carey. *The Russian Elite. Inside Spetsnaz and the Airborne Forces*. London: Greenhill, 1993.

Schwarzkopf, Gen. H. Norman, written with Peter Petre. *The Autobiography: It Doesn't Take A Hero*. New York Bantam, 1992.

Scott, MGen. Winfield. *Infantry Tactics: Or, Rules for the Exercise and Manoeuvers of the United States Infantry*. New York: George Dearborn, 1835.

Sheehan, Neil. *A Bright Shining Lie: John Paul Vann and America in Vietnam*. New York: Random House, 1988.

Sherman, Gen. William T. *Memoirs of General William T. Sherman*. New York: The Library of America, 1990.

Simmons, BGen. E.H. *The United States Marines: The First Two Hundred Years. 1775–1975*. New York: Viking Press, 1976.

Simpkin, Richard. *Race to the Swift: Thoughts on Twenty-First Century Warfare*. London and New York: Brassey, 1985.

Slim, Viscount Field Marshal. *Defeat into Victory*. London: Cassell, 1972.

Snepp, Frank W. *Decent Interval*. New York: Random House, 1977.

Steuben, MGen. Baron de. *Regulations for the Order and Discipline of the Troops of the United States*. Albany, NY: Backus and Whiting, 1807.

Summers, Col. Harry G. *On Strategy: A Critical Analysis of the Vietnam War.* Novato, CA: Presido, 1982.

—— *On Strategy II: A Critical Analysis of the Gulf War.* New York: Dell, 1992.

Sun Tzu. *The Art of War.* Trans. with Intro. by S.B. Griffith. London: Oxford University Press, 1963.

—— *The Art of War.* Trans. with Intro. by Roger Ames. New York: Ballantine, 1993.

Taber, Robert. *The War of the Flea.* London: Paladin, 1970.

Taylor, Gen. Maxwell. *Swords and Plowshares.* New York: Norton, 1972.

Thompson, Sir Robert. *Defeating Communist Insurgency: The Lessons of Malaya and Vietnam.* New York: Praeger, 1966.

—— *Make for the Hills: Memories of Far Eastern Wars.* London: Leo Cooper, 1989.

Thompson, W. Scott, and Donald D. Frizzell. (Eds.) *The Lessons of Vietnam.* New York: Crane, Russak, 1977.

Thucydides: *The History of the Peloponnesian War.* New York: Penguin, 1954.

Trinquier, Roger. *Modern Warfare: A French View of Counterinsurgency.* London: Pall Mall Press, 1964.

Upton, Bvt MGen. Emory. *Infantry Tactics: Double and Single Rank (Adopted to American Topography and Improved Fire Arms).* New York: D. Appleton, 1868.

U.S. Army, FM 100–5, *Operations.* Washington, D.C.: USGPO, 1986.

U.S. Army. SH21–76, *Ranger Handbook.* Fort Benning, GA: US Army Infantry School, 1987.

U.S. Army and U.S. Air Force. FM 100–20, *Military Operations in Low Intensity Conflict.* Washington, D.C.: USGPO, 1990.

U.S. Department of Defense. Joint Publication 1, *Joint Warfare of the U.S. Armed Forces.* Washington, D.C.: USGPO, November 1991.

U.S. Department of Defense. *National Military Strategy.* Washington, D.C.: Department of Defense, 1992; 1993.

U.S. Marine Corps. FMFRP 2–12, *Marine Air–Ground Task Force: A Global Capability.* Washington, D.C.: HQMC, April 10, 1991.

U.S. Marine Corps Small Wars Manual. 1940. Washington, D.C.: GPO Reprint, NAVMC 2890, 1985.

U.S. Marines in Grenada, 1983. Washington D.C.: History & Museums Divisions, Headquarters, U.S. Marine Corps, 1987.

U.S. Marines in the Persian Gulf, 1990–1991: Anthology and Bibliography. Washington, D.C.: History & Museums Division, Headquarters, U.S. Marine Corps, 1991.

U.S. Marines in the Persian Gulf, 1990–1991: With the I Marine Expeditionary Force in Desert Shield and Desert Storm. Washington, D.C.: History & Museums Division, Headquarters, U.S. Marine Corps, 1993.

U.S. Marines in the Persian Gulf, 1990–1991: With the 1st Marine Division in Desert Shiel and Desert Storm. Washington, D.C.: History & Museums Division, Headquarters, U.S. Marine Corps, 1993.

U.S. Marines in the Persian Gulf 1990–1991: With the 2d Marine Division in Desert Shield and Desert Storm. Washington, D.C.: History & Museums Division, Headquarters, U.S. Marine Corps, 1993.

U.S. Marines in the Persian Gulf, 1990–1991. With the 3d Marine Aircraft Wing in Desert Shield and Desert Storm. Washington, D.C.: History & Museums Division, Headquarters, U.S. Marine Corps, (in preparation).

U.S. Marines in the Persian Gulf, 1990–1991: With the 1st Force Service Support Group in Desert Shield and Desert Storm. Washington, D.C.: History & Museums Division, Headquarters, U.S. Marine Corps, (in preparation).

U.S. Marines in the Persian Gulf, 1990–1991: Marine Forces Afloat in Desert Shield and Desert Storm. Washington D.C.: History & Museums Division, Headquarters, U.S. Marine Corps, (in preparation).

U.S. Navy. FTP-167, *Landing Operations Doctrine, U.S. Navy.* Washington, D.C.: Navy Department, 1938.

U.S. News and World Report Staff. *Triumph Without Victory: The Unreported History of the Persian Gulf War.* New York: Random House, 1992.

Van Tien Dung, Gen. *Our Great Spring Victory: An Account of the Liberation of South Vietnam.* New York: Monthly Review Press, 1977.

Vo Nguyen Giap, Gen. *People's War, People's Army.* New York: Praeger, 1964.

——— *How We Won The War.* Philadelphia: Recon Publications, 1976.

Wagner, Arthur Lockwood. *Organization and Tactics.* Kansas City, MO: Hudson-Kimberly, 1894.

Walt, Gen. Lewis W. *Strange War, Strange Strategy.* New York: Funk & Wagnell, 1970.

War Department *Training Regulation NO. 10–5.* Washington, D.C.: War Department, December 23, 1921.

Watson, Bruce W. (et. al.). *Military Lessons of the Gulf War.* London: Greenhill, 1993.

Westmorland, Gen. W.C. *A Soldier Reports.* New York: Dell, 1980.

Williamson, Porter B. *Patton's Principles.* Tucson, AZ: MSC Inc., 1979.

Wills, Brian Steel. *A Battle from the Start: The Life of Nathan Bedford Forrest.* New York: HarperCollins, 1992.

Woodward, Bob. *The Commanders.* New York: Simon & Schuster, 1991.

The Words of Command and Direction for Exercising the Musket, Bayonet, and Cartridge. London: William Breton; Boston: D. Henchman, March 26, 1733.

Wyeth, John A. *Life of General Nathan Bedford Forrest.* New York: Harper & Bros., 1899; Dayton, OH: Morningside Bookshop, 1975

Xenophon. *The Persian Expedition.* Trans. by Rex Warner. London and New York: Penguin, 1979.